TRADITIONAL

Crafts & Skills

FROM THE COUNTRY

Books by Monte Burch

Ultimate Bass Boats
Field Dressing and Butchering Deer
Field Dressing and Butchering Upland Birds, Waterfowl, and Wild Turkeys
Field Dressing and Butchering Rabbits, Squirrels, and Other Small Game
Field Dressing and Butchering Big Game
The Field & Stream All-Terrain-Vehicle Handbook
Denny Brauer's Jig Fishing Secrets
Denny Brauer's Winning Tournament Tactics
Black Bass Basics
Guide to Calling & Rattling Whitetail Bucks
Guide to Successful Turkey Calling
Guide to Calling & Decoying Waterfowl
Guide to Successful Predator Calling
Pocket Guide to Seasonal Largemouth Bass Patterns
Pocket Guide to Seasonal Walleye Tactics
Pocket Guide to Old Time Catfish Techniques
Pocket Guide to Field Dressing, Butchering & Cooking Deer
Pocket Guide to Bowhunting Whitetail Deer
Pocket Guide to Spring & Fall Turkey Hunting
Guide to Fishing, Hunting & Camping Truman
The Pro's Guide to Fishing Missouri Lakes
Waterfowling: A Sportsman's Handbook
Modern Waterfowl Hunting
Shotgunner's Guide
Gun Care and Repair
Outdoorsman's Fix-It Book
Outdoorsman's Workshop
Building and Equipping the Garden and Small Farm Workshop
Basic House Wiring
Complete Guide to Building Log Homes
Children's Toys and Furniture
64 Yard and Garden Projects You Can Build
How to Build 50 Classic Furniture Reproductions
The Indoors and Out
The Home Cabinetmaker
How to Build Small Barns & Outbuildings
Masonry & Concrete
Pole Building Projects
Building Small Barns, Sheds & Shelters
Home Canning & Preserving (with Joan Burch)
Building Mediterranean Furniture (with Jay Hedden)
Fireplaces (with Robert Jones)
The Homeowner's Complete Manual of Repair and Improvement (with three others)
The Good Earth Almanac Series
Survival Handbook
Old-Time Recipes
Natural Gardening Handbook

TRADITIONAL
Crafts & Skills
FROM THE COUNTRY

FROM THE GARDEN TO THE KITCHEN, AND FROM RAISING CHICKENS TO WOODWORKING,
A FRESH AND EASY-TO-FOLLOW APPROACH TO COUNTRY WISDOM

MONTE and JOAN BURCH

LYONS
PRESS

Guilford, Connecticut

An imprint of Globe Pequot, the trade division of
The Rowman & Littlefield Publishing Group, Inc.
4501 Forbes Blvd., Ste. 200
Lanham, MD 20706
www.rowman.com

Distributed by NATIONAL BOOK NETWORK

British Library Cataloguing in Publication Information available

A previous paperback edition was catalogued by the Library of Congress as follows:

Burch, Monte. Country crafts and skills : more than 100 easy projects / Monte and Joan
Burch. Guilford, Conn : Lyons Press, c2003.
   vi, 262 p. : ill. ; 28 cm.
   TX147 .B84 2003
   ISBN: 1585748730 (pbk.)
LC record available at https://lccn.loc.gov/2004271876

ISBN 978-1-4930-6198-3 (paper : alk. paper)
ISBN 978-1-4930-6199-0 (electronic)

Contents

TRADITIONAL

Crafts & Skills

FROM THE COUNTRY

PART ONE

Livestock

Livestock were an essential part of yesterday's homesteads and can still provide home-raised food for today's homesteaders. And nothing need ever be wasted. For instance, the family cow produces milk and meat, while sheep provide wool for clothing as well as mutton for the table.

Cattle

Cattle were and still are a very important part of many farms and ranches. Raising cattle can consist of five different operations: backgrounding, or raising calves to feeder size; feedlot feeders; cow/calf herds; simply raising a calf for beef; or keeping a family milk cow. (We won't discuss dairies because they've become "big" operations.) In the old days, farmers quite often raised a few cattle from birth to slaughter, slaughtering for their family use and selling off the excess. The family dairy cow was also used to produce the family beef. These days many farms and ranches specialize in the various operations. Beef cattle are well suited to farms that have adequate amounts of forage and roughage. The amount needed depends on the number of animals and the operations involved.

Cattle Breeds

The first question is whether to raise purebred or grade cattle. If you intend to produce breeding stock you may choose to raise purebreds. This requires a higher initial investment, and quite a bit of work in maintaining registration papers and records. For the farmer raising just a few head, however, the profits can be higher than with grade cattle. If you intend to produce feeder calves for sale, or finish calves out yourselves, you will probably wish to purchase grade cattle. Regardless, "it takes the same amount of land to produce a good cow as a poor cow," my granddad used to say.

Choosing a breed for a purebred herd is mostly a matter of choice. In my grandfather's day only a handful of beef cattle breeds were available. These days the number has proliferated. Each breed has unique requirements and produce different types of animals.

Grade cattle can be of mixed breeds or, preferably, a three-way cross, which produces animals with the greatest vigor and, with luck, the benefits of each of the crosses. For example, an Angus cow might be bred to a Polled Hereford bull to produce a "black-baldy" cow. The cow might then be bred to a black Limousin bull to produce a "black-baldy" calf.

Purchasing

The first step is to purchase breeding stock. Several options include a heifer calf, a bred heifer, an open heifer ready to breed, or a mature cow. A heifer calf requires the least initial investment, but requires additional cost in raising to breeding age. It will normally take more than two years for you to realize any income from your investment. An open heifer is a bit more costly in initial investment, but less cost in the time it takes to realize the investment. You will also have to own or rent a bull or utilize artificial insemination. A bred heifer eliminates the immediate need for breeding. A mature cow allows the quickest return on your investment. The best choice in a mature cow is either a cow ready to calf within three or four months or a cow with a calf by her side. Sometimes you can purchase a bred cow with a calf at her side, but this is also the most expensive initial investment.

Make sure you get the best you can afford. When purchasing mature cows, you're sometimes actually buying someone else's culls. It's also important to purchase a cow of the right age. Most beef cows reach maximum production in seven years, with the most productive years between four and nine. Some cows can produce at fourteen years of age or older. If possible, check the calving records. A good beef cow will produce a calf every eleven to twelve months.

Although each breed has different conformations, some general rules can be followed for all of them. For the most part, the body should

CATTLE ARE ONE OF THE MORE POPULAR LIVESTOCK. THEY DON'T TAKE AS MUCH WORK AS SOME LIVESTOCK, BUT THEY DO REQUIRE MORE LAND AND FEED.

be broad and deep and moderately low set. The top line should be straight and the flanks full. Appearance should be smooth. Fleshing should be ample, considering breeding performance, age, and feeding level. Females should have excellent mothering abilities including a sound, correct udder and teats. Bulls should have a pronounced masculinity, including a moderately swollen neck. They should also have a correctly placed sheath and no scrotal faults. Semen tests and scrotal measurements are also important.

Whichever breed you purchase, make sure the individual animal is in good health. Within thirty days of purchase, the animals should be tested and found free of brucellosis (Bangs disease or infectious abortion), leptospirosis (a bacterial disease), and tuberculosis. Purchase only from reputable breeders.

Feeding

Different types of animals and animals raised for different purposes have different feed requirements. Feeding may be for maintenance, growth, fattening, lactation, or pregnancy. Pasture forage is the main key to animal feeding. Depending on soil fertility and forage species, from one to five acres of pasture are required for each cow. The pasture should provide adequate grazing for nine months or longer. A mineral mix and salt should also be kept available at all times. Winter requires supplemental feeding. Grass hays make up the "bulk" of winter feed. Make sure the hay is of good quality. Normally, one-third ton of hay is required per cow per month. The total amount of hay required, however, depends on the length of the season and the quality of the hay. If the hay doesn't provide adequate protein, you may have to supplement with a protein such as cottonseed meal, soybean meal, or a commercial protein supplement. Silage may also be fed, but it may tend to overfatten older cows.

Herd Health

It's important to control diseases and parasites, both internally and externally. Your vet is the best tool for setting up a total herd health program suited to your particular needs. Insects such as flies, lice, and ticks can be controlled with several tactics including a high-pressure sprayer and insecticides, backrubs or dust bags, and cattle insecticides. The latter should be placed at points frequented by the animals. Near a water source is an excellent location.

Breeding

Grouping calves in a sixty- to ninety-day calving period allows for better herd management, and a more uniform calf crop, with higher market values. Do not run a bull with the herd all year. Some cattlemen prefer spring calving; others prefer fall calving. Spring calves require less harvested feed, such as hay, and are normally sold in the fall. Those born in January or February should have some sort of shelter to prevent chilling and freezing. I like to split the herd with calving in both periods. It's a bit more work, but creates a wider range of ages of market animals.

Calving

Make sure you mark the expected calving dates on your calendar. Then begin watching the cows carefully a few days before the expected calving dates. A sign of upcoming calving is a cow that begins to stay away from the herd. Her udder will begin to swell. Her vulva will become enlarged, and the area near the tail head and pin bones will shrink. First calf heifers may have more difficulty than mature cows and should be watched very carefully. A small pasture near the house is the ideal location for the herd ready for calving.

A calf is normally delivered head and front feet first. Several factors may cause a difficult delivery, including a small pelvic opening in the cow, calves having unusually large heads and shoulders, and a posterior or backward delivery. Under normal calving, no assistance is needed. If the delivery hasn't been made within two hours of labor, you should call a veterinarian or experienced cattleman.

Once the calf is delivered, clear any membrane from around its nostrils. If the delivery has been difficult and long, hold its head down immediately upon birth. Holding the calf's head down will clear fluids from the nasal passages and throat. Even a calf that appears dead can sometimes be revived with artificial respiration.

Apply iodine to the navel cord. Some cattlemen like to band male calves for castration at this time. I used to do this, but sometimes the testicles haven't dropped in a newborn calf, resulting in more severe castration problems later.

Allow the cow to dry the calf by licking it. In most instances, the calf will stand and begin to nurse on its own. If the calf doesn't nurse within three to four hours, provide assistance. Watch the cow and if she doesn't shed the membrane within twenty-four hours, call your veterinarian.

Raising the Calf

Except when raising purebred breeding stock, bull calves should be castrated. Not only does this make them easier to handle, there is also no chance of accidental breeding of heifers and prices at the market are better for steers than for bull calves. Some cattlemen castrate when the calves are two to four weeks old. Calves are easier to handle at that age and there are fewer setbacks from the operation. Others castrate at three months. Knife castration is the preferred method at these times. In recent years, a new form of castration has been developed. Delayed castration is an advanced form of banding that is done from three to six months of age. This allows more and faster gains and doesn't create nearly the stress or possibilities of problems of knife castration.

Horned cattle used for commercial purposes are usually dehorned. Horned cattle fight others in the pasture or feedlot and can inflict serious injury. Barnes-Tubes, available from local farm or vet supply, are the most common form of dehorning. For the most part, this is a vet job unless you are experienced.

Calves are normally weaned or removed completely from the cows around seven to eight months of age. The weaned calves should be placed in a sturdy lot with good grass or hay, fresh water, and minerals. I also like to feed a calf rations until they are "started," and then they are turned out to pasture. Both calves and cows will bawl for a few days, and it can be an infernal noise. Calves should be vaccinated, treated for worms and external parasites, and fly tags placed in their ears.

Marketing

Some producers like to jerk the calves off the cows and send them to market. The animals are pretty well stressed at the time and do not bring as good a price as when they are "conditioned," which usually takes about thirty to sixty days. The buyers at the market are primarily "backgrounders." They purchase calves at 300 to 400 pounds and then raise them on grass to feedlot size, which runs from 500 to 700 pounds. You can do your own backgrounding and again garner more gains if you have the available pasture. (This is my basic method.) You can also feed out the animals. This will take another year of fattening rations and is the most time-consuming and expensive of the operations. You will need about a ton of grain and around three tons of hay per animal. You can, however, usually earn greater income again, especially if you market the grain-fed beef for slaughter yourself. This is an especially effective way for small landowners to gain in profits; just don't name the calves. Finishing beef cattle means feeding enough grain in the rations so the cattle are able to attain a quality grade of choice. Finishing rations are fed to the British breeds from 600 pounds to a market weight of 1,000 or 1,100 pounds. Charolais and large-type breeds can be fed from 500 pounds to 1,200 to 1,300 pounds. Finishing rations usually contain maximum amounts of grain and a minimum amount of roughage. Finishing rations can be corn silage or ear corn with grains such as milo or barley. One of the traditional rations is "corn-fed" using shelled corn. Once the cattle are on the corn program, they should not have access to roughage. Farmland Industries research on no-roughage, whole corn, shows a calf with a weight of 652 at the start, weighing 1,036 at the finish for a daily gain in pounds of 3.58. This requires 604 pounds of feed per 100 pounds of gain. The feeders should be kept full of corn at all times. Provide no less than three inches of feeder space per head. Follow good management practices and provide daily attention to feed intake and animal conditions. Commercially prepared feeding rations are also available. With a small herd, this can be fairly profitable.

Bottle Calves

One very common practice on small farms with limited space is purchasing baby calves, normally dairy calves. This is an easy way to acquire beef without the hassle of raising it. Our kids raised baby calves throughout their high school years, with over twenty-five in the barn one winter. Raising "bottle" calves, however, isn't without problems.

Calves should be kept in a dry, draft-free building maintained at a comfortable temperature. They should be separated by partitions to prevent them from licking or sucking each other. Sanitary housing and feeding equipment are essential to control the spread of contagious diseases. Fly control is very important to prevent the spread of diseases and promote good growth of baby calves. Residual insecticides should be used in the building prior to housing the calves. Clean and disinfect feeders and waterers frequently and thoroughly. Ear tags or sprays can be used.

RAISING A BUTCHER CALF IS FAIRLY EASY, EVEN ON A SMALL FARMSTEAD.

Purchase only calves that appear to be healthy, bright-eyed, and alert. A large calf will generally make a better stocker calf. If at all possible, calves should be at least four days old and have received sufficient colostrum milk. Calves with enlarged or infected navels should never be purchased. Take the temperatures of all calves. A temperature of 101° to 102°F is considered normal for a young calf. Do not purchase calves with elevated or depressed temperatures.

The day of purchase, disinfect all navels with iodine. Inject all calves in the muscle with one cc of injectable vitamin A and D. Vaccinate calves for red nose or IBR (infectious bovine rhinotracheitis) and P13 (parainfluenza type 3). Inject all calves in the muscle with the label-recommended dosage of antibiotics. Repeat this procedure each day for three to five days depending on the appearance of the calves.

Caution should be taken not to overfeed calves. Feed calves milk replacer twice daily following the directions on the label. Drinking temperature of the restored milk replacer is 100°F. For proper, fast, and complete mixing of the milk replacer, use water at a temperature of 100° to 120°F when mixing. Offer the calves a free choice of 16 percent protein calf starter beginning the second or third day.

When using nipple bottles or buckets to feed the milk replacer, the nipple should be eighteen to twenty-four inches off the floor when the calf nurses. Once-per-day feeding is an acceptable program after calves are two weeks of age. Calves must be observed twice each day, however.

Take the temperature of each calf once per day. Inject any calves with elevated temperatures over 102.5°F, or under 99°F with the recommended antibiotic. Although this procedure is time consuming, it will pay big dividends. When once-a-day feeding is practiced, the milk replacer may be fed in the morning and the calves' temperatures taken in the afternoon.

Offer free-choice, high-quality legume hay when the calf is consuming about one pound of grain mixture daily. Offer free-choice water at all times. Do not, however, allow calves to consume large amounts of water following the milk feeding.

In the event of calf scours, reduce the amount of milk replacer in the liquid mixture about 50 percent for that calf. Keep the total liquid intake the same. About one day after scouring ceases, gradually work back to the previous level of milk replacer.

Feed milk replacer until calves are eating one and a half pounds of calf starter daily and have started on hay. This method requires approximately twenty-five pounds of milk replacer per calf. Most calves will usually eat one and one-half pounds of starter between five and six weeks of age.

After weaning from the milk replacer, feed one pound of calf starter for each month of age or one-fourth pound for each week of age. Make high-quality legume hay available free choice and provide salt or minerals. Consult your veterinarian for a complete vaccination and parasite-control program.

The same tactics can be used for home-raised baby calves, whether dairy breeds, calves rejected by their mothers, or orphaned calves. At birth, disinfect the navel with iodine. Immediately after birth, the calf should nurse approximately one quart of colostrum milk, preferably from its mother. Eight to ten hours later, the calf should nurse more colostrum milk. The minimum quantity of colostrum should be equivalent to 5 percent of the calf's body weight consumed during the first twelve hours of life. Inject into the muscle one cc of injectable vitamin A and D. Change to milk replacer when the calf is four days of age. If the mother's colostrum can't be used, substitute colostrums are available.

Raising the Beef Calf

The same basic steps are used in raising a beef calf for home use. You can grow your own, or purchase a started, conditioned calf. Or you can purchase a bottle calf. If you have the space and money, it's best to purchase two or more calves. Cattle are quite social and do best in a small "herd." You can then sell off the other calves and pay for your "beef."

The length of time you fatten the calf depends on the type of meat preferred. Prime beef that is well marbled with fat must be kept on feed until at least two years old. A large, well-fed calf of that age should weigh between 1,000 and 1,500 pounds and will yield 600 to 700 pounds. These days many prefer less marbled beef, called "grass-fed." If you have the pasture, run a spring calf on pasture until the second winter, and then grain feed the last few months. A yearling calf, called "baby beef," will run from 800 to 1,000 pounds and with less fat has lower cholesterol. It is also extremely tender meat.

RAISING A BOTTLE CALF IS ONE WAY OF GETTING A BEEF COW FAIRLY ECONOMICALLY, BUT IT DOES TAKE DAILY WORK UP TO WEANING TIME.

You will need a lot or corral and perhaps a barn or stall for inclement weather. Water and free-choice minerals should also be provided. During the winter months, free-choice hay should also be available until the final fattening phase. Calf starter rations should be used with weaned calves and feedlot starter rations used with fattening rations at the beginning of that phase.

The Family Milk Cow

In days past the family milk cow was an important part of country life. The cow provided both milk products and meat in the form of the calves she raised. The family milk cow can still do those things, but she's a rarity, even on most family farms. One reason is the time involved. During the milking season, she must be milked twice a day, morning and night. Although not particularly hard or time-consuming, it is a task that ties you to a strict schedule. As a kid growing up on a family farm in Missouri, it was my task from the day I became old enough until I graduated from high school.

Although any dairy breed will work, the smaller breeds, such as the Guernsey or Jersey breeds, are the most popular. They don't require as much feed but don't give as much milk as the larger breeds, such as the Holsteins. And, the milk is higher in butterfat than that of some of the other breeds.

The dairy cow should be gentle, healthy, and not have any bad habits. You don't want a kicker or one that must wear a yoke to prevent her from breaking fences. Her udder shouldn't have any hardened tissue or lumps. It's best to see the cow milked by hand or milk her yourself before purchasing. Draw several streams of milk from each teat onto a close-woven black cloth stretched over a container. Examine the milk for flakes, clots, or strings of blood. Make sure she is free of tuberculosis, brucellosis, as well as leptospirosis. These diseases can all be transmitted to humans. A veterinarian should have tested the cow no more than thirty days prior to purchase.

During the summer months, provide plenty of quality pasture. During the winter months, a smaller cow such as a Jersey will need at least ten pounds of hay a day. She will also need a pound of grain for each two to four pounds of milk she produces. Commercial mixes may be used or make your own of ground corn and wheat bran. Soybean oil meal or linseed oil meal may also be added for protein. Provide mineralized salt and water free choice. In cold climates, provide shelter. This can be a sunny, comfortable shed, or even a box stall. The art of hand milking is fairly easy. Confining the cow in a stanchion for milking is easier on her—and you as well. Place her feed in the feed box in front of the stanchion and she will enter readily.

Keep the cow gentle by handling her sensitively and quietly. Brush her daily to remove manure from her flanks and thighs. Before milking, make sure the udder and flanks are free of dirt or manure that might drop into the milk bucket. Wipe the udder and flanks with a clean, damp cloth before you begin milking. Make sure your hands are clean and dry and your fingernails short. Use a consecutive squeezing motion, starting with your forefinger and thumb, and working outward through your fingers. At the same time, pull down gently. Milk with both hands to draw the milk as quickly as possible into a small-topped milk bucket.

Artificial insemination is the best method for breeding a single cow, although you may be able to take the cow to a neighbor's bull. Family milk cows are usually bred so they calve and freshen in twelve-month intervals. The cow should be allowed to dry up for a month or six weeks before she calves again. This provides better milk production. Reducing feed and gradually discontinuing milking forces her to go dry.

Raising the milk cow calf is much like that described earlier. Once the calf has had initial

THE FAMILY MILK COW WAS A MAINSTAY OF OLD-TIME FARMS. A MILK COW NOT ONLY PROVIDES MILK PRODUCTS, BUT A BUTCHER CALF EACH YEAR, AS WELL.

colostrum, my dad and granddad allowed the calf to have half the milk for the first couple of weeks, then gradually weaned some of the milk away and placed the calf on grain feed. Even after a full milking, we often let the calf "strip" the cow or finish off a little milk. The calf must be kept separate from the cow except when allowed to nurse. Make sure the building housing the calf is sunny, ventilated, and well sanitized.

Swine

Back in the old days, most farms kept a few sows and raised some hogs. The hogs were primarily raised for family use, with the extras going as market or slaughter hogs. Pig raising these days is big business, with facilities raising thousands of pigs. Very few family farms raise hogs for market; however, a good number still raise a butcher pig for family use. Raising a pig or two is relatively simple and doesn't require much in the way of money, space, or effort. If you do the butchering yourself, it's an economical method of raising meat.

Buying

The easiest method is to purchase feeder pigs at about forty to sixty pounds and then feed the pig out to 200 or 250 pound slaughter weight. An alternative is to purchase a bred sow and raise a litter of pigs. This requires a great deal more work, money, space, and equipment. And, last, you can purchase gilts or unbred females, a boar, and begin a hog operation. This, of course, requires even more effort, money, and equipment.

Equipment and Space

Just about any small unused building can be used to house a hog or two. A small portable house or shade that can be pulled around a pasture is ideal. This allows for rotation of pasture forages and helps prevent disease problems. The most important factor in housing is shade and ventilation. Pigs can't sweat since they have no sweat glands. That is the reason they like to wallow in mud—not because they're "dirty" animals, but because the mud helps cool them down. Always provide plenty of shade in hot weather. If raising pigs in areas with high temperatures, you'll need a "wallow" kept wet, or a sprinkler system.

For farrowing, you'll need a farrowing house or farrowing crate. The latter contains the sow so she doesn't lie on her babies, a common hazard.

The biggest problem with pigs is fencing. Pigs can and will root under or through just about anything, and mature pigs can push or break even stout boards. Wooden pens can be used for fencing off lots adjacent to permanent housing. Woven or "hog" wire fencing, which is usually thirty-six inches high, is commonly used for permanent pastures. A strand of barbed wire needs to be strung on the bottom to help prevent rooting. Portable fencing consists of 36-inch high by 16-foot long welded wire "hog panels." Steel posts are driven in the ground and the

Pigs are more economical than beef and provide pork products. Growing a butcher pig is fairly easy if you have a good, strong pen. The author's son is showing a registered show pig.

panels wired securely in place to the posts. One alternative is electric fencing. Hogs are smart, and once they experience an electric shock, they won't cross an electric fence.

Sow and Litter

If purchasing a bred sow to produce a litter, the first decision is whether to purchase a pure-bred or a crossbred animal. If starting a hog operation, you should consider a purebred. A number of excellent breeds are available. If purchasing primarily to raise butcher hogs, sell-ing the extras as market hogs, a crossbred sow is more economical, but can be just as good quality. Regardless, it's important to purchase a sow that is sound and healthy. The animal should have a negative blood test for brucellosis and leptospirosis and should be vaccinated for Erysipelas. It should also be free of internal and external parasites.

Once you have the animal home, keep a close watch for thirty days or so for signs of any illness. If in doubt, a temperature check should be made. If the temperature is over 103°F, call your veterinarian.

Feeding

In the old days hogs were fed "slop" which was a mixture of water and ground grain such as corn. This "slop" was fed in pig troughs. Table scraps were also often fed—a porker is a great way of disposing garden waste such as cab-bage and lettuce leaves, beet tops, and vegeta-ble trimmings. Dry feeding, however, is actually the best method.

Pasture forages during the growing season can also provide a food source. Even with that, you should offer supplemental feed. Corn is the universal "pig feed" and the backbone of a feed ration, whether homemade or purchased. Corn by itself, however, does not provide a balanced diet. You can mix your own feed from different materials, but for a small herd the best method is to purchase ready-mixed feed. These contain the correct proteins, vitamins, and minerals. Some ready-mixed feeds do contain antibiotics and if

you're into raising "organic" pork, you may need to mix your own feed. If so, you should consider planting several acres of corn as a base for the mix. Different rations are needed for the differ-ent ages. The University of Missouri chart illus-trates the percentages of different materials.

Chart Title Sample Ration for Sows and Gilts

Ingredient	% in Ration
Corn[1]	77.3
Soybean meal	17.5
Alfalfa meal	2.5
Trace-mineralized salt	.5
Bonemeal or dicalcium phosphate	1.1
Limestone	1.1
Vitamins[2]	+
Calculated	
Protein	15.1
Ca	.8
P	.5

[1]Additional fiber may be incorporated into the ration by re-placing 5 to 10 percent of the corn with oats or other fiber containing by-product mill feed.
[2]Add vitamin premix.

Limit sows' and/or gilts' feed during gesta-tion to prevent them from becoming too fat. Four pounds of 15 percent protein ration a day is a good general suggestion. During the last one-third of the gestation period, increase the feed to six pounds per day. Make sure calcium and phosphorus are available free choice. Equal parts limestone with salt and steamed bone meal, or equal parts dicalcium phosphate and salt may be used. Allowing sows or gilts access to good pasture can increase litter size, save on feed costs, and also result in larger pigs at birth, as well as more weaned pigs.

Although growing or market pigs can be fed a specific amount of ration each day, the best method is free choice. Pigs tend not to over-eat as do some animals and self-feeders are not only effective, but they also cut down on labor time and costs. Just make sure the pigs have free choice of clean water at all times as well.

Farrowing

The gestation period for pigs is 114 days, although this may vary somewhat with individual pigs. You should know the date bred in order to estimate the farrowing date. About a quarter of all pigs die before they are five months old, and most of those die during the first two weeks. Several important steps can be taken to lessen your losses. A few days before the farrowing date, wash the sow and clean off all lice and mange. Move the sow into a clean, disinfected area or onto clean ground. A boiling-hot lye solution followed by boiling rinse water was the traditional method of disinfecting farrowing quarters in the old days. Be extremely careful when handling lye. Follow the instructions on the container explicitly. These days, less dangerous disinfectants are available. Once the farrowing house or quarters have been disinfected, do not allow visitors and keep a footbath of disinfectant at the door for disinfecting boots. Provide clean bedding such as straw, and make sure you have all necessary medications and equipment needed to care for the sow and piglets on hand.

Make sure the farrowing house is free of drafts but is well ventilated. Keep the temperature of the farrowing house between 40° and 80°F. A temperature of 85°F is ideal for newborn piglets.

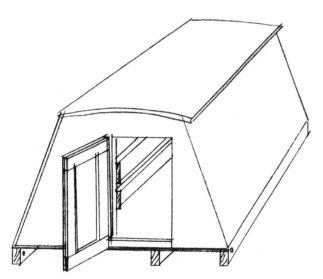

IF BREEDING AND RAISING PIGS, YOU'LL NEED MORE EQUIPMENT, INCLUDING A FARROWING HOUSE.

Most growers utilize infrared heat lamps over the farrowing area or crate.

Farrowing pens or crates should have a guardrail or separate area the piglets can crawl under and away from the sow. One of the most frequent causes of death is the sow rolling over on the piglets. The heat lamp draws the piglets away from the sow and into the safer area when they are not nursing.

Sows will become restless and begin to make a nest of bedding just before farrowing. Be on hand when the sow farrows, although, in most instances, the piglets are born without problems; they pop out fairly easily. Help with farrowing only if needed. If the sow is in labor ten to twelve hours with no results, she probably needs help. Unless you have an experienced person on hand, call your veterinarian. In most instances, you can insert your hand into the vagina (wearing a plastic vet glove) and provide gentle assistance. Dip the navel of newborn pigs in iodine. The four needle or wolf teeth should also be clipped to prevent pigs from injuring each other. A pair of side cutters makes the chore easy and it's a fairly easy and painless operation at this time.

The old-timers allowed the sow to eat the afterbirth, but with modern rations, it's not necessary. And, eating the afterbirth may lead to the sow eating her own pigs. Any dead piglets should be immediately removed and disposed of properly.

After farrowing, check the sow's temperature every twelve hours for the first couple of days. Call a veterinarian if the temperature is high or low.

Before the pigs are two weeks old, castrate the boar pigs if they are not to be used for breeding purposes. Although not difficult, it is a two-person job: one to hold the piglet, and one for the operation. Again, an experienced hand can be valuable for this operation. Castration is done with a sharp scalpel, or better yet, a razor-blade knife. In the most common method, one person holds the piglet by the rear legs with the head down. The area between the hind legs is thoroughly cleaned and disinfected. The testicles are located and massaged down toward the pig's head until they are exposed. With continued downward pressure, make an incision directly over and into the testicle. The incision must be between one and a half and two and a quarter inches in length for easy removal of the testicle as well as proper drainage. Use the thumb and forefinger to apply pressure to squeeze the testicle through the incision. With the cord held taut, slip the membranes back into the incision and cut the cord as close as possible to the body. Repeat for the other testicle.

Make sure you apply a fly repellent to the skin around the incision. Keep the piglets on a clean dry surface for two to four days. Do not allow them to wallow or get into places with excess moisture. Be alert at all times for disease and contact a vet immediately if the piglets display any unusual symptoms.

After about a week, offer a starter ration creep feed and plenty of water to the piglets. With a litter of normal size, gradually increase the sow's feed for the first couple of weeks after farrowing until she is on full feed.

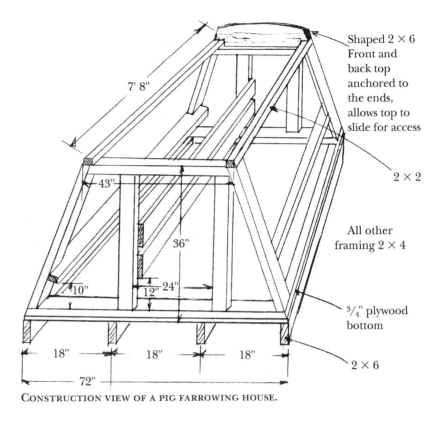

CONSTRUCTION VIEW OF A PIG FARROWING HOUSE.

Weaning

Piglets should be weaned between six and eight weeks, but no later than at eight weeks. This consists of simply removing the piglets from the sow. The best tactic is to place the piglets far enough from the sow that they can't see or hear her. It's a good idea to decrease the sow's ration by a fourth a couple of days before weaning. Once weaning has been done, increase the roughage in the sow's ration to help in drying up the udder.

Raising to Market

Regardless of whether raising pigs from your own sows, or purchased, weaned feeder pigs, the basic steps are the same. You must provide a well-balanced nutritious ration, control internal and external parasites, minimize feed waste, and isolate sick animals in a separate pen.

Newly weaned pigs are normally placed on a grower ration, as determined by the prior chart. Regardless of whether confined or on open range, make sure they have the proper amount and kinds of food, as well as water, available at all times.

If fattening a pig for home use, one tip is to fatten two pigs instead of one. Pigs are fairly social and two seem to gain better than just one. If you have several pigs to fatten, group them according to size since they will fight for feed.

If purchasing feeder pigs, buy from a reputable individual or organization that has been in business for some time. Don't buy bargain pigs. They may have disease problems. Make sure you determine what treatments have been given. Watch for signs of scours (an E. coli infection characterized by diarrhea) and other diseases and treat immediately in cooperation with your veterinarian.

It's important to know and understand the various swine diseases. Several books are available listing the common diseases and how to recognize or treat them. Feeder pigs should also be vaccinated against serious diseases. Contact your veterinarian for suggested treatments.

You may wish to start purchased pigs out on feeds with antibiotics for the first week or two after purchase. The first week to ten days is when more than half of the death loss from purchased feeder pigs occurs. After the pigs are ten days old, you can worm them. Make sure you check on your pigs daily to catch problems quickly. Make sure all pens and shelters have been disinfected and treated for lice and mange. Always supply plenty of water and provide shade in pastures or pens.

For confinement feeding you'll need four square feet per hog less than 100 pounds and nine square feet per hog to market weight. The general rule of thumb for pastures is one 25-pound to 40-pound growing and finishing pig per acre. If using self-feeders, allow one opening for each four heads. Again, you can buy a formulated mixed feed or mix your own.

Marketing

In many instances, you'll be growing pigs for your own table. Extra market hogs can be sold at hog markets, but the best tactic is to contact local slaughter plants and offer to sell the market hogs. They won't buy them, but most slaughter plants have customers who will.

Goats and Sheep

Goats and sheep were common sights on the settler's homesteads. They are still popular animals with many small property landowners.

Goats

Goats are relatively easy to take care of, yet they can provide both milk and meat. Goat's milk is easier to digest than cow's milk, and is often suggested for infants and invalids. The butterfat in goat's milk is softer and the texture is more like homogenized cow's milk than raw cow's milk. Goat's milk can easily be made into tasty butter, cheese, and high-quality ice cream. The meat from goats is also delicious, especially when barbequed. Called "chevon," the meat is primarily from milk-fed young goats.

Goats are available in a number of different breeds. Choosing a breed is important, but the most important factor is the availability of specific breeds in your area. Unless you intend to exhibit your goat at a fair, you don't need to purchase a registered animal. Choose a particular animal that is sound, in good health, and if a milking goat, with good dairy characteristics. If purchasing a mature dairy goat, get a record of the animal's milk production and the production of its offspring. A good producing doe should average 1,800 pounds of milk in a ten-month lactation period. This comes out to about three quarts a day, but will vary a great deal throughout this period. The doe should have a feminine head, thin neck, sharp withers, and well-defined backbone and there should be wideness to the ribs and a roomy barrel with a fairly wide chest. The udder and teats are also important. The udder should be large when full of milk, but quite a bit smaller when empty. The teats should be well shaped, but not too large nor too small.

Housing

A goat doesn't need an elaborate barn or house. Any small shed about four by six feet will suffice for a single dairy goat. Although the floor should be dirt, rather than concrete, it should be kept clean. They also need an exercise yard. It must be well fenced with either woven wire or boards and between forty-eight and fifty-four inches high. A goat quickly learns to jump or climb over fences, so never teach her to jump. When taking her in and out, lead her through a gate. If she does learn to jump, you'll have to place a wire top over the pen.

Milking

Milking supplies include a pail and cloth for washing the udder, a brush, and a milk pail. The easiest method of milking is with a milking platform. This should be kept away from the goat's living quarters to keep the milk sanitary.

Before milking, brush the animal and then wash the udder. Thoroughly wash and sanitize all milking utensils and storage containers and be careful to keep the milk sanitary after milking.

GOATS AND SHEEP ARE EXCELLENT LIVESTOCK CHOICES FOR THE SMALL HOMESTEAD. BOTH ARE FAIRLY EASY TO CARE FOR. GOATS CAN PROVIDE MEAT AND MILK; SHEEP, MEAT AND WOOL.

Feed

Running your goat on pasture is a great way of feeding her. An excellent choice is alfalfa or native grasses, but the best bet is a fairly large pasture with a variety of forages. You should also make sure she has clean water at all times. The milking doe should also have a minimum of one pound of a grain mixture for up to two quarts of milk per day. For each additional two quarts of milk, add one pound of the grain mixture. For a dry doe, feed one pound of mix per day. You can use commercial dairy cow or dairy goat feed, used according to the goat's stage—growth, lactating, or dry.

At birth, the kid needs two feedings of colostrum, the mother's milk. This provides vitamin A and also helps prevent disease. You can allow the kid to nurse at birth or bottle-feed it.

One good method is to allow the kid to nurse for three days, and then bottle or pan feed after that. Make sure all utensils are thoroughly washed in scalding water and sanitized before using. The milk must also be heated to 100°F. The kid will refuse to drink cold milk.

Provide good quality leafy hay. The kid will start eating it after a few days. As soon as the kid will accept it, feed a high-protein calf starter. By three weeks, the kid should be eating pasture forage, hay, and calf food, as well as nursing and drinking water from a pan. By eight weeks, the kid should be eating and drinking well on its own and milk feeding can be stopped.

The doe should have a two-month drying period before kidding again. To dry up the doe, stop milking her for seven days and then at the end of the week, milk her one more time.

Breeding

The doe should be bred once a year. Milk goats will often have two kids at one time, sometimes as many as four. Goats can be breed as young as eight months if healthy and well fed. The most common breeding period is from August through March. The doe will usually freshen about five months after the service.

Just before the doe is to kid, clip the hair on her udder, hindquarters, and tail to ensure cleanliness. Provide her with a kidding stall and clean bedding. She should not be given cold water nor tied just before kidding.

Cut down on her feeding a few days before she is due. Feed a laxative feed such as beet pulp or bran. You will know when she is ready to kid because she will have a rising tailbone, loose to the touch, with sharp hollows on either side. She will also be restless, pawing at the bedding and bleating plaintively. The udder will rapidly fill and turn shiny and pink. The vagina will issue a mucus discharge.

Caring for Your Goat

Regular care is needed for a healthy, productive animal. The hoofs must be trimmed regularly or they can cause serious lameness. Check and trim the hoofs at least once a month. The bottom of the hoof should be trimmed, from the heel to the toe, so the bottom is parallel with the top. By trimming often, you won't need to trim as much of the pad. If you do need to trim the pad, do it gradually. When the pad turns slightly pink, stop trimming. The first cut should be made to remove the outer wall. Next, level the heel and pad so the foot will sit level.

Kids that develop horn buds should be dehorned. A disbudding iron is the safest and easier method of dehorning. (Two irons are best—you can have a second ready for the second horn without excess time and stress on the animal.) Heat the iron to cherry red. Place it on the horn bud and use a circular motion with light pressure. This will normally take five to ten seconds to burn down to the clean skull. Apply petroleum jelly to each disk immediately after disbudding.

Male goats that are not to be used for breeding should be castrated between one and fourteen days of age. Using a sharp, disinfected knife, cut off the lower one-third of the scrotum, force the testicles out, and with a firm grip, pull them down and out with the attached cords. This should be a steady, but firm motion. Cut the cords and apply a disinfectant to the wound.

Control external parasites with an animal insecticide. Do not spray when the doe is milking because the spray might get into the milk. Make sure you follow all safety and environmental regulations and rules for the particular insecticide used. Keep the area clean to cut down on fly development.

Watch carefully for disease and contact your vet if you suspect any. Common goat diseases include: ringworm, pink eye, foot rot, foot abscess, digestive disorders, scours, joint conditions, infectious dysentery, enterotoxaemia, and mastitis.

Some diseases can also be transmitted to humans through the goat's milk. These include listeriosis, leptospirosis, brucellosis, and tuberculosis. It's a good idea to work with your local vet for a complete health program.

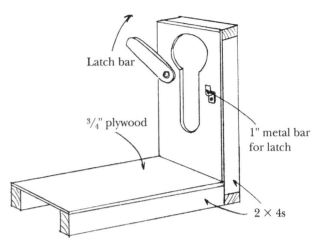

A MILKING PLATFORM MAKES IT EASIER TO MILK.

Sheep

Sheep were a very important livestock for the early settlers and old-timers. Sheep produced wool for clothing as well as meat for the table. Raising a few sheep is still a profitable enterprise, especially for those with smaller acreages than is feasible for other livestock, such as cattle. An average ewe requires about three quarters of a ton of hay per year. Good quality land may produce between four and five tons of hay per acre. Half of this should be in grazing or pasture land. You should have hay or silage for winterfeed.

Sheep do, however, need more care than most other livestock. This is not especially hard labor, but is often quite time consuming. Timing is extremely important in sheep raising; you have to continually keep watch on them to be a good shepherd. You will need sturdy, solid barns to house the sheep in the winter. These should, however, be open and cold, rather than closed and humid. With their wool coats, all sheep, except baby lambs, do well in the cold. Shade must also be provided in the summer months. Pastures need to have solid woven wire bottoms with barbed wire tops to hold the animals and to help keep out predators such as wild dogs and coyotes. You will also need corrals for sorting, equipment for tail docking, ear tagging, and perhaps shearing. These days, hired sheep shearers are more common than the owners doing the chore.

A fairly wide variety of sheep breeds is available. Some are better wool producers, others better meat producers, and some breeds can produce both. Sheep's milk is even higher in fat than goat's milk and is very good for making feta cheese. Sheep's milk is very popular in some parts of the world and there is also increasing interest in the United States. It's important to choose the breed most suited to your needs, as well as management desires. For instance, Merino produces fine wool, Suffolk are fast growers for meat, and the Corriedale and Columbia breeds are good choices for both wool and meat.

Sheep can produce from one to more than three lambs per year depending on the management system chosen. One of the more traditional old-time management systems is early lambing. The ewes are bred to lamb in January or February and the lambs raised as "hot-house" for the Easter market, or raised to 100 pounds to sell in early summer. Late-lambing, or in April or May, allows maximum use of summer forage, but has several disadvantages, including a greater risk of parasite and predator problems. Another system is accelerated lambing. Each ewe lambs three to five times a year for two to three years. This system naturally requires a lot more management skills.

SHEEP ARE FAIRLY EASY TO KEEP, ESPECIALLY ON THE SMALL FARMSTEAD. THEY CAN PROVIDE BOTH WOOL AND MEAT.

Most sheep flocks are started with sheep purchased from local breeders. It is extremely important to buy sound, healthy animals from a reputable breeder. Do not buy older sheep or those more than seven years of age. Do not buy overly fat ewes, as they may not be good breeders. But also don't buy an extremely thin ewe because this may indicate disease or parasites. Look at the teeth. Missing teeth can indicate a poor feeder. Look for obvious health problems, which can include any sort of eye damage indicating pink eye. Examine the udder to determine if there are any lumps, which can indicate mastitis. A limp may indicate untrimmed feet or hoof disease. Runny droppings may indicate internal parasites. Examine the wool carefully. If the fleece is ragged and patchy, the animals may be infested with external parasites. The wool should not extend too far down the legs or over the face since it causes problems during shearing. The latter can cause wool blindness, which prevents eating as well as mothering.

One of the reasons for the popularity of raising sheep is they can get most of their nutrients from pasture and hay, more so than many other animals, including goats. Sheep eat the pasture right down to the ground, including weeds, and will even eat poisonous plants. Pasture rotation is an extremely important facet of sheep raising, not only because of their close grazing habits, but also because of their susceptibility to parasites. With proper pasture management, however, sheep can actually boost native pasture production. If the pasture is sufficient, no additional grains are needed. If good pasture is not available, feed a legume hay free choice along with about two pounds of a high grade of mixed grain daily. Pasture forage and hay must also be supplemented with concentrated feeds, especially for ewes during the latter portion of pregnancy and lactation. Commercial dairy feeds are an excellent choice. Mineral and salt supplements must also be fed free choice. Copper, however, can be toxic to sheep. A clean water source is also necessary.

Breeding and Lambing

Ewes come into heat every twenty-one to twenty-six days, and the gestation period is five months. During pregnancy, the ewe should have about one and a half pounds of good grain a day along with free-choice alfalfa or legume hay. About a month before lambing, increase the grain so the ewe begins to gain weight slightly. About one to two weeks before lambing the ewe will show udder development. Clip the wool away from the udder in order for the lambs to find the teats more readily. As lambing time approaches, the ewe will move more slowly and begin to lie down more often. She will seek out a quiet corner and may refuse feed. When she throws out strings of mucus and begins to grunt and strain, she is in labor. After about fifteen minutes the water bag should come out followed by two feet, toes pointed down. Once the legs are out past the knees, the nose will appear, and then the head and shoulders and finally the rest of the lamb will be expelled. Most ewes will have twins; some will have triplets. The ewe should then clean the lambs until they are dry and fluffy. Within an hour, they should be on their feet and nursing. If the ewe labors for more than an hour without producing a lamb, a veterinarian should examine her for problems.

Proper care of baby lambs is also extremely important. Small lambing pens are necessary. These are basically temporary pens of wooden panels tied together, about five to six feet square. When the ewe is ready to lamb, she is placed in the pen. This keeps the lambs with their mother and prevents the other ewes from bothering her or her lambs. In cold weather, you may also wish to add a heat lamp over the pen, but make sure there is no danger from fire.

It is not unusual for a ewe to reject her lamb. She will absolutely have nothing to do with it, butting and kicking it. Placing a bit of Vicks VapoRub on both the ewe's and lamb's noses may prevent her from smelling the lamb and she may allow it to nurse. In many cases, however, the lamb must be bottle-fed. The lamb must be placed in a warm, draft-free pen. Feed one to two ounces of goat's or cow's milk at least every four hours around the clock for the first week after birth. Gradually increase the amount of milk to eight ounces per bottle at each feeding. If the lamb experiences diarrhea, cut back the amount of milk to half and provide a dose of Kaopectate. Try to get the lamb to nibble calf pellets with mixed grain, as well as good legume hay.

One of the most common management practices in the United States is docking the tails of lambs. This prevents dampness and the risk of maggot infestation caused by long tails. Lambs should be docked about one to two weeks after birth. The chore can be done with an axe or knife, but an emasculator crushes the blood vessels and makes the chore more bloodless. The tail should be docked leaving only about an inch on the lamb. Immediately dip the stump in an

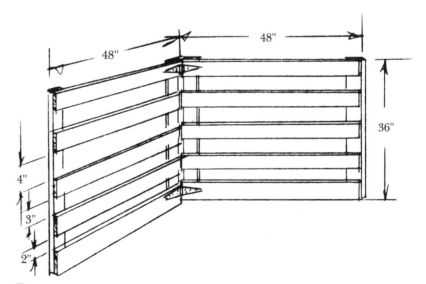

TEMPORARY PENS OF WOODEN PANELS SHOULD BE USED DURING LAMBING TO KEEP THE BABY LAMBS WITH THE EWE AND TO PREVENT OTHER SHEEP FROM BOTHERING THEM.

antiseptic to prevent infection. A shot for tetanus, as well as an antitoxin, should be given at the time of docking.

All ram lambs that will not be kept for breeding should also be castrated. It's a good idea to do the castration at the same time as docking to cut down on stress. Some growers use rubber bands for castration, but surgical castration is the best method. Keeping the testicle forced against the bottom of the scrotum, make an incision at the bottom of the scrotum over each testicle. Pull out the testicle and tunic (whitish membrane surrounding the testicle) until the cord breaks. This causes little bleeding, but if you cut the cord, it can be bloody. Repeat for the second testicle. Again, a tetanus shot is advised.

Both internal and external parasites are extremely common problems with sheep. A management plan for parasite control is extremely important. Check with your local veterinarian for a flock management plan.

You can shear one or two sheep with a hand shear and a lot of hard work, along with a few not-so-nice words. Shearing more than one or two sheep is a chore best left up to the experts. Both you and your sheep will be better off and you'll end up with better quality wool.

Poultry

The chicken house was a standard feature of the old-time farm. As a kid I hated chickens—except when it came time for the Sunday dinner of fried chicken. My job was to gather the eggs, which often resulted in a pecking from a hen that was trying to "sit" her eggs. Or the rooster might chase me. But the worst job was the annual cleaning of the chicken house. This was dusty, dirty, smelly, and a lot of hard work. I did, however, thoroughly enjoy and look forward to the yearly arrival of day-old chicks, fresh from the hatchery and delivered to our country mailbox. Baby chicks have a "sweet" smell all their own, and their fuzzy little bodies were fun to handle.

These days, most folks living in the country don't keep chickens. Chickens, however, can provide both eggs and meat for those willing to work for them. Given free-forage of your yard, chickens will also keep down pests such as ticks and chiggers. Of course, they will leave their calling card when they do. Chicken manure is one of the highest nitrogen manures and excellent for growing many plants. And, there's also ducks, geese, and turkeys.

Chickens

The first step is to decide whether you wish to have egg producers or meat chickens. Some breeds are best for specific uses, others are somewhat in-between. Breeds such as the White Leghorns are the most productive egg producers. The hens will weigh about four to six pounds during their production period, and should produce about 200 eggs a year. They are, however, a bit skinny and small for eating. On the other hand, young roosters are a bit larger and are delicious table fare.

CHICKENS WERE A TRADITION ON THE OLD FARMSTEADS. THEY DON'T TAKE A LOT OF WORK, YET PROVIDE EGGS AND MEAT.

23

POULTRY INCLUDING CHICKENS, TURKEYS, AND EVEN DUCKS AND GEESE WERE A VERY IMPORTANT PART OF OLD-TIME FARMSTEADS. RAISING CHICKENS IS FAIRLY EASY AND THEY CAN PROVIDE BOTH MEAT AND EGGS.

The meat breeds, including Jersey Giants and others, can weigh up to fourteen pounds. These birds actually get too big for frying, but are great for roasting. The more common and popular in-between breeds include the Plymouth Rock, one of the most traditional breeds. They not only produce large brown eggs in fairly good quantities, but they also make great fryers, roasters, and broilers.

It's best to start out with a flock of 100 birds. This allows for accidents, disease, and predation. You can purchase pullets ready to start laying, already started chicks, or even mature birds. The latter are often sold in farmer's markets. One traditional method is purchasing day-old chicks.

These can sometimes be purchased at local hatcheries, but they can also be bought mail order. When buying from a hatchery, make sure you purchase from a reputable source and that the chicks have been tested for typhoid and pullorum diseases. Hatcheries "sex" chickens to determine the pullets and cockerels. With this method, you can specify which or how many of each you desire. If it is meat you prefer, you'll want cockerels since they grow more quickly and are larger than pullets.

The chicks must be started in a brooder house or under a brooder heat source as soon as you get them home. In the old days, every farm had a brooder house just for that purpose. Then the chicks were moved to a general-purpose hen house. Any dry, warm building without drafts will suffice if you use a brooder heat source. The building must be thoroughly cleaned and disinfected before use. A galvanized washtub can easily be made into a brooder or you can purchase a commercial brooder. Cover the floor with newspaper. Create a guard about a foot high around the brooder and about two feet away in all directions. Leave the guard for the first day or two, and then gradually move it farther away each day. After about two weeks, the guard can be removed. Chicks tend to cluster together and any square corners will trap them, causing them to smother each other.

Place starting mash or finely chopped corn in paper plates for the first week. Next, switch to feeding in small troughs. Keep at least two non-tippable glass water fountains filled with clean water available. Discard the paper plates three times each day and thoroughly wash and sterilize the water fountains several times each day. Some growers like to place the fountains up on a platform covered with hardware cloth screening to help prevent droppings from fouling the water.

Commercial chick starter or mash should be fed until the chicks are about four to six weeks old. You should also provide some fine grit, such as sand, in a shallow pan. After about eight weeks, switch to a commercial growing feed or a combination of grain and growing mash. Make sure grit is available at all times. You can gradually switch

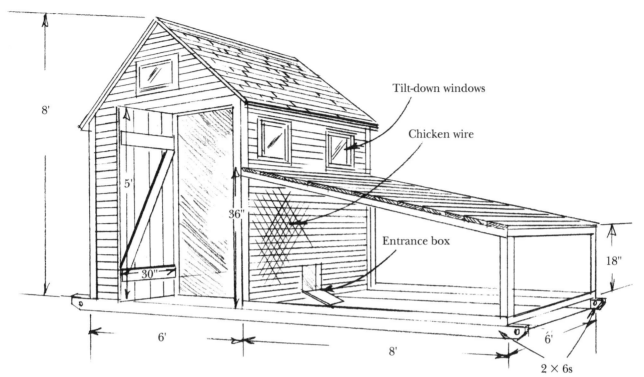

CHICKENS SHOULD BE HOUSED IN A DRY, BUT VENTILATED BUILDING. A NUMBER OF SMALL HOUSES HAVE BEEN DESIGNED FOR RAISING CHICKENS FOR EGGS OR MEAT. SHOWN IS A COMBINATION PORTABLE BROODER/GROWER/LAYING HOUSE/RANGE SHELTER.

to grain, such as chopped corn, wheat, oats, or barley, which is more economical. Most small farm growers these days prefer to purchase commercially mixed feeds. If you have the space, the chicks can also be given free run to forage after they are about six weeks old. Make sure all are back in the house and penned up for the night or you'll have many predation problems.

The all-purpose birds will usually start laying at about twenty-four weeks of age. As they begin to lay, replace the growing mash with an all-mash laying diet. You should also keep a steady supply of grit and oyster shells. The latter supplies the calcium necessary for normal eggshells. You will need about 100 pounds of feed per bird per year for layers. The chickens can be fed daily in feed troughs that have dividers. Clean water must be kept available at all times in self-waterers.

Laying chickens or those being raised for slaughter can be kept in almost any shed or build-

ing that provides protection from the weather, yet has adequate ventilation. Over the years, a great number of specialty chicken houses have been designed. Most are set up on blocks or rocks to help prevent dampness. They all feature some sort of

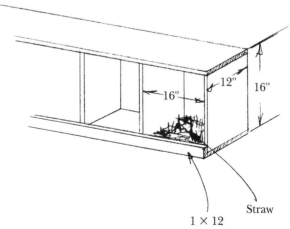

YOU'LL ALSO NEED NEST BOXES. THEY CAN BE MADE OF 1-×-12 MATERIALS.

screened opening in the front that may have drop-down doors for cold weather. A small chicken entrance with a ramp leading to the entrance is often used. And, finally, they have an entrance door leading into the house. There should be from three to four square feet of space per bird. You will also need nests for the hens to lay eggs. Roosts should be constructed at the back of the house and away from drafts. The roosts should be about three feet above the floor and ten to twelve inches apart. Apply an absorbent litter of chopped straw or wood shavings on the floor. When the litter becomes damp, renew to help remove parasites and disease organisms.

Cleanliness is critical for a healthy flock. Keep all waterers and feeders clean with a regular washing and disinfecting. Completely clean and disinfect the entire building at least once a year. If you suspect disease, isolate the diseased birds from the rest of the flock. Burn or bury any dead birds.

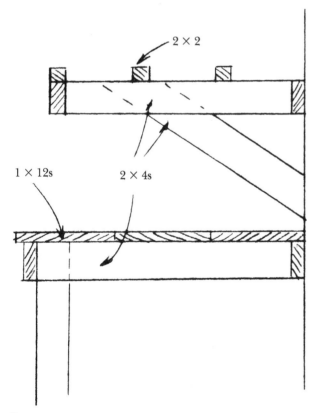

ROOSTS PROVIDE A PLACE FOR THE BIRDS TO SPEND THE NIGHT AND A SHELF COLLECTS THEIR DROPPINGS.

With proper care and feeding, your flock should produce quality eggs. The eggs should be gathered twice a day. Wipe them off with a damp cloth and keep them stored at between 45° and 55°F. My granddad kept his eggs in a cellar, the perfect temperature.

Quite often an enclosure or pen was used to keep the chickens from wandering too far. But in the old days, chickens were more often free-ranging. They will quickly learn to return to the house each night, and it should be closed off to prevent Br'er Fox from gathering his chicken dinner.

Turkeys

Raising Thanksgiving dinner is a bit more complicated. A handful of turkeys were often part of the old-timer poultry flock, but they are a bit harder to raise than chickens. Turkeys should be kept separate from all other poultry. They should not be kept in any housing or even open range that has been used by any poultry for at least three years prior to prevent them from contracting diseases such as blackhead. Turkeys must be kept separated by age or size or the larger turkeys will kill the smaller or younger ones. Young turkeys must also always be kept dry and warm. The same type of equipment and housing that is used for chickens can be used for turkeys, although special turkey houses that can be frequently moved around a pasture are the best option. Turkeys may be grown to maturity as roasters. Smaller types may be butchered at about twenty-four weeks, large hens at twenty to twenty-two weeks. If purchasing day-old poults, make sure they are from a breeding flock free of typhimurium, sinusitis, and pullorum-typhoid. Feeding and brooding is basically the same as for chickens.

Ducks and Geese

Both geese and ducks require less care in raising than chickens or turkeys. Ducks and geese are primarily raised for their meat, but the old-timers kept them for their down as well. It takes little in the way of housing and/or equipment for either breed. Both can free-range quite easily and will take care of themselves. Although ducks will readily take to a pond, they will also do quite easily with a shallow pool (such as a child's wading pool) kept filled with clean water. Ducks and geese should, however, be kept away from chickens.

You can begin a small flock with day-old ducklings, brooding and rearing them in the same manner as for chickens. As duck hens are not particularly good mothers, the old-timers often used a broody hen to raise ducklings from duck eggs.

Probably the easiest poultry to keep is geese. Geese are great garden "weeders," preferring weeds to many of the vegetables. They're also extremely hardy, needing nothing more than a shelter with an open entrance and a floor to prevent dampness. Geese do great free ranging, but should be kept away from the rest of the poultry. They will graze a pasture to the ground, so you should keep pastures in rotation to allow them to grow. Geese can be raised and grown in the same manner as for other poultry, but they should have fresh greens daily as well as plenty of clean water. One caution: ganders can be quite pugnacious, especially during the breeding season. They will attack anything that gets close, as more than one farm youngster has learned the hard way in days past when geese were common farm fowl. Geese are quite messy as well. They do, however, make great "guard-dogs" announcing any visitors quite noisily.

Bees

Bees were traditional on most farmsteads, including my granddad's. Beekeeping is also a great hobby the entire family can enjoy. Bees are interesting, fun to watch, and can provide lots of golden, sweet-smelling honey, as well as a very valuable commodity of the old-timers, beeswax. Bees are also necessary for pollination of many flowers, vegetables, and pasture forage, as well as orchards and berries. Getting started in beekeeping is not particularly expensive or hard to do and, because of the interest in beekeeping, numerous organizations, magazines, and books are available for more information than can be provided here.

The Basics

Start with one colony of bees. You will need a beehive. The best hive for the beginning "apiarist" is the dovetailed hive, or movable frame hive. The hive should have extracting supers rather than section supers. The latter are used by more experienced beekeepers. You will also need a bellows smoker as well as a bee veil. The smoker is basically a small canister with a bellows attached. It is filled with a material that will smoke when ignited. The bee veil can be made from any stiff and wide-brimmed hat. Sew a five- to six-inch strip of black nylon screen wire to the brim of the hat. To the bottom of the screen-wire, sew a strip of cloth to tuck into your collar to keep the bees out. Other clothing is simply a long-sleeved shirt and pants along with gloves and boots to overlap and keep out bees. You will also need a scraper, wide chisel, or hive tool to pry the hive apart. In addition, you will need something to put the honey in as well as comb foundations for starting straight combs. Beekeeping suppliers offer complete kits with the hives and all the equipment needed for beginners. A bee colony is made up of one queen, or the mother of the hive; thousands of worker bees or sexually undeveloped females; and a few drones, or males who mate with the queen. Bees for the hive can be obtained by purchasing a swarm from a nearby beekeeper or from mail-order sources.

Place the beehive in any small, out-of-the-way corner of the garden or orchard. The bees should be placed in an area so as not to disturb people, or be disturbed themselves. The hive should face either the south or east. Until the beekeeper gains experience he should remove the honey with an extractor or by cutting the honey and comb out, then replacing it with comb starter.

You probably won't be able to work a hive without getting an occasional sting. The stings can be dangerous to some people more than others. Some people may, in fact, have an allergic reaction. Be aware of the problem and how to deal with it. Yet, the occasional bee stings that occur even with proper hive management are only annoyances to experienced beekeepers. (My granddad, however, never got stung as long as I can remember.) Bees seem to be

attracted to perfumes as well as the odor of sweat. Wear light-colored, tight, but smooth-textured clothing that covers your entire body. Gentleness is the key to being a good beekeeper. When you open the hive, go slowly. Don't over-smoke the bees. Be very careful not to harm or irritate the bees while handling them. Don't try to work the bees on windy or stormy days.

Starting the Bee Colony

You can start a bee colony from a neighboring apiary, but make sure the bees have been inspected and come with a certificate of health. If purchasing mail order, packaged bees normally come delivered to your location in packages of two to five pounds. A good starter package is three pounds. This should provide a colony large enough for a steady honey flow during peak nectar time as well as build the colony up to fifty thousand bees. The packaged bees come with the queen bee shipped inside a private little box or cage. It takes about eight weeks for a

BEEKEEPING IS A FUN, INTERESTING HOBBY THAT CAN PRODUCE PLENTY OF SWEET-TASTING HONEY, AS WELL AS AID IN POLLINATING FLOWERS, VEGETABLES, AND FRUITS.

YOU'LL NEED BEEHIVES. THESE CAN BE PURCHASED OR YOU CAN CONSTRUCT THEM YOURSELF.

colony to build up to a good harvesting capacity. Most bee sellers know the dates for the best timing across the country and ship accordingly. After assembling the beehive in the proper location, fill the frames with comb foundation. You may have to provide sugar water at the initial installation of the colony to get them started.

Beekeeping is based on seasonal management. If attention is not given at specific times of the season, the bee operation will not be successful. Following is a general listing. The timing will vary across the country according to weather and the seasons from north to south.

Normally on the first warm spring day in late March or early April the bees will emerge from the hive and begin flying. In the fall, the entrance hole should have been reduced in size to keep the hive warm and prevent mice from entering. At this time, the entrance hole should be opened and cleaned. A few weeks later unpack the colonies and inspect the hive. Check for diseases, dead bees, lack of food, and whether or not there are eggs from the queen. Make sure there is plenty of room for the queen to lay eggs and expand her nest upwards. Otherwise, the bees will swarm to a new location. If necessary, feed the bees honey or sugar water until a good flower bloom, such as clover, exists.

By the last of June when full clover honey flow begins, move the queen to the lowest chamber. Place a queen extruder and a super of drawn combs well shaken to remove bees on top; otherwise, the brood will develop in the honeycomb. Next, place the hive body with the brood on top of the super. Ex-amine the hive about every two weeks during the clover honey flow.

In late July or early August remove and extract the clover honey and return the supers to the hive for the fall honey flows.

In the latter part of September remove and extract the surplus honey and store the supers for the winter. Remove the supers and queen extruders. Reduce each colony to no more then two hive bodies. The top hive body or second brood chamber should be left full of honey for the bees to use over the winter.

Some beekeepers start over each spring, but the beginning beekeeper, keeping just enough bees for family use, can carry a colony over the

OTHER BEEKEEPING EQUIPMENT YOU'LL NEED INCLUDES LIGHT-COLORED CLOTHING, BEE VEIL, GLOVES, AND A SMOKER.

winter fairly easily. In this case, only the supers are removed for honey, leaving the brood chamber full. Slightly close down the entrance hole to prevent mice from getting in. In northern latitudes, you will also need to provide a windbreak and possibly even insulation. Straw makes a good insulation; use about two inches of straw piled around the sides. Don't over-insulate because this allows the cold in, but does not allow the hive to warm up during the day.

The Farm Pond

Water has always been a major factor in homesteads. Most settlers looked for land with springs or along creeks or rivers. In later years the farm pond served many different uses. A well-designed and constructed pond can be a water source for livestock, a family recreation area, and a source for producing food. Ponds can be used for raising a variety of fish. Bass and bluegill are the most common fish stocked, along with channel catfish. Catfish can also be stocked by themselves in ponds for fish farming.

Constructing a Farm Pond

If you don't already have a suitable pond, the first step is to construct one. Pond location, design, and construction are fairly complicated. The best tactic is to contact the local Soil Water and Conservation Service in your county seat. They have engineers who can help with all these steps.

Once your pond has been constructed and filled, it's ready for stocking. The recommended stocking is with purchased fingerlings. This should consist of 100 largemouth bass, 500 bluegill, and 100 channel catfish per surface acre of water. Do not use wild fish caught and transplanted to the pond. The bass and bluegill will reproduce; the channel catfish must be restocked regularly.

If managed properly, even a small pond can produce catfish for the table. Up to 500

A POND CAN BE AN INVALUABLE RESOURCE FOR YOUR HOMESTEAD, PROVIDING FOOD AND RECREATION.

pounds of fish per surface acre of water per year can be produced if the fish are fed a pelleted fish food. Catfish are one of the most efficient sources of protein. Fed a high-protein diet of pelleted fish food daily, catfish can produce one pound of fish for each 1.8 pounds of food.

Ponds used for raising catfish should be at least eight feet deep with the edges sloping at a sharp angle to prevent weed growth. All debris must be removed from the pond basin. Use a turndown drainpipe to allow for drawing down the pond for harvest.

If the catfish are fed daily or on-demand, stock with four- to six-inch fingerlings at a rate of 500 per surface acre. If fed occasionally, stock with 300 fish per surface acre. You can use either floating or sinking catfish feed. The floating pellets allow you to monitor the amount of feed needed per day by observing the amount of feed consumed within fifteen minutes of feeding. The fish can be harvested with hook and line and bait or the pond can be drawn down and the fish removed at one time.

THE MOST COMMONLY STOCKED FISH ARE BASS, BLUEGILL, AND CHANNEL CATFISH. CHANNEL CATFISH CAN ALSO BE GROWN BY THEMSELVES IN SMALL PONDS AS A MAJOR FOOD SOURCE.

PART TWO

Gardens and Orchards

The old-timers gardened big time. They had to garden to survive. But these days, gardening is fun, it's good exercise, and you benefit from all the delicious food you raise.

Orchards may be hard work, but it's also very satisfying outside work and you can grow bushels of luscious fruits.

Gardens

My granddad had a full acre garden, and when we moved back to the country in the early seventies we also had big gardens. In fact, at one time we had four gardens: one acre of sweet corn, a potato garden, a general-purpose garden, and a "wildlife" garden.

Starting Seeds Indoors

Many plants do best if the seeds are started indoors, well in advance of the actual planting date. These plants include tomatoes, peppers, cabbage, broccoli, cauliflower, and even cucumbers, squash, cantaloupes, and watermelon. Seed starting is fairly easy and it's a fun task for late winter/early spring. Most plants do best if they're started six to eight weeks ahead of their planned planting date, which should be after the last frost for plants such as tomatoes. Other, hardier plants that do best in cool weather should be planted earlier. These include broccoli and cabbage.

I start most seeds in wooden flats. These are basically one and a half inches deep, made of white cedar. It's hard to water seedlings from the top and watering from the top also sometimes causes damp-off. Therefore, I water with a wicking system. A piece of half-inch soft nylon rope is coiled in the bottom of the seed flat with about eighteen inches of the rope left hanging out. Once the starting soil has been placed in the flat

RAISING VEGETABLES, BERRIES, AND FRUITS IS AN OLD-TIME SKILL MANY OF TODAY'S MODERN GARDENERS ENJOY.

and the seeds planted, I insert the hanging end into a fruit jar filled with water. This is a very simple and easy way to keep the flat watered without under- or overwatering.

You can purchase seed-starting mixtures or make up your own. There are basically two methods that can be used. Some gardeners like to start seeds in rich compost mixed half and half with good garden soil. Another mix is one-half potting soil and one-half good garden soil. In this case, the plants are often left in the mix until they are planted in the garden. Another method is to start the seeds in a mixture of equal parts perlite, milled sphagnum moss, and vermiculite. In this case, the seeds are started in the mixture and then transplanted into a growing mixture. Both methods work depending on the seeds. I like to start peppers, tomatoes, broccoli, and cabbage, as well as tiny flower seeds in the latter. In the case of cucumbers, watermelon, and the like, the seed is started in the compost/garden soil mix in peat pots, and then planted directly into the garden, pot and all.

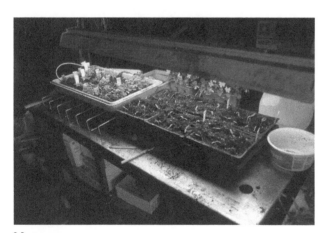

MANY SEEDS CAN AND SHOULD BE STARTED INDOORS. BOTTOM HEAT AND A FLUORESCENT LIGHT CAN STIMULATE GROWTH.

Place a double layer of newspaper in the bottom of the flats. Fill the flats with the starting mixture and tap water until the mixture is well soaked throughout. Allow the soil and water to sit for a few hours to assure the water is well distributed. The next step is to plant the seeds. Follow the instructions on the seed package label as to the depth they should be planted. Some seeds must be covered to germinate; some need light and are simply pressed down to ensure contact with the soil. I like to start the seeds in tiny rows in the flat. I make little furrows by pushing a thin wooden stick down into the soil about one-quarter inch. The seeds that need light are then dropped into place and pressed with the stick. Those seeds that need covering are covered to the depth of the furrow. Planting in rows also makes it easy to identify the plants. I often start as many as a dozen different varieties in one flat. I make plastic markers from discarded cottage cheese and margarine tubs. Simply cut about half-inch wide and two-inches long strips and use a pen to identify each section or row. I used to then place a piece of plastic wrap over the flat and sit it in a warm sunny location with temperatures around 65° to 70°F. For the past dozen or so years, however, I've started plants under a shop light with fluorescent bulbs. I also provide bottom heat with a seed-starting warmer mat placed beneath the flat. This is especially effective for slow-starting seeds such as peppers. Once the seeds begin to sprout, remove the plastic.

When the seedlings have acquired two sets of leaves, transplant them into individual containers. I use recycled purchased, divided plastic seed flats. I've also used plastic and paper coffee cups for planting individual seedlings. A growing

A SIMPLE WOODEN SEED FLAT WITH A JAR OF WATER AND SOFT ROPE FOR A WICK PROVIDES STEADY MOISTURE.

or potting soil should be used for the transplants. Again, you can purchase or make up your own mixture. A simple mixture consists of equal parts sifted compost and vermiculite or perlite. A richer version is one part compost, two parts potting soil, and one part well-rotted manure. Mix well together, and then place in the containers. I like to set the containers in a deep pan and water until the soil is well soaked. I punch holes in the bottom of the containers. This prevents overwatering and allows for bottom watering.

Allow the soil to soak for a few hours to equalize, and then push a pencil or small stick down in the center of the container. Wiggle the pencil around to create a large enough hole to insert the seedling. Use a wooden Popsicle stick to gently pry the seedling out of the starting mix. Grasp the seedling with a leaf and lift up gently. Then place in the growing mix, and use the pencil end to gently press the soil around the seedling.

The seedlings should be kept in a greenhouse, cold frame, or other warm location to receive filtered, but not direct sunlight. You can also continue to grow them indoors under the grow lights. Cold frames are a simple way of holding seedlings until they can be planted in the garden, and are also great to harden off the seedlings. Cold frames can be made of discarded storm windows and a few boards. Place the transplanted seedlings in the cold frame and after a few days, when the days warm up, open the lid slightly to allow in cooler air. As the weather continues to grow warmer, you can gradually open the cold frame wider until they're full open all day. Close the cold frame at night until after the last frost. If you don't have a cold frame, about a week before you intend to plant them, sit the seedlings outside on the north side of the house or under shade. The seedlings should also be protected from wind, as it tends to dry the tender plants out. On the first day allow the plants only about an hour of exposure and then bring them back indoors. Continue adding time outdoors during the week until the plants can withstand full exposure.

ONCE THE SEEDS HAVE GERMINATED AND GROWN TRUE LEAVES, THEY'RE TRANSPLANTED INTO SMALL INDIVIDUAL CONTAINERS. THE SEEDLINGS ARE THEN GROWN ON A SUNNY WINDOWSILL OR GREENHOUSE UNTIL THEY CAN BE PLANTED IN THE GARDEN.

Transplanting

Although each plant has different transplanting requirements, a few general rules should be followed. Transplant late in the afternoon or early in the evening. This lessens the shock of full sun and wind exposure in the garden. Make sure you dig a hole large enough for the seedling as well as all the soil in the container and the root ball. Turn the container upside down and gently rap on the bottom to loosen the root ball. At the same time, hold your hand beneath the container to catch the loosened seedling and root ball. Place the plant in the hole, making sure all roots are spread out evenly. Fill the hole around the plant with loose soil and gently press the soil in place. Leave a slight depression around the plant to gather water. Sprinkle at least a quart of water around each transplant.

Planning Your Garden

A successful garden requires a good site, although with diligent work you can turn a poor site into a productive garden. Drainage is the most important factor. A well-drained area is best. A low-lying site, which holds standing water, is a poor site. Normally, a well-drained site will have suitable soil. Sites in low, flat areas may have clay or be hard-panned because of the standing water. The presence of run-off water and clay in the soil does not allow the roots to breathe, and it's hard to build up organic materials in this type of soil.

The best garden soils are loose and friable with few rocks. Unfortunately, our hillside Ozark garden has plenty of rocks. We simply work around them, removing a few each season. Adding compost each year to the garden helps build-up organic matter. We also mulch much of our garden with old hay, which also helps build up the soil. Regardless, it is necessary to take a soil test to determine soil fertility and pH. Take the soil test to your local Extension Service office. In about a week, you'll have the results indicating pH and fertilizer requirements. Most plants do best with a pH of around 7. In many instances, you will have to add lime to adjust the pH, and then add the fertilizer as indicated by the soil test.

it to catch rainwater. Turn the pile once a week with a pitchfork and it should be rich black compost in a couple of months. A power shredder can speed up the process by breaking the materials into smaller pieces before placing in the pile. If the pile is correctly made it will heat up, causing rapid breakdown of the organic materials. Temperatures may reach as high as 150°F. If the pile doesn't heat up in a couple of days, add more nitrogen in the form of manure.

If you have a large garden that needs compost, you can make sheet compost. This is done by spreading the organic materials on the garden plot itself. Turn them under to decompose right where they are. Include plenty of nitrogen-rich natural fertilizers. You can use the compost in just about any way in your garden and orchard to add nutrients and humus to the soil. It should not, however, be used by itself as a potting soil for flowers or vegetables, or for starting seeds.

Compost

Compost is the main ingredient in a successful garden. It's easy to make, and a great way of disposing of unwanted organic materials. Just about everything from grass clippings to leaves and twigs can go into the compost pile. Although compost can be created in a large garbage can, the best method is in a compost bin, which is a simple wooden bin 5 by 5 by 5 feet in size. Leave one side open to work the materials. Layer the materials in the bin, for instance, a layer of twigs and branches, a layer of leaves and grass, a layer of manure, a layer of leaves or grass, a layer of manure, a layer of garden soil, a layer of wood ashes, and so forth, until you have the bin almost full. Soak the pile thoroughly with water. Add a bit of garden soil on top and create a depression in

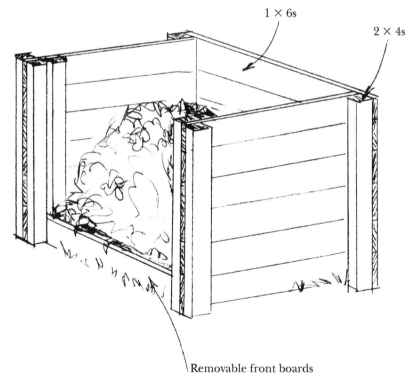

1 × 6s

2 × 4s

Removable front boards

COMPOST IS EASY TO MAKE AND CAN ADD TO THE PRODUCTIVENESS OF YOUR GARDEN OR FLOWERS. IT IS ALSO A GREAT WAY OF GETTING RID OF GARDEN REFUSE. A COMPOST BIN WITH A REMOVABLE FRONT MAKES THE CHORE EASIER.

Another method of adding soil fertility is to grow green manure crops during the off-gardening season. Green manure crops are started in the fall. They protect the soil from erosion and compaction from raindrops. About three weeks before planting time, turn the crop under using a rotary tiller or plow. A green manure crop can reduce fertilizer needs by one-half. Good plants for a green manure crop include sweet clover, winter wheat, and rye.

It's a good idea to plan your garden well in advance of the season. Draw a simple graph showing where you want to plant what. Many plants do best if rotated from one spot to another each year because this cuts down on pests and diseases. Keep a garden record book each year of the varieties used and how successful they were.

Plant Selection

In the olden days, most gardeners saved their seeds for use the following season. In some instances, they were limited in the varieties they could grow, but a wide variety of plant species are available for today's gardener. Following are tips on the most common plants.

Asparagus: A well-drained site with rich soil is needed for asparagus because the roots will grow five or six feet into the soil. Dig a trench eighteen inches deep and fill the bottom with compost. Next, cover with three inches of good garden soil. Set the crowns twelve to eighteen inches apart. Spread out the roots and cover the crowns and roots with two inches of soil. As the plants develop, gradually fill the trench with soil. Each spring feed the plot with three pounds 12-12-12 or similar fertilizer per 100 square feet. Make sure to thoroughly work the fertilizer into the soil before growth starts. Remove the tops of the plants in the fall in the south. In the north, remove the tops in the spring. Asparagus should only be harvested very lightly the second year of growth. A full crop can be harvested the third year.

Beans: Snap pod, shelled, and dried beans are garden favorites. Beans prefer a well-drained soil of average fertility. Bean seeds are cold sensitive. The soil must be at least 70°F for snap beans and 75°F for lima beams to germinate. Beans mature within two months. Successive plantings every third week can provide a constant supply. Plant bush beans two to three inches apart. Plant pole beans in hills three to four plants to a hill and spaced about three feet apart.

Beets: Beets prefer a well-drained sandy loam soil. Sow the seeds directly in the garden as soon as the soil warms. Soaking the seeds overnight in water before planting will help increase germination. Beet seeds are actually made up of a cluster of three to four seeds. The seedlings must be thinned to two inches apart to prevent overcrowding. Use the thinnings for greens. Make sure the soil doesn't dry out, as water is essential for growing beets. Sow seeds from May through July, every three weeks, for a continuous supply of beets into November. Use a high potash fertilizer to side dress the plants once the bulbs start forming.

Broccoli: The best broccoli heads are grown in cool weather. The seeds may be started in late winter and the plants set out in early spring. Cover the plants during any late frosts. An alternative is to direct seed in early summer for a fall harvest. You can also start seeds indoors and transplant them outdoors, spacing them twelve to eighteen inches apart. Use a complete fertilizer to side dress the plants once a month. Use about one pound of fertilizer to each twenty-five-foot row.

Brussels sprouts: Grow as for broccoli.

Cabbage: Cabbage can be direct seeded, but it does best when transplanted. Seeds can be started in late winter and transplanted in early spring, again, as long as you are prepared to cover the tender young seedlings in case of frost. Economical covers can be made of discarded plastic milk jugs, by cutting off the top. Early summer plantings can also be made for fall harvesting. Side dress with nitrogen when the plants are about half grown.

Carrots: A plot free of stones and with a sandy loam is best for carrots. Raised beds that receive minimum compaction are also good choices. Germination is slow. As the seed is very fine, thinning is necessary to prevent overcrowding. As the plants grow, add loose soil around the root crowns to prevent green tops. Fertilize the plot before planting with one pound of general fertilizer per fifty-foot row. Side dress with nitrogen when the plants are half grown.

Cauliflower: The best cauliflower heads are grown rapidly and mature in cool weather. Seeds can be direct seeded, but they do best when transplanted. Once the heads become about the size of a golf ball, they should be blanched by gathering the leaves around the head and tying at the top with twine. Seeds can be planted in July for a fall harvest. Cauliflower can overwinter in the south.

Cucumber: Very sensitive to cold, cucumbers must be planted well after the last frost date. You can also protect the plants with row covers if planted earlier. Work in a gallon of well-rotted manure or compost at each hill before planting. Make sure the seeds do not come in contact with the manure. Once the seeds sprout, place mulch around them to cut down on weeding chores. Cucumbers will also easily grow up a trellis making them easier to grow in limited spaces. Space the plants six inches apart in a single row. A cattle panel bent into a U shape is an excellent trellis.

Eggplant: Start the seeds indoors eight to ten weeks before transplanting. Eggplant prefers a rich, sandy loam soil. Do not plant in areas that have had tomatoes, peppers, potatoes, strawberries, or another eggplant crop, for several years.

Lettuce: A wide variety of lettuce species is available and they are all fairly easy to grow. We like to grow lettuce in raised beds. It's planted in rows, which makes it easy to keep the weeds out. By sowing every two weeks throughout the spring, we can keep a steady supply of vitamin-rich lettuce through the summer.

Muskmelon: If you have a short growing season, seed the melons in peat pots indoors a couple of weeks before transplanting outdoors or you can direct seed in the garden well after the last frost date. The young plants must be protected from the wind until they become hardened.

Okra: Okra prefers hot, humid weather. The seeds germinate better if soaked before planting. Plant seeds an inch deep in rows that are three feet apart. Keep well watered.

Onions: Onions can be grown from sets, bulbs, or seeds. Onion sets can provide the first crop if planted as soon as the ground can be worked. Onions are fairly frost resistant and grow best in cool weather. A quart of sets will plant about fifty feet. Plant the onion sets about one to two inches deep and three inches apart. Fertilize at planting time, then again when the plants are about six inches tall. Onion plants are young onions that have already sprouted. They should be set four inches apart and about one inch deep. Put out plenty, and thin, using them as green onions. You can also start onions from seeds.

Peas: Peas should be planted as early in the spring as the soil can be worked. Peas will germinate in temperatures ranging from 60° to 65°F. Many varieties require trellising because the vines grow long. Some smaller bush varieties are also available. You can also plant late varieties for fall harvest. You can get better success by using an inoculant, which provides the proper live bacteria needed to help legumes take nitrogen from the air. Plant two inches deep in rows two feet apart. Thin to two-inch spacing after the seeds germinate.

Peppers: Regardless of whether sweet, hot, or in-between, all peppers are grown the same way. Peppers like warm weather and they should be started indoors six to eight weeks before transplanting. Pepper seedlings should not be transplanted in the garden until nighttime temperatures do not fall below 60°F. Peppers will grow with moderate fertilization. Mulching increases production. Black plastic mulch can help maintain soil temperature and moisture. After many years of growing peppers, I finally got smart and grow them in the same manner as tomatoes, with a soaker hose and mulch. The peppers are also staked to prevent them from falling over. Peppers like a lot of water, at least once a week.

FOR BIGGER, BETTER PEPPERS TRY STAKING AND TYING THEM, WITH A SOAKER HOSE RUN BENEATH A LAYER OF MULCH.

Potatoes: Seed potatoes are first cut into chunks about one to one and one-half inches in size, with at least one eye for each chunk. Before planting, apply well-rotted manure, or ten pounds high phosphate fertilizer per fifty-foot row. Dig a furrow and place the cut potato pieces cut-side down about twelve inches apart in rows two feet apart. You can also grow potatoes in an old tire ring. Place a tire on the ground, fill it with soil, and plant the pieces. As the plant grows, add another tire and more soil. Continue doing so until the plants mature.

Pumpkins: Easy to grow, these fall favorites were often planted by the old-timers as a com-panion crop to sweet corn. They are planted in hills in the corn rows as soon as the soil warms. You can also plant them separately; however, they do take up a lot of space. Pinch back excessive vine growth and pinch off all but two pumpkins per vine.

Radish: A quick, easy-to-grow crop, radishes should be planted in loose, well-cultivated soil so they can grow quickly. They can be sown as soon as the soil can be worked. Sow at three-week intervals to provide a long-lasting crop.

Rhubarb: Rhubarb can be planted in spring or fall. Space the plants about three feet apart. Place the crowns one and a half to two inches below the soil surface. Keep well watered and cultivated. Use ample compost the first year for generous feeding. Do not harvest the first year. Harvest very lightly the second year.

Spinach: Plant as early in the spring as the ground can be worked. You can also plant in the fall and the seeds will overwinter for an early-spring harvest in some areas.

Summer squash and **winter squash:** Summer squash is easy to grow. You can plant the seeds indoors in peat pots and transplant to the garden after all frost danger, or direct seed in the garden. Winter squash takes longer to mature, but is planted and grown in the same manner. Some winter squash have long trailing vines that require quite a bit of growing space.

Sweet corn: Today's sweet corn is far removed from the corn cultivated by the early Native Americans. Most species these days have a single recessive gene known as Sugary-1. This enables it to produce and retain more sugar. Several different genetic classes are available: Normal Sugary (su) is the standard sweet corn grown for many years. It loses its sweetness fairly quickly after harvesting and will germinate in soil 50° to 55°F. Sugary Enhance (se), has a modified gene that increases the level of sugar and slows the conversion to starch, which extends the flavor. Most se corns grow best at 60°F soil temperature. Supersweet or Extra Sweet (sh) corn has a shrunken gene that raises the original level of sugars even further and extends the

SWEET CORN IS A VERY POPULAR VEGETABLE AND IT'S EASY
TO GROW. TODAY'S "SWEETER SPECIES" ARE BETTER TASTING
AND LAST LONGER IN STORAGE.

MINERAL OIL DROPPED INTO THE SILKS AT TASSEL TIME
CAN HELP PREVENT WORMS FROM GETTING TO THE EARS.

flavor over a longer period of time. The sh corn must be planted in soils of at least 70°F for good germination. They should also be isolated from all other corns to prevent cross-pollination. All classes of seeds are available in white, yellow, or bicolor species.

Corn should be planted about twelve inches apart in rows three feet apart, and in blocks of at least three rows. Short, solid blocks are better than three long rows for good germination. As soon as the seeds sprout, fertilize with a general-purpose fertilizer. Side dress with nitrogen when the plants are six inches high and again when

they begin to create silks. One trick my dad used to prevent worms in the ends of the corn was to place a drop of mineral oil in the tip of each ear just as the corn began to tassel.

Sweet potatoes: Create a large ridge about twelve to eighteen inches high. Set the plants ten to eighteen inches apart. Place the roots well in the ground, but do not cover the bud. Pour a bit of water around each plant and firm it up. Mulch well. Black plastic mulch is a great way of growing sweet potatoes. Create the ridge and place the plastic on it. This can be done a couple of weeks before planting time and will help warm the soil. In late afternoon cut slits about twelve inches apart in the plastic and transplant the plants. Water well.

Swiss chard: An easy-growing plant that provides edible leaves and stalks. Plant and grow like spinach.

Tomatoes: Almost everyone's favorite, tomatoes are easy and fun to grow. My granddad and dad were both tomato "freaks," and I sort of inherited the passion for growing tomatoes. We often put out a hundred or more plants and can lots of tomato juice, whole tomatoes, taco sauce, and spaghetti sauce, as well as salsa. Over the years, I've used some of my dad's tricks and added a few of my own. Start tomatoes indoors about six weeks before they should be transplanted in the garden, which is after the last chance of frost. You can plant earlier with protective covering. Don't start tomato plants too early in the year, as they will become leggy and long if they are held for some time before transplanting. After the first true leaves appear, transplant to individual containers and hold until transplanting in the garden.

My tomatoes are grown two to a cage, but first a soaker hose is laid on the ground. A hole is dug on each side of the soaker hose and the plants placed in the holes, where I've dropped a teaspoon of Epsom salts. The plants are transplanted as deeply as possible, carefully bending the plant so much of the stem is buried as well. Once the plants reach about a foot in height, mulch is placed around them and the cages placed over them. The cages are made of hog wire and are about twenty-four inches in diameter. These are sturdy and will hold the plants, yet allow for easy picking. Every third cage also has a stake driven by it. The cages are all tied together at the top and to the stakes to prevent the wind from blowing them over. Tomatoes should not be overwatered, so I water once a week with the soaker hose. They should also not be over-fertilized, especially with nitrogen fertilizer. Superphosphate, bone meal, and muriate of potash are all good tomato fertilizers.

YOU CAN GROW BUSHELS OF TOMATOES USING MY SYSTEM OF 24-INCH DIAMETER HOMEMADE CAGES OF "HOG-WIRE" AND GROWING TWO PLANTS TO A CAGE. A SOAKER HOSE RUN BETWEEN THE PLANTS AND A THICK STRAW MULCH PROVIDES MOISTURE. ADD A SELF-FERTILIZING FEEDER TO THE SOAKER HOSE FOR EVEN MORE PRODUCTIVITY.

Turnips: A very easy to grow plant, turnips are normally sown in the fall, but can be sown early in the spring for a summer harvest. Turnips do not tolerate extreme heat. Make successive plantings for a longer season.

Watermelon: The seed can be started indoors about four weeks before transplanting. Start the seeds in peat pots and transplant pot and all after the last frost date. Or you can direct seed into the garden. Mulching around the plants helps cut down on weed problems. Black plastic mulch can increase harvest, as well as grow earlier and healthier plants.

Bugs and Disease

The healthier your soil, the fewer problems you'll have with bugs, worms, and disease. Broccoli, cauliflower, and cabbage are all susceptible to worms. Dusting with Sevin solves the problem quite easily, however. Tomato worms can be picked off and destroyed. As a kid I got a penny from my granddad for every worm I could find.

One old-fashioned method of helping reduce garden pests is companion plantings. Some plants can be beneficial to others. For instance, garlic will keep the cabbage lopper away from cabbage plants. Garlic planted with potatoes helps prevent potato blight. Horseradish planted near potatoes keeps away potato bugs. In fact, onions and chives and garlic will help keep away many garden pests. But you can't just stick any plants together. You should plant deep-rooted and shallow-rooted plants together, rather than two deep-rooted or two shallow-rooted plants. This prevents the plants from competing with each other. Height is also important. For instance it is unwise to plant corn and sunflowers together since they would compete for the sun. Alternating rows of plants, rather than planting a big block of the same variety also helps prevent bug infestation and disease.

Following are some companion suggestions: Beans can be planted with potatoes, cabbage, cauliflower, cucumbers, or carrots. Turnips and peas get along well. Corn goes well with beans, cucumbers, pumpkins, potatoes, squash, and peas. Beets can be planted with onions or kohlrabi. Carrots can be planted with onions, lettuce, chives, and peas. Cabbage can be planted with potatoes, dill, onions, and sage. Cauliflower can be planted with dill, potatoes, onions, and sage. Peas do well with turnips, radishes, carrots, cucumbers, beans, or corn. Cucumbers can be planted with corn, peas, sunflowers, or beans. Broccoli can be planted with potatoes, dill, onions, sage, beets, or onions. Tomatoes can be planted with carrots, parsley, or chives. Onions and garlic do well with lettuce, beets, and summer savory. Radishes can be planted with cucumbers, lettuce, or peas. Potatoes can be planted with corn, cabbage, beans, or horseradish. Lettuce can be planted with radishes, cucumbers, or carrots.

Many herbs can also be helpers. Sage and rosemary will help keep away the cabbage maggot and cabbageworm. A border of winter savory, marjoram, the mints, or tansy around your garden can keep many harmful insects away.

You can also plant flowers around your vegetable garden. A border of marigolds discourages soil nematodes, the whitefly, and Mexican bean beetles. Homemade pest deterrents can also be used. Ground up cayenne or other hot peppers can be mixed with finely ground garlic and the dust applied early in the morning after the dew has dried. It repels tomato worms, keeps rabbits from nipping young plants, and keeps away other pests. Mix together equal parts wood ashes and flour with salt added and dust on broccoli, cauliflower, or cabbage to keep the cabbageworms away.

Berries

Berries were invaluable assets to most old-timers. Strawberries, blackberries, blueberries, and raspberries were very important foods. Many of these berries were foraged from the wild, but industrious old-timers would often propagate the wild berries for their homestead.

Strawberries

You can grow strawberries, and the difference between store-bought, mealy, dry berries and big, luscious homegrown strawberries is unbelievable. It does, however, take some time to grow strawberries, and plenty of work. My dad was also passionate about strawberries and raised an abundance each year. The entire family enjoyed his efforts and he also enjoyed giving berries away to friends and neighbors.

Strawberries do best in a soil with good drainage and protection from cold air. A gentle southern exposure slope is ideal. The shallow roots of strawberries also require a soil that stays moist but not soggy. The soil should have plenty of organic matter.

Don't till up a patch of turf and plant strawberries. You're only asking for lots of work in keeping out the weeds such as quack, crab, or Bermuda grasses. The bed should be begun in early summer. Plow the bed and leave it fallow. In the fall plant a cover crop of rye and then in early winter turn under the cover crop. A good idea is to spread two bushels of well-rotted manure or compost per 100 square feet of row space. Till the manure in well before planting the berries. Strawberries require fertilization and adding a bit of general-purpose fertilizer at time of planting can also increase production.

Planting is usually done in early spring, about the same time you set out cabbages. For a home garden producing both fresh berries and berries for preserving, you'll need from fifty to a hundred plants. Strawberries are planted in one of three different methods: the hill system, the matted-row system, and the spaced-row system. The hill system is best for those with limited space. Plants are set from twelve to eighteen inches apart in all directions and all runners are removed as they form. This method grows extremely large berries and bears heavily for several years. The beds can be mulched with black plastic in cold climates.

In the matted-row system, plants are set twelve to twenty-four inches apart, in rows four

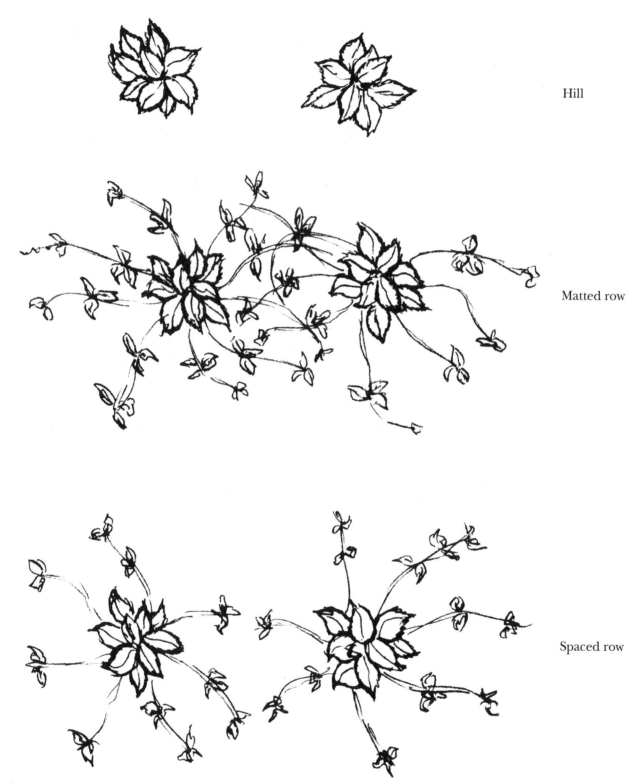

Hill

Matted row

Spaced row

STRAWBERRIES CAN BE GROWN IN ONE OF THREE SYSTEMS: HILL, MATTED ROW, OR SPACED ROW. SPACED ROW IS THE MOST COMMON FOR HOMEOWNERS.

to four and a half feet apart. Runners are allowed to form, but are trained outward to create a wide row. Although yields are not as abundant, this is the easiest and least time-consuming method.

The method recommended for most home gardens is the spaced-row system. In this method, the plants are set as for a matted row, but only the early runners, which make the most vigorous plants, are kept. Any runners formed after early to mid June are removed. Space the runners about seven inches apart and thin out the extras. This method also produces yields of high-quality fruit.

It's important to properly place the plants in the ground. The roots should be spread out as much as possible. The soil should be firmly seated against the plant and the roots, leaving no air space. The crown of the plant must be above ground level. It's best to plant strawberries as soon as you get them. A still, overcast day is the best time for planting. Don't let the roots dry out. One method is to set the plants in a bucket of water, take each out one at a time and plant. Water well. Some gardeners like to trim off a third of the roots and some of the leaves before planting. Keep well watered until the plants are settled in. Strawberry plants require water regularly. If rainfall falls short of one and a half inches per week, the plants should be watered. Sprinklers, soaker hoses, or drip irrigation may be used.

Weed controls can make all the difference between shining success and dismal failure. You must keep down the weeds. The first step is to apply Dacthal in a band over the row of newly set plants; this is effective for forty-five to sixty days in controlling grass and broadleaf weeds. Summertime weed control in the aisles is mostly by shallow cultivation. In late August, an application of Norex or Tenoran will control fall germinating weeds in the aisles.

Pinch off all strawberry blossoms the first year. In late fall apply maintenance fertilizer or compost. Mulch the patch with some type of mulch without weed seeds. Straw, sawdust, wood

chips or shavings, pine needles, or even dry leaves may be used.

The second year, watch for frost and be ready to cover the plants if it threatens. You're now ready for a feast. Strawberries again need lots of water, especially during bloom and harvest. Irrigation is necessary in dry climates.

You can either till in the plants after one bearing season, or renovate the bed. Renovation is not hard to do. Immediately after the last picking, mow the old foliage as close to the ground as possible without injuring the crowns of the plants, usually one to three inches above the crowns. Set your mower height so the old leaves are removed, but the new expanding leaves are not cut.

In a small patch, rake out the leaves and old mulch if there is any insect problem. If the soil is dry and irrigation is available, water the soil well. Then treat the bed with a maintenance fertilizer of one pound of 13:13:13 per 100-foot row.

Narrow the beds to eight to twelve inches. You can use a cultivator to narrow the rows, or remove one half the bed one year and the other half the next. Stretch a string where you want your bed to be and cultivate on one side. This will result in a nice straight row. Clean out the narrowed rows and thin the remaining plants, preferably by hoeing. Thin plants to about nine inches apart in rows. Apply herbicides such as Dacthal for weed and grass control. Irrigate after the patch has been renovated. If delayed by more than ten days after the last picking, it is better to only slightly narrow the rows, yet cultivate between them thoroughly. Late mowing of green active leaves can set the plants back. Severe narrowing of the rows too long after harvest leaves insufficient time for new runner plants to establish for the next crop.

Brambleberries
Both blackberries and raspberries freely grow wild. In fact, we've never planted either species because of their abundance. Both are available

Raspberries require cutting the fruiting canes to prevent spreading out of control and making the plant put energy into fruit rather than growing new canes. On yellow and red raspberries, cut off the fruiting canes in the fall after they have produced a crop. Pick out the heaviest canes to save. They should be spaced about four to six inches apart. These will then produce next year's crop. On purple and black raspberries, cut the new growth in the spring, cutting the canes back to eight to twelve buds. Prune to leave the canes from six to eight inches apart. All raspberries do best on a trellis or other support.

BRAMBLE PLANTS MUST BE PRUNED PROPERLY FOR GOOD PRODUCTION. BLACK RASPBERRIES SHOULD BE PRUNED IN THE SPRING, CUTTING THE CANES BACK TO EIGHT TO TWELVE BUDS AND SPACED SIX TO EIGHT INCHES APART.

Gooseberries and Currants

Gooseberries and currants do best in soil that is rich in organic materials, cool, and moist. In areas where summers are mild, these berries can be planted in full sun. In hot, dry areas, plant them in partial shade. Set the plants at the same depth as from the nursery and five feet apart in rows eight feet apart. Cut the stems back to half their original length. Add one cup of fertilizer to each plant each spring and prune out old, weak wood and unproductive branches older than three years early in the spring before any growth starts. The berries are produced on one-year-old wood. Mulch heavily and do not cultivate.

as domestic plants and are fairly easy to grow. Brambles do best in deep, well drained, and loamy soil with a lot of organic matter. They do not do well in soils that do not drain, leaving moisture around the roots. When planting, set the plants at the same depth they were at the nursery. Cut the tops back to about six inches. Blackberries should be spaced about five feet apart in rows eight to ten feet apart. Raspberries can be spaced more closely, from two to three feet apart in rows three feet apart. Apply a good general-purpose fertilizer, such as 12:12:12 at the rate of one pound per each 100 square feet. Remove the buds so the canes won't set fruit the first year. Water thoroughly, and then use mulch around the plants to maintain moisture and prevent weed growth.

Blueberries

Blueberries must be planted in well-drained porous soil and should have full sun most of the day. They require a pH of 4.5 to 5.5. If your soil is neutral or alkaline, add aluminum sulfate. Since the roots are extremely shallow, the

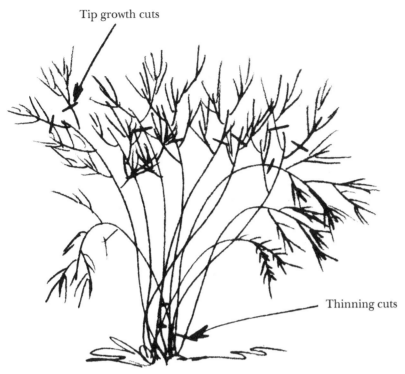

Tip growth cuts

Thinning cuts

AFTER THE SIXTH YEAR, PRUNE BLUEBERRIES LEAVING SIX TO EIGHT OF THE MOST VIGOROUS TWIGS. PRUNE IN EARLY SPRING WHILE THE PLANTS ARE STILL DORMANT. PRUNE OUT THE LATERALS.

have an abundance of organic materials. The best tactic is to lay out rows east to west, which reduces the shade cast by the trellis and successive rows. Work in a good amount of compost or well-rotted manure before planting. Cut back the tops to two buds above ground level. Set the plants eight feet apart in rows spaced ten feet apart. During the first year, allow the main stems to grow unchecked. The vines should be trained to grow on a trellis. The trellis consists of two wires; one wire is three feet and the second wire is five feet off the ground. Following a hard frost, but before winter sets in and while the plants are dormant, prune the old canes from the main stem. Leave four new canes, the shoots that started to grow the previous spring. Cut back the new canes to six to eight inches and with three to four buds. These buds will produce the new shoots that bear leaves and grapes the following year.

plants should be well mulched and watered in dry times. The plants should be spaced about four feet apart in rows eight to ten feet apart. Set the plants just a bit deeper than at the nursery. Make sure you incorporate lots of organic matter into the soil at planting time. Mulch well, but do not cultivate. Once the plants begin to produce, after the fifth or sixth year, prune out all but six to eight of the most vigorous canes early each spring while the plants are still dormant. Also, prune out twiggy stems and weak laterals. Blueberries also produce on one-year-old wood.

Grapes

Grapes were and are a very important food source. Grape jelly, jam, fresh grapes, juice, and wines are all from this popular plant. Grapes should be planted in a location that offers protection from strong winds as well as late frosts. The soil should be well drained, but

GRAPES REQUIRE TRELLISING AND PROPER PRUNING. AFTER A HARD FROST, PRUNE THE OLD CANES BACK FROM THE MAIN STEM. LEAVE FOUR NEW CANES AND SHOOTS THAT STARTED TO GROW THE PREVIOUS SPRING. CUT BACK THE NEW CANES TO SIX TO EIGHT INCHES WITH THREE OR FOUR BUDS.

The Home Orchard

My granddad, my dad, and now my wife and I have all had big orchards. We have about forty trees, including apples, pears, apricots, cherries, and peaches. Growing an orchard is hard work but not so much time consuming. Just remember that certain chores must be done at specific times to realize any fruit.

Fruit Trees

Many fruit trees are available as dwarf, semi-dwarf, and standard size. These days you can have an orchard much easier, faster, and using less space than with the old-time orchards. With dwarf trees, you can plant six trees on a ten-by-twenty-foot space. An orchard even this small can have apples, peaches, pears, and cherries and provide plenty of fruit for pies, canning, or just plain delicious fresh eating. Dwarf trees normally grow from six to eighteen feet high and usually produce fruit in the second growing season. You can expect from three to four bushels of apples from a dwarf tree. Semi-dwarf trees take up more space. They usually produce in two to three years and produce more fruit than dwarf trees. Standard trees must be spaced twenty to thirty-five feet apart in all directions, depending on the variety. They will grow up to twenty-five feet tall and produce in four to five years. A standard apple tree can produce up to twenty bushels of apples.

Many new fruit tree varieties these days are more insect and disease resistant than the trees of the past. Another advantage is that a number of varieties can be planted over a wider geographic region. These days, you can grow just about any fruit tree in any part of the country. Just be sure to check the zone map suggested by the nursery before purchasing.

Fruit trees are permanent fixtures. I know because I've planted fruit trees in places I later wished I hadn't. Make up an orchard or garden plan. Use a tape measure and measure the plot. Then, using a grid paper, locate the positions of the trees you want to plant. Remember, some trees are self-pollinators; some require pollinators. Most nurseries offer spacing charts for the different varieties and dwarf or standard size trees. You can reduce spacing for some trees by planting smaller trees between larger ones.

When planting, make sure you don't allow the roots to dry out. Follow planting instructions

MANY FRUIT TREES ARE AVAILABLE AS DWARF, SEMI-DWARF, OR STANDARD SIZE. THE FIRST STEP IN GROWING FRUITS IS SELECTING THE PROPER SIZE TREE TO FIT YOUR SPACE.

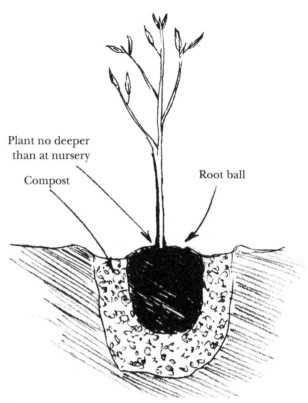

Plant no deeper than at nursery

Compost

Root ball

FOLLOW THE PLANTING INSTRUCTIONS THAT COME WITH YOUR PURCHASED TREE. MAKE SURE YOU DIG A LARGE HOLE, ADD COMPOST, AND WATER WELL.

that come with the trees you purchase. Make sure the planting hole is large enough so that the roots aren't crowded. The planting hole should also be deep enough that the tree can be set at the same depth as its nursery line. It's a good idea to dig the hole about twice as deep and twice as large as needed. Then fill the hole with half good-quality topsoil and half compost. Avoid clay soils, which can hold water around the roots, or prevent percolation from rainwater. Trim off all damaged roots before planting. Do not add powder or liquid fertilizer at the time of planting because it can burn the roots. Tree fertilizer tablets or time-released fertilizers can, however, be used.

Position the tree in the hole and if the roots are bare, spread the roots out well. Add several inches of soil around and over the roots and pack the soil firmly to remove any air pockets. Water well and allow it to soak in. Then add more soil, pack, and water again. Once completed, the hole should be one inch lower than the surrounding soil. This moatlike channel allows water to stand and soak into the soil, rather than run off. Mulch with hay, pine bark, or wood chips and keep well watered the first year.

Pruning

"Pruning trees is like raising kids," says pomologist Dr. Miklos Faust of the Agricultural Research Center at Beltsville, Maryland. "Start caring early or you're in trouble later." Dr. Faust points out that each kind of fruit tree demands a distinct pruning technique, but the key, for all trees, is to begin early, at planting or in the first spring. Following are his suggestions for the two most popular fruit trees grown by home gardeners.

Apple Trees

1. For apple trees, start with a four-foot sapling. Select lower scaffold branches. These should be located one and a half to two feet above the ground. Prune out all but about five of these branches,

PROPER PRUNING IS ONE OF THE MOST IMPORTANT ASPECTS OF SUCCESSFUL FRUIT GROWING. DIFFERENT TREES REQUIRE DIFFERENT PRUNING TACTICS.

APPLE TREE: CONE-SHAPED PRUNING METHOD.

spaced evenly around the trunk. This will form the first scaffold level.

2. Leave three more branches about one and a half feet above the lower scaffold. Clip all other branches back to the trunk.

3. Prune the center branch (leader) to form a cone with the two levels of scaffolds. This cut releases growth hormones for the scaffold branches.

4. Second year pruning: Prune each scaffold branch as a separate tree; that is, into a cone with each original branch as the leader.

   All pruning up to this point outlines the scaffold framework for the rest of the tree's life. All subsequent pruning is corrective in nature. "These cuts are the most difficult to decide," cautions Dr. Faust.

5. Prune all branches that oppose your scheme of scaffolding: those that grow too low, grow straight up, or cross over scaffolding branches.

6. Thin branches that may block light from fruiting limbs because apples form on the inside of the tree. (Peach trees fruit more toward the outside.)

7. The four- to six-year-old tree: Place braces between the trunk and any branches that form at angles less than 45 degrees to the trunk. The braces will help form an open framework, saving injury to, and providing light for, developing fruit. (Make braces from one by ones. Drive a nail halfway into each end. Cut off the nail heads. These points can then be sunk into the tree to hold the braces firmly in place.)

8. Place braces before spring pruning but not when wood is frozen. Longer braces can replace outgrown ones as your tree responds to spreading. Two years is usually sufficient for proper training.

   "Braces are absolutely necessary for spur-type apple trees because these are more upright than nonspur-types," says Dr. Faust. "Spurs, short interior shoots, bear large, gray fruiting buds (unlike smaller, brown leaf buds on longer shoots). Pruning the wrong buds will set fruiting back a year since buds begin to form in the June or July period prior to spring blossoming the following year.

"Apple trees are pruned heaviest in the early, formative years. Very little is necessary later to stimulate fruit development," says Dr. Faust, who prescribes just the opposite for peaches.

Peach Trees

1. The first year: Select scaffold branches to form wide angles with the trunk. This will help develop a strong, winter-hardy tree.
2. Prune down the central leader considerably in the first year and thereafter to eliminate it. This will allow growth to develop a basket shape.
3. Encourage fruiting by pruning the tree regularly. Look for branches bearing mostly non-fruiting, single-leaf buds. Fruiting buds are the outer pair of bud triplets.
4. Each year, bevel or clean up the middle of the tree so light can enter. After the second growing season, only light thinning is necessary to keep the center open and scaffold branches well spaced.
5. Watch to see that fruit-laden branches don't reach the breaking point. Each year fruiting wood tends to grow farther out on the branch ends. The basket shape can thus become too wide causing branch splitting. Keep the branches trimmed back yearly.

   Note: All pruning must be done in early spring, before the tree breaks dormancy.

PEACH TREE: BASKET-SHAPED PRUNING METHOD.

Fertilizing

Avoid over-fertilizing fruit trees. Too much fertilizer allows them to put all their energy into growing branches and leaves instead of fruit.

Insects

Next to pruning, the most critical factor in cultivating a productive orchard is insect control. Some insects can be controlled organically by removing diseased and dead limbs, picking up fallen fruit, and keeping the ground beneath the trees free of litter that harbors insects. One of the most important steps is applying dormant oil spray while the trees are still dormant and before their buds begin to swell. This oil smothers hibernating pests and their eggs. Peaches, nectarines, and apricots also require a fungicide applied with the dormant oil. This prevents a disease called "peach leaf curl."

A full orchard spray program can also be used to increase production. This is utilizing a purchased general-purpose fruit-tree spray. The spray is usually applied beginning with a dormant spray, then green tip, pre-bloom, full pink, blossom, petal fall, first cover, and second cover to harvest. For some fruits, the process may be repeated every ten days. For other fruits, the process may be repeated every fourteen days. It is important to carefully read the instructions supplied with the spray, not only for effective control of insects and disease but also for safe application and prevention of environmental hazards.

Nut Trees

Nut trees, including walnuts, pecans, butternuts, chestnuts, hazelnuts, and almonds, can also add to your home orchard. Many of these trees are also excellent shade trees. They grow best in full sun and in a well-drained soil and they should be planted in the same manner as described for fruit trees. Nut trees are normally not bothered by the pests and diseases of fruit trees. Almonds, however, are susceptible to peach leaf curl and should be sprayed with dormant oil. Most nut trees are also self-pollinating, although some require a pollinator. Make sure you check pollination requirements with varieties selected.

Starting Trees

Many trees and bushes can be propagated from cuttings. Hardwood tree cuttings are normally taken in the late autumn after the leaves have fallen from the deciduous plants.

1. Cut twigs from the ripe new wood of the past season. The twigs should be about six to eight inches in length. The cuttings should be cut straight across the bottom leaving a node or bud just above the cut.

AN INSECTICIDE SPRAY PROGRAM CAN INCREASE PRODUCTIVITY. MAKE SURE YOU FOLLOW ALL ENVIRONMENTAL AND SAFETY RULES LISTED ON THE MANUFACTURER'S LABEL.

The top should be cut on a slant, leaving a bud just below the cut.

2. Tie the cuttings in bundles and bury them butt ends up, outside in the soil and below frost line. You can also bury them in sand in your basement or cellar. If you keep the cuttings inside, make sure to keep the sand moist and cool.

3. When spring arrives, remove the cuttings, prune off the lower buds, dip in rooting medium, and plant in pots with a good potting soil. Cover the pot with a plastic bag and keep the cuttings in a cool place with filtered sunlight. Alternatively, you can plant the cuttings about six inches apart in your cold frame.

4. After the first growing season, transplant the tiny sprouts into a permanent nursery location.

Below frost level

YOU CAN START TREES FROM CUTTINGS. ONE METHOD IS TO BUNDLE THE CUTTINGS AND BURY THEM OUTSIDE IN THE SOIL. DIP IN ROOTING MEDIUM IN THE SPRING AND PLANT IN A COLD FRAME.

Brambles can easily be grown from cuttings. Just before the ground freezes solid, cut four-inch sections from roots that are about the thickness of a pencil. Place the root cuttings in sand and keep moist in your cellar or basement. Keep moist but not wet, and plant the root cuttings the next spring.

PART THREE

From the Woodlot

Timber was an extremely important material for the old-timers. And wood is still important to today's "homesteaders." A woodlot or timberland can supply materials for many things, including: logs for building homes and out-buildings; lumber for constructing and trimming buildings; lumber for furniture and other projects; firewood for heating; and a variety of materials for other projects, such as crafts.

Chainsaw Basics

The pioneers felled trees with crosscut saws and axes. It was and is hard work, and it takes a lot of time. Chainsaws make it much easier these days to gather wood. Just like any other tool, a chainsaw must be treated with respect both in the manner of safety as well as maintenance.

Safety Tips

Today's chainsaws are a far cry from those I used forty years ago on my father's farm. Today's saws are much safer and easier to use. But, you must follow a few safety rules.

1. Always make sure the chain is sharp. A dull chain causes you to put pressure on the saw and leaves you off guard should something unexpected happen.
2. Make sure the chain has the proper tension, and the clutch is properly adjusted. Check the chain brake to make sure it is working. The chain should not move while the saw is idling. If the chain moves while the saw is idling, you can get a nasty cut by falling on it, or brushing it against your body.
3. Start the saw on a firm surface, preferably the ground. Make sure nothing obstructs the guide bar and chain. Place your foot in the saw handle to make sure the saw sits securely on the ground while starting.

AXES AND CROSSCUT SAWS WERE THE WOODLOT TOOLS OF THE OLD-TIMERS. THESE ITEMS WILL STILL DO THE JOB, BUT IT TAKES A LOT OF WORK.

CHAINSAWS MAKE IT MUCH EASIER TO WORK WITH THE WOODLOT OR TIMBER. TODAY'S CHAINSAWS ARE ALSO EASIER AND SAFER TO USE.

ALWAYS WEAR SAFETY GEAR WHEN USING CHAINSAWS, INCLUDING EYE AND EAR PROTECTION, A SAFETY HELMET, LEATHER GLOVES, AND PROTECTIVE CLOTHING.

4. Always turn off the saw, or manually operate the chain brake before moving to make another cut.
5. Carefully plan your cutting chore. Examine the tree that is to be felled or the limbs to be removed to make sure they won't fall on power lines, buildings, equipment, or people. Avoid hazards such as dead limbs, roads, power lines, and bystanders. (Work at a safe distance, but never alone). Examine the lean of the tree to be felled and evaluate the wind direction.
6. Protect against kickback. Never remove or modify the chain brake. It is designed to reduce kickback and possible injury.
7. Clear all debris away from the cutting area. This is especially important when felling. If necessary, cut brush or saplings out of the way to create an escape route.
8. Never stand directly behind a tree you're felling. The butt of the tree can kick back up and injure or kill you.
9. Maintain a stable stance while cutting. Do not cut above chest height. Don't reach far out to make cuts.
10. Always refuel on the bare ground in an area where there is nothing flammable.

Prevent spilling fuel, and then move the saw a few feet from the fueling area before starting it.
11. Wear protective gear. This includes a hardhat, eye protection, and hearing protection. Logger's helmets combine these safety features. You should also wear leather gloves and protective chaps.

Don't let the precautions scare you. If used properly a chainsaw can be a very valuable tool.

Cutting Trees

In most instances, three steps are involved in collecting wood: felling the tree, limbing, and bucking or cutting the tree into the desired log lengths. It is important to carefully follow safe methods for all three.

Felling

First, examine the area around the tree to make sure the falling tree won't damage property, and keep other people and pets out of the area. Move your vehicle some distance away. (Many folks have dropped a tree right on top of their pickup.) Next, examine the lean of the tree. Most trees will have indications of the lean. This

TREE FELLING IS A VERY COMMON USE OF A CHAIN SAW. FOLLOW ALL SAFETY PRECAUTIONS. FIRST DETERMINE THE LEAN OR NATURAL "FALL" OF THE TREE.

may be the visible angle of the trunk. If in doubt, stand off about thirty feet and sight the trunk with a plumb bob. Do this from several sides. One side of the tree may have more or larger limbs than the other sides and this will also cause the tree to fall in that direction. If possible, fell the tree with the lean. You can change the direction to some degree, but it's difficult unless you're a pro. Determine the wind direction and force. Strong, gusty winds can push a tree in an unintended direction.

Next, examine the landing area, or where you intend the tree to fall. Examine surrounding trees to determine if there are other ones that may catch the falling tree and create a "hanger." Make sure nothing is around the base of the tree to impede your work, or prevent your escape. Locate at least two escape routes on the opposite sides of the tree from the intended felling direction. Make sure these paths are clear of obstacles that may trip you.

Two methods can be used for felling. The most common uses an undercut notch to help direct the fall of the tree. This is basically a V-shaped

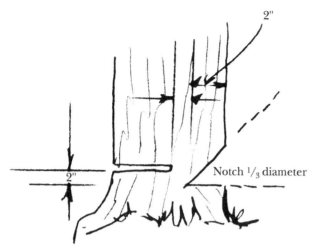

THE MOST COMMON FELLING METHOD IS THE "NOTCH" CUT.

notch cut on the fall side of the tree. Usually a
first cut is made parallel to the ground, and then
a slant cut from the top to create the notch. In
recent years a different type of notch, called an
"open face," has been used quite often. This consists of two slanting cuts, creating a 90-degree
angle rather than a 45. This allows the tree to fall
farther before the notch closes and provides a bit
more of a safety factor. The notch should be
about two-thirds the thickness of the trunk. Then
cut from the back of the tree towards the notch
and about two inches above the center of the
notch. Don't cut all the way through, but leave a
bit of wood between the notch and the back cut.
This acts as a hinge and helps prevent the tree
butt from jumping back and up in the air. Never
cut through the hinge because this prevents control of the fall. The width and angle of the hinge
can also act as a felling control. If an angle hinge
is used, the tree will start to fall on the narrow portion of the hinge.

As soon as the tree starts to fall, shut off the
saw and get away from the area as quickly as possible. If necessary, leave the saw behind.

For trees larger than the length of the saw
bar, another method is used as shown.

If the tree hangs up on another tree, do not
walk under it. Use a tractor, winch, or other means
to pull out the butt of the tree to release it.

MAKE A CUT PARALLEL TO THE GROUND ABOUT A THIRD OF
THE WAY THROUGH THE TREE.

MAKE A SLANTING CUT TO MEET THE FIRST CUT AND REMOVE
THE "WEDGE."

MAKE A THIRD CUT ABOUT TWO INCHES ABOVE THE NOTCH AND FROM THE BACK.

DO NOT CUT ALL THE WAY THROUGH TO THE NOTCH. LEAVE A "HINGE" OF WOOD, WHICH HELPS DIRECT THE FALL OF THE TREE AND PREVENTS THE BUTT FROM DANGEROUSLY JUMPING BACK AND UPWARD.

Limbing

The next step is to "limb," or remove the limbs from the tree. Always watch that you cut in such a manner that the tree won't sag and pinch or bind the saw chain, and always stand on the uphill side of the tree when cutting on sloping ground. Otherwise, when a limb is released, the tree may roll over on you. Never limb above your shoulders. This causes you to reach out, holding the saw at arm's length, and puts you in a dangerous position. Before limbing, examine the area to make sure saplings are not bent over and trapped under the limbs. When released, these saplings can spring back with deadly force.

Examine the other trees around the felled tree. Are there dead branches that may have been loosened and could fall in the area? They may not fall during the tree felling, but a few minutes later. These are called "widow makers" for a very good reason.

If cutting the limbs for firewood, start at the top of the tree and the outer ends of the limbs.

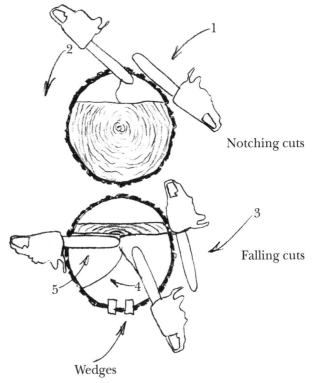

LARGER DIAMETER TREES REQUIRE A DIFFERENT METHOD.

THE NEXT STEP IS TO REMOVE THE LIMBS. DON'T STAND ON THE DOWNHILL SIDE. CUT ON THE OPPOSITE SIDE WHERE POSSIBLE. MAKE SURE YOU CUT SO THE SAW DOESN'T BIND FROM PRESSURE AS THE LIMBS BEGIN TO PART.

Also, start on the top limbs and work your way down. This eliminates cutting close to the ground with the saw. On limbs that are over your head, cut them off at the trunk first. If possible, cut from the opposite side of the log. This provides additional protection since it places the log between you and the saw. Cut the limbs off as close to the trunk as possible. This will make the log easier to move or roll for future operations. It is important to cut the limbs from the proper direction so they won't close up and bind the saw chain. Watch that the tree doesn't roll over on you when cutting lower limbs that may be under pressure.

Bucking

Cutting the log into usable lengths for either sawmill or firewood is called "bucking." Quite often bucking, especially on smaller trees that are being used for firewood, is done at the same time as limbing. In the case of a saw log, bucking is commonly done after the limbs and "top" are removed. For saw logs, a trim allowance must be made for final trimming at the mill. On eight-foot logs, for instance, a four-inch trim is normally added to the length. If the total length of the log is on the ground, the biggest problem in bucking is avoiding running the chainsaw into the ground. If the log is suspended in any manner at one end or the other, bucking becomes

more difficult. In this case, an over-cut is normally made one-third the diameter of the trunk, followed by an undercut to release the trunk. If a log has one end unsupported, the first cut is an undercut, followed by an over-cut.

Again, stand on the uphill side of the log when cutting. On smaller trees and logs, you can place the log over something to raise it off the ground and prevent the chain from digging into the ground. If you're cutting a large log into lengths for firewood, cut all lengths almost all the way through, but don't allow the chain to go completely through and into the ground. Then, using a log peavey, roll the log over and complete the cuts on all pieces to remove them.

BUCKING IS CUTTING THE TREE LIMBS OR TRUNKS INTO THE LENGTHS DESIRED. AGAIN, FOLLOW SAFETY RULES AND CUT TO PREVENT BINDING THE SAW.

Sawmills

Logs can be transported to a sawmill for milling into planks or lumber for any number of uses. Commercial sawmills most often do the sawing of logs into lumber, but these days portable, one-man sawmills are available. Portable mills, such as the TimberKing model shown below, have become increasingly popular. Not only can these mills be towed to the log, but they are also much safer and easier to use than circular mills. Rather than a huge, dangerous spinning blade, these machines utilize a heavy-duty band saw blade. The thin band saw blade doesn't waste as much material, and if you're cutting for rough projects, the wood surface is smooth enough for use without further work. The log can be cut into planks (lumber) or posts and beams for either type of construction.

THESE DAYS, ECONOMICAL ONE-MAN, PORTABLE, BAND SAW MILLS, SUCH AS THE TIMBERKING MODEL SHOWN, MAKES IT EASY AND FEASIBLE TO GAIN HIGHER PROFITS OR MORE WOOD PRODUCTS FROM YOUR WOODLOT.

Curing and Drying

If the wood is to be used in rough-sawn projects, construction beams, planking, or fencing, it is sometimes air-dried for a month or two, or even used immediately. Wood to be used for fine furniture, house trim, and other projects must first be dried. Most woods for this purpose must be dried down to 6 percent moisture. As with sawmills, commercial kilns can also kiln-dry woods for you. The simplest drying method, although the most time-consuming, is air-drying. This is an age-old method. I have air-dried many board feet of lumber in the loft of the barn. All that's required is a dry area with plenty of ventilation. It does, however, take quite a bit of time. Soft woods, such as cedar or pine, can air-dry in a couple of years. Hardwoods, such as oak or walnut may require from four to ten years, depending on the thickness and species. Air-dried wood should be conditioned for several months in your home or shop before using it.

SMALL LOGS, SUCH AS THIS WALNUT, WOULD BE "WASTE" IN A NORMAL LOGGING OPERATION. THE LOG SHOWN CAN BE USED FOR FURNITURE OR EVEN POST-AND-BEAM CONSTRUCTION.

The first step is to coat the ends of all boards with paraffin or boiled linseed oil. Then stack the wood on a perfectly flat surface with "stickers" or one-half by two-inch flat pieces of wood placed between the planks. These "stickers" prevent the boards or planks from twisting and warping, but allow the air to circulate and gently dry the wood cells.

Small quantities of wood can also be cured and dried at home with small kilns, including solar models. A number of small kiln designs are available on the Web from the Department of Forest Products, Virginia Polytechnic Institute and State University Extensions. A good deal of this information is linked through www.woodweb.com. Most of these kilns will dry woods such as walnut or oak in two to three months.

ROUGH PROJECTS CAN USE THE SAWN PLANKS AS IS. FOR BETTER RESULTS, THE PLANKS SHOULD BE DRIED. AIR-DRYING IS AN AGE-OLD METHOD. STICKERS MUST BE PLACED BETWEEN THE BOARDS TO PROVIDE CIRCULATION.

You will also need a moisture meter to determine the moisture percentage of the wood. The Lee Valley Tools Timber Check model is an excellent economical choice. Woodcraft Supply also has several models.

Once the wood has been properly cured and dried, it must be kept stored in a dry area and stacked perfectly flat. It can then be planed to the correct thickness. You can also create your own special molding for a very distinctive project or home office.

Log Construction

Log construction was one of the earliest forms of home and building construction. These days, log construction is still very popular. Some traditional log construction methods are still being used; other, newer methods have also been developed.

Hand Hewing Logs

Hewing logs to flatten their sides for building stacked-log or post-and-beam structures appears complicated but really isn't. It is, however, fairly hard work. If possible, the logs should be hewn while still green. The first step is to position the log up off the ground and onto short sections of wood. Fasten the log securely in place with log dogs so it won't roll. Then temporarily drive nails into the ends of the log on the side to be hewn. Snap a chalk line between the nails to create two lines to hew to. Turn the log with the side to be hewn facing outward. Then stand on the log and, with your feet well spread, use a scoring axe to make scoring cuts every six inches or so. Be sure of your footing, your axe control, and that the log is well secured.

Standing on the opposite side of the log from the scored side, use a broad axe (which has an offset handle) to cut from scored line to scored line. Wear steel-toed shoes and loggers' chaps to protect against an accidental cut. Use

LOG CONSTRUCTION IS TRIED AND TRUE AND AS POPULAR TODAY AS IN THE PAST.

69

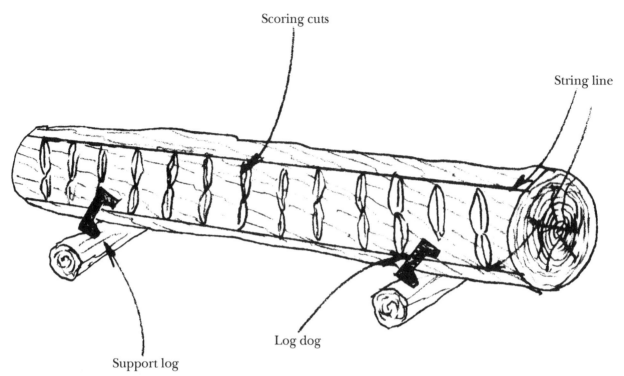

Scoring cuts

String line

Log dog

Support log

HEWN LOGS CAN BE USED FOR LOG-HOME BUILDING OR POST-AND-BEAM CONSTRUCTION. HEWING LOGS IS FAIRLY EASY. FIRST, THE LOG MUST BE DOGGED IN PLACE SO IT WON'T ROLL. THEN IT IS SCORED WITH AN AXE OR CHAIN SAW.

A BROAD OR HEWING AXE IS THEN USED TO CUT AWAY THE CHIPS BETWEEN THE SCORED LINES TO PRODUCE A "FLAT" SIDE.

short, controlled chops. You can shorten the process by first making the scoring cuts with a chainsaw. Logs can also be hewn using a foot adz, but the process is slower.

Stacked-Log Construction

Stacked-log construction of buildings can be of hand-hewn or peeled round logs. The hand-hewn logs normally utilize chinking between the logs. Round logs may either be chinked, chinkless, or splined. A variety of joints can also be used for log-home construction, depending on whether the logs are square hewn or round.

Log-home construction is fairly simple, but backbreaking hard work. It is, however, a method that can be done one step at a time, or rather one log at a time, over a period of time, rather than having to do all the construction at once as with other building methods. A home-built log home creates a great deal of self-satisfaction.

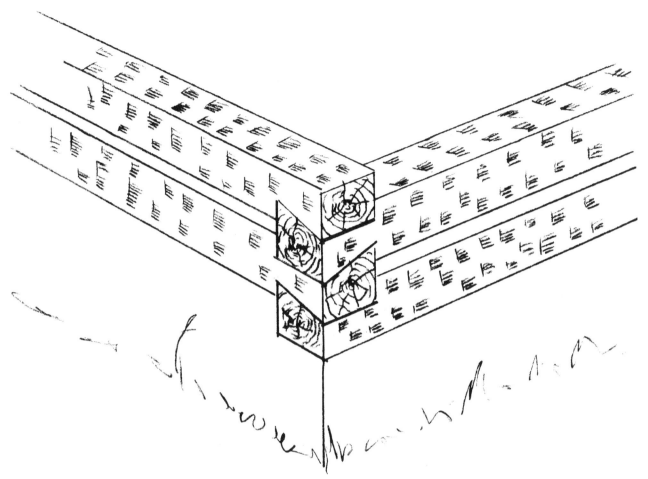

HAND-HEWN STACKED LOG CONSTRUCTION.

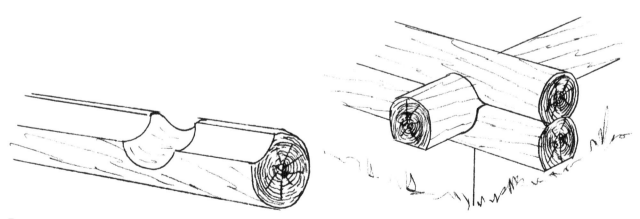

ROUND-LOG STACKED CONSTRUCTION.

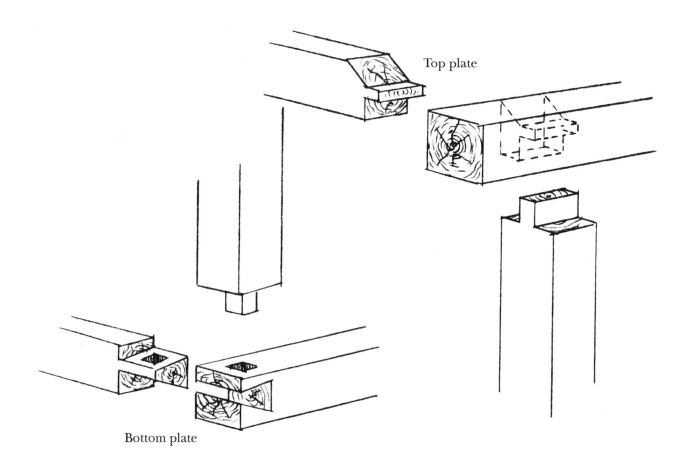

Top plate

Bottom plate

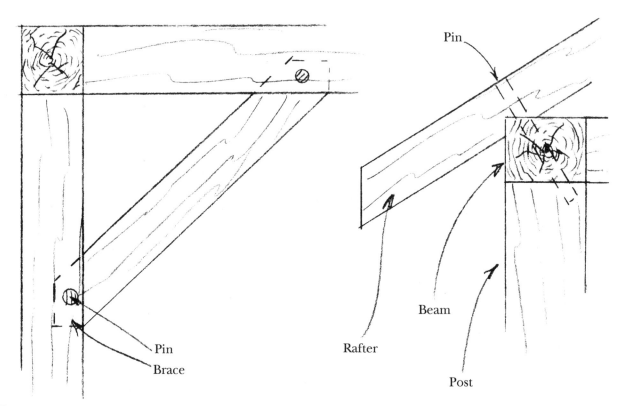

Pin

Pin

Brace

Rafter

Beam

Post

POST-AND-BEAM LOG CONSTRUCTION.

72

Post-and-Beam Construction
Hand-hewn or milled-square posts-and-beams can also be used to construct homes and outbuildings. Shown on previous page is a typical construction design.

Splitting Shakes and Shingles
If you have access to white oak, cypress, or white cedar you can create your own shakes or shingles. Shingles are sawn with a taper; shakes are split. You must have a clear, straight grained trunk at

YOU CAN ALSO MAKE YOUR OWN WOOD SHINGLES. A PART OF A LOG OR "BOLT" IS FIRST QUARTERED, AND THEN SHINGLES ARE SPLIT OFF USING AN OLD-TIME FROE.

least eighteen to twenty-four inches in diameter and the length desired, which is normally sixteen to eighteen inches. The logs are first sawn into lengths, called "bolts." Use a splitting wedge and maul to split the bolts into quarters. A large log should be further split into eighths. Place a froe about one-half to five-eighths inches from the edge of the grain of the block, following the radial lines of the grain. Drive the sharpened edge of the froe into the end of the block using a maul. Then turn and twist the handle to pry the shake away from the bolt. Once you have split a shake from the bolt, turn the bolt end-for-end and split off another shake. Work on the same face from which you cut the first shake. You will end up with a variety of shake widths.

Splitting Logs for Rails
No one can appreciate one of the great qualities of Abraham Lincoln until they have built a split-rail fence. It is hard work, but very rewarding. You'll not only have created a traditional piece of history, but also probably the most unusual fence in your neighborhood.

If you have a woodlot that needs thinning, you have a natural supply of logs for splitting into rails. Incidentally, selective thinning of many forests will create a healthier forest, and provide more habitat for wildlife. And, the meandering, brush-filled zigzag split rail fences that once covered much of Eastern North America were great wildlife havens. Woods such as cedar, white oak walnut, and locust split well and make long-lasting fences. The logs should be eight or nine feet long and seven to eight inches in diameter. You will need a heavy hammer or maul and a couple of log splitting wedges.

1. Drive a metal wedge directly into the center of the large end of the log to start the split.
2. Drive the second wedge into the split created on the log length, about eight inches from the first wedge.
3. Once the first wedge falls out from the crack created by the second wedge; move

Logs can be split into rails for fences. Beginning at one end, drive in a wedge to start the split, then "leap frog" a pair of wedges to create the split.

the first wedge down in front of the second wedge and drive it in until the second wedge becomes loose enough to remove.

4. Simply continue leap-frogging the wedges until you reach the end of the log.
5. The log should split in half as you reach the end. If it splits only on one side, turn it over and use the wedges to split that side as well. It may also be necessary to use an axe or hatchet to complete the split and separate some of the fibers.
6. Next, split the half logs into quarters in the same manner.
7. Place a large rock at each fence connection. Next, start laying the fence, overlapping each rail onto the next one. Continue until the fence is four or five rails high. The old-timers said the first rows or rails laid on the rocks should be laid in the light of the moon, so they wouldn't sink into the ground. If you wish to secure the rails together, simply drive 16-penny nails into the joints.

Split-rail fences are fairly easy to build and quite decorative.

Firewood

Wood is a very plentiful and accessible fuel. It comes from a renewable resource and when burned properly, is relatively clean. The value of the wood as a fuel depends on the type of wood, its density, and moisture content.

Choosing the Best Firewood

Any wood will burn, but the highest BTU per cord comes from heavier or denser woods. The moisture content of the wood is also important. Dense, air-dried hardwoods produce the greatest amount of heat. Dense hardwoods are best because they burn more slowly and produce more BTUs of heat volume than lighter, less-dense hardwoods. Dry wood delivers more usable heat because less energy is needed to drive out the wood's moisture while burning. Some of the best woods for burning include the oaks, the hickories, honey locust, black locust, Osage orange, mulberry, and sugar maple. The next best are ash, walnut, coffee tree, hackberry, the elms, and sycamore, which are moderately dense. The poorest hardwoods include soft maple, catalpa, cottonwood, willow, and box elder. Generally, evergreen species should be avoided due to their resin contents. These resins cause unwanted deposits in chimneys and flues, making them difficult to clean and subject to chimney fires.

When cutting firewood, available drying time should be considered before choosing species. All green trees store water in woody tissues. Some trees, such as cottonwoods and willows, contain more water than wood. Green cottonwood contains more moisture than wood, while other trees, such as green ash, are only about one-half moisture in standing trees. Trees with low natural moisture contents are the best choices for firewood use when limited drying time is available.

CUTTING YOUR OWN FIREWOOD WILL WARM YOU TWICE, AS THE OLD SAYING GOES, BUT IT'S PLEASANT WORK. AIR-DRIED HARDWOODS MAKE THE BEST FIREWOOD.

Generally, it takes up to nine months for firewood to dry to the normal 20-percent moisture content that is considered optimal for burning. This poses a problem for the user who waits until late in the year to replenish a woodpile. There is a trick, however, to help speed the drying process while allowing the cutter to wait for cool weather for the actual bucking and splitting chores. This involves cutting down whole, green trees during the growing season to allow the wilting leaves to pump moisture from the woody tissue. Once the trees are down and dead, they can be cut into firewood in a somewhat dried state.

Otherwise, cut and split as early as possible to hasten the drying process. Twelve-inch diameter round wood should be at least quartered for the fastest drying time. Cut more than you need and you can carry over a supply of dried wood for the following year, and also ensure the best heating wood.

Splitting and Bucking

If the logs haven't been cut into firewood lengths, a sturdy saw buck can be used to hold the logs up off the ground for easier cutting into the lengths needed.

LARGER PARTS SHOULD BE SPLIT USING A MAUL, OR WEDGES.

Splitting is an age-old job that requires little knowledge but a strong back and lots of work. Splitting wood will sure tone up those muscles. Don't try to hand split woods such as elm. You'll only end up spewing words your family shouldn't hear.

Wood splits much easier as soon as it is cut, rather than after it has cured. Using a splitting maul also makes the chore easier. A splitting maul is a heavy, wide-angled axe that really provides the weight and leverage needed for splitting logs.

Take a firm stance, make sure there is nobody or nothing to hit or hurt overhead or behind you, look directly at where you aim to strike, and swing with force. If you look carefully at the end of the wood chunk before starting to split it, you'll notice how the grain runs. Splitting with the grain is much easier than against it.

Of course, a powered wood splitter can take much of the chore out of splitting firewood.

A POWER SPLITTER MAKES THE CHORE QUICK AND EASY.

Storing Firewood

Stack the wood in loose piles up off the ground to allow as much air circulation as possible. A wood shed that allows plenty of sunlight but is covered to protect the wood from rewetting is the best choice.

PART FOUR

Old-Time Country Crafts

In the old days, crafting was not just a hobby; it was necessary to create utilitarian items. Yet, some of these "utilitarian" items were also objects of beauty around the homestead—quite often the only beauty available to the homesteaders. A few crafts *were* simply great fun, but most served a necessary purpose. Many of these same crafts can be as valuable to today's "homesteaders" as they were to the old-timers.

Basketry

Making baskets is an age-old skill that is just as much an art as it is a craft. Some of the most beautiful and valuable ancient works of art are handmade baskets.

Coiled Basket

One of the simplest baskets is the Native American coiled basket. The Native American baskets were made of grasses, leaves, wood strips, roots, and fibers. A coiled basket is made much like a coiled clay pot. A bundle of grasses or leaves is wrapped with a lashing of tree roots or cane. This wrapped bundle is then formed into a coil with the bottom of the basket started with a spiral. After the first spiral is started, the lashing is wrapped around the outside of the bundle, then laced though the next inside coil and pulled tightly to hold the coils together. A small bone or wooden awl was used to thread the cane through and tie the pieces together. A leather awl can also be used for the chore. As more grasses are added to the coil, it is wrapped with the cane, lashing the coils together as the material is wrapped.

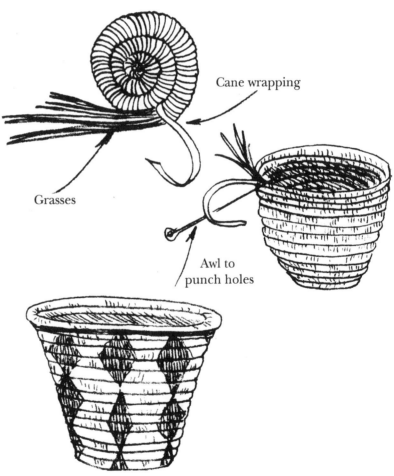

Cane wrapping

Grasses

Awl to punch holes

NATIVE AMERICANS MADE COILED BASKETS FROM GRASSES, LEAVES, ROOTS, AND FIBERS.

When the bottom is completed, the coils are started up to make the sides.

Willow or Cane Basket

Baskets can also be made entirely of cane or semi-rigid pieces of thin wood strips such as willow. The baskets were made in the manner of coiled baskets, however, instead of stitching into the previous coils, the cane is woven in and out in a variety of patterns.

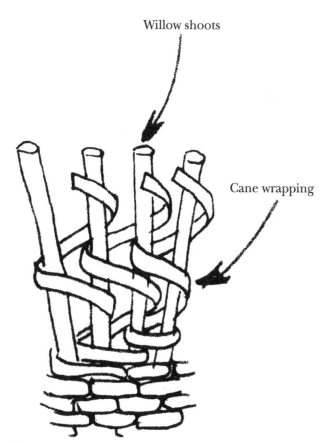

Willow shoots

Cane wrapping

BASKETS CAN ALSO BE MADE OF SEMI-RIGID PIECES SUCH AS WILLOW.

Wicker and Willow Baskets

Both willow and wicker, along with thin roots of plants such as buckbrush, were also woven into baskets. In this case, the bottom of the basket was often wood with spokes placed in holes bored in the wood base. The willow or wicker was then woven around the spokes to create the weave.

The top was finished off with a decorative border design.

Weaving Rush Baskets

Using rushes found in the wild, the old-timers also wove rush baskets. Other leaves, including iris, can also be used for baskets. The rushes must be dampened before use. Lay them out flat in a shady spot and sprinkle them with a watering can. They should not, however, be waterlogged. Roll the pieces in a piece of cloth such as an old sheet and leave overnight. Before using, flatten the rushes and then wipe each rush with a damp cloth. Remove any weakened tips.

The basket shown utilizes a simple check or single weave pattern of under one, over one. You'll need twenty rushes about one-half inch in diameter and forty inches long for the stakes. You'll need a dozen rushes one-half inch in diameter and full length for the side check weaves. You will also need finer rushes for the pairing weave. The basket is woven around a mold using a clay or plastic flowerpot approximately five inches across at the base.

- Insert a fine rush around the first stake, bending it in half at the stake. This creates weavers one and two.

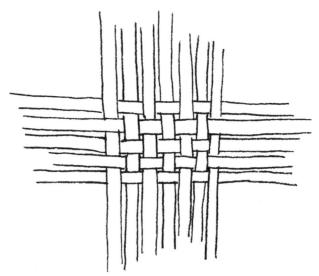

RUSH BASKETS WERE ALSO POPULAR WITH THE OLD-TIMERS.

- Pass weaver one over weaver two in front of the first stake, then behind the second stake.
- Pass weaver two over weaver one, in front of the second stake and behind the third stake. Weave the weavers alternately until you have completed two rounds.
- To add weavers, push another thin end of rush in place on the underside where it won't show and work the doubled weaver for two or three strokes. Keep the stakes evenly spaced as you work.
- With the third round separate the stakes and work them singly. With each subse-quent round, separate more of the stakes. By the time the bottom of the basket is large enough to fit the base of the flowerpot, all stakes should be single.
- Slip the base over the flowerpot and tie in place with soft string. Continue weaving in and out, over and under, to create the height needed. To finish off the top, draw the weavers back under four rounds using an awl. Trim the ends and allow the basket to dry thoroughly on the flowerpot.

Methods of making split baskets are covered in Part VII.

Corn Crafts

In the olden days, when everything was utilized, the corn patch was put to many uses. Mattresses were often made of sacks stuffed with dried corn shucks. They probably didn't last but one winter, but a new supply was readily available each fall. In the days before mechanical corn pickers, the corn ears were hand picked and the corn was fed on the cob or run through a hand-cranked corn sheller to produce shelled corn for both livestock and human use. The corncobs were saved in a dry place and used as fire starters, to make corncob pipes, as striker holders for turkey calls, and for any number of other household uses. After the corn was picked, the corn stalks were cut and tied into shocks to dry for livestock food. These days a corn-shock makes a great fall yard ornament and when fall passes, the stalks can be chopped up and added to your compost pile.

CORN WAS UTILIZED FOR MANY PUPROSES BY THE OLD-TIMERS, INCLUDING FOOD FOR HUMANS AND LIVESTOCK.

Corn Broom
One of the more unusual crafts was making brooms of "broomcorn." These brooms have become extremely popular at modern day craft shows. The first step is to purchase some broomcorn seed, which is available from lawn and garden specialty seed companies. Broomcorn is grown much like ordinary corn, only the seeds are planted more closely together. The plants grow rather tall, so plant the seeds at the back of your garden or next to a fence. In the fall, the seed heads will fill out. While the stalks are still quite green, cut off the top straw portions of the seed head. Place these gathered heads in a dry place in the sun and allow them to cure for a few days, and then shake and rake out the seeds. Use

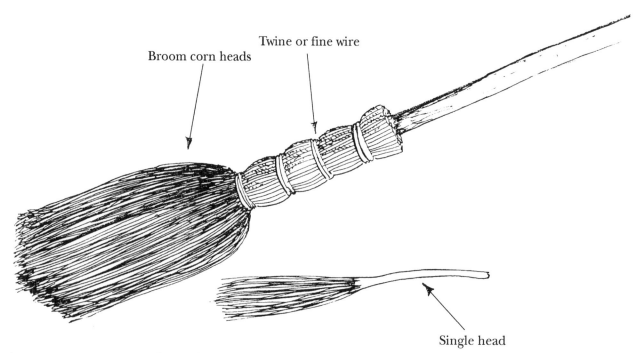

Broom corn heads

Twine or fine wire

Single head

A CORN BROOM, MADE FROM "BROOM" CORN HAS BECOME INCREASINGLY POPULAR AT MANY CRAFT SHOWS. YOU CAN GROW YOUR OWN BROOM.

an old fine-toothed handsaw or a coarse animal hair comb to rake out the seeds. You will need a cured wooden sapling of about three quarters of an inch in diameter, or a purchased wooden dowel, for the handle. Position the broom heads around one end of the handle and wrap tightly with fine wire or twine. Tie or twist to secure the heads tightly in place. Trim off the ends of the straws so they are even on the bottom end. You can also make a short hearth broom by eliminating the handle. Merely tie the broom heads tightly together in a bundle, wrapping the bundle the entire length to form a short handle, and then trim the bottom edges.

Corn Husk Doll
Making corn husk dolls was also a favorite pastime of pioneer children and it can be just as much fun for your children and grandchildren today as it was then. Save the husks or shucks from your garden corn and allow them to dry for

a couple of days or until they have a light, papery feeling. The corn silks can also be saved and used as "doll hair."

- Grasp a handful of husks and dampen them with water to make them pliable. Tie them tightly together at the top with string. Then fold the husks back over the tied end with the string inside. This creates the head. Tie around this with string to form the neck.
- Braid husks together to create the arms and tie at each end to make the hands. Place the braided arms through the husks below the neck and tie a string around the husks below the arms to create the waist. For little girl dolls, clip off the husks on the bottom end to create a skirt. For little boy dolls, separate the husks below the waist to create legs, braid and tie off to create feet.

THE HUSKS AND SILKS WERE UTILIZED TO MAKE CORN HUSK DOLLS BY THE PIONEERS. IT'S AN EASY AND FUN PROJECT ALL CHILDREN ENJOY.

- Draw eyes, nose, and mouth using a crayon. Use white glue to glue the dried corn silks in place for hair.

Once you've shown the kids how to make cornhusk dolls, give them a handful of husks, stand back, and watch the fun.

Candle Making

Candles were a necessity for our ancestors, but are probably more popular today than when they were actually needed. Today candles are a part of almost every decor with scented, decorative candles found in almost every home. Dinner candles should, however, always be unscented.

Hand-Dipped Candles

You can easily make hand-dipped candles the same way your grandmother did. It's easy and fun and requires very little in the way of equipment.

1. The first step is to make dipping frames. These can be made from sturdy metal coat hangers. Bend the coat hangers into a square frame. Tie four pieces of soft cotton twine vertically to the top and bottom of each frame. Special candle wicking is also available for purchase.
2. Wax for the candles must be melted using a double-boiler arrangement. One method is to suspend a discarded metal square gallon can in a home canner. The tops of the metal can edges are fastened to two sturdy wooden strips with screws. Be aware that both the inside and outside pans will probably be ruined for any other purposes.

   Caution: Above all else, never melt wax over an open flame. The wax can easily ignite and cause a dangerous fire. It's a good idea to wear a long-sleeved shirt, rubber gloves, and face goggles to prevent burns from wax that might splash or drip on you.
3. Break up enough paraffin or candle wax to almost fill the square center can. This should take about ten pounds of wax, which will make about sixteen candles. Add two or more crayons to color the wax or add candle coloring. You can also add scents such as vanilla. An old-fashioned way of scenting candles was to crush bayberries and boil for ten or fifteen minutes. Strain through a cloth and allow to cool. Then remove the wax from the top of the bayberry liquid and add to the candle wax. Heat the wax to 175°F using a candy thermometer to check the temperature.
4. Dip the dipping frame down into the wax. Slowly remove the frame and hang in a cool spot. Be careful handling the hot wax. Do not allow it to splash on you,

and hang the dipped frame in a place where the dripping wax won't harm anything. Allow to cool for five minutes.

5. Repeat the dip after the wax has cooled. After ten dips, every other dip should be about half way up on the candle to produce the taper. Approximately thirty dips altogether should produce a nicely tapered candle.

6. The last step is to clip the candles from the bottom of the frame and allow them to hang for two days. Store in a cool, dry place.

Decorative Candles
You can also easily create decorative candles using a variety of techniques.

Sand Candle
One of the more unusual and beautiful candles is a sand candle. These are great natural-appearing candles that go well with rustic decor. Coloring and scents can be added as desired. This is a some-

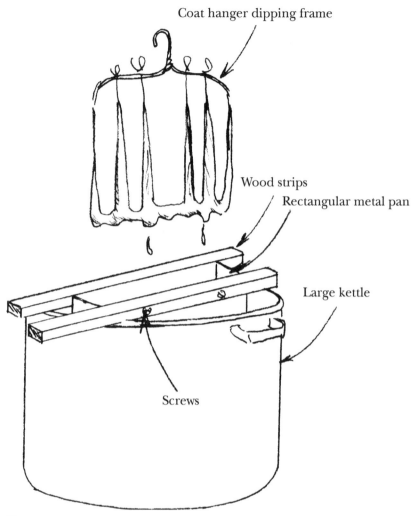

Coat hanger dipping frame

Wood strips

Rectangular metal pan

Large kettle

Screws

HAND-DIPPED CANDLES CAN BE MADE THE SAME WAY YOUR GRANDMOTHER MADE THEM. YOU'LL NEED CANDLE WAX, COLORING, WICKS, A DIPPING FRAME, AND A DOUBLE-BOILER ARRANGEMENT TO DIP IN.

what messy chore that is best done outside.

1. Fill a large bucket or tub with damp sand. The sand should be damp enough to mold in place with your hands. Scoop out a bowl-shaped depression in the center of the sand. If you wish, you can press some pretty rocks, shells, buttons, and so forth partly into the depression.

2. Tie a piece of candle wicking to a stick and place the stick across the top of the

tub or bucket. Allow the wick to hang down to the bottom of the depression. Tying the wick around a small washer or some decorative item will help hold the wick in place in the bottom of the candle.

3. Melt wax in a double-boiler arrangement and add scent and coloring as desired. One method is to suspend a metal gallon can inside a larger pot. The tops of the metal can edges are fastened to two sturdy wooden strips with screws. Be aware that the inside and outside cans or

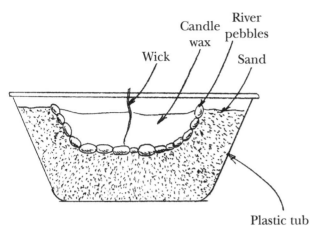

Candle wax
River pebbles
Wick
Sand
Plastic tub

SAND CANDLES ARE ALSO FUN AND EASY TO MAKE. MELTED WAX IS POURED IN A MOLD OF DAMP SAND.

pans will probably be ruined for any other uses.

Caution: Again, never melt wax over an open flame. The wax can easily ignite and cause a dangerous fire.

4. Wearing long-sleeved shirt, rubber gloves, and face goggles, carefully pour the melted and very hot wax into the mold. Allow to cool.

5. Gently lift out the candle and dust off the loose sand. The candle can be flattened on the bottom in order to sit properly or a leather sling can be made to hang the candle.

Stalagmite Candle

Another very unusual candle is a stalagmite candle. Merely coat the outside of a fruit jar with vegetable oil, then pour melted wax that has partially cooled over the jar and allow it to run down and form drips. Continue adding runs and drips to the jar until a solid form is built up. Remove this form from the fruit jar when completely cooled and place small votive candles inside the bowl created. This candle is especially pretty when a number of different colors of wax are used to form the bowl and is a good way to use up small, leftover portions of colored wax.

STALAGMITE CANDLES CAN BE MADE BY DRIPPING HOT WAX OVER AN UPTURNED, WELL-GREASED JELLY JAR. WHEN COOL, SIT UPRIGHT AND PLACE A VOTIVE CANDLE INSIDE.

Molded Candles

One great way of making candles is to copy items such as small statuary or cut glassware. Make a mold of the object using rubber-molding compound found at art supply stores. Follow the directions with the rubber-molding compound to make a mold sturdy enough to hold wax. Remove the rubber mold, add a wick, and fill with wax. Tie the candle wicking to a small washer to hold the wick in place in the bottom of the mold. Wrap the top end of the wick around a small stick suspended over the top of the mold and trim the wick after removing the candle from the form. To use these molds more than once, the candle will have to be easily removed from the mold.

Making Soap

With a little work, you can make your own soap, a very important product of the early settlers. The soap can be made from lard (pork fat), tallow (beef fat), fat from meat trimmings, or fat from a bear, a common source in the early days. You can also use a mixture of fats to create the soap.

Step by Step

For six pounds of tallow or lard, you'll need two and a half pints of cold water and one thirteen-ounce can of lye (in flake form).

1. Save all the trimmings from meat, as well as animal fat cooking grease. Keep this refrigerated or frozen until you have collected enough to make a batch of soap. Heat the fat, allowing all the impurities to settle to the bottom and then pour the clean grease off the top. Any fats or grease used in soap making must be free of dirt, lean meat, and must not be "spoiled."

2. Dissolve the can of lye in the water in a glass mixing bowl. Wear a long-sleeved shirt, rubber gloves, eye protection, and a facemask. Do not breathe in the vapors. Stir very slowly and be very careful. The lye is caustic and can cause bad burns. If you should splash lye on yourself, immediately wash with plenty of cold water.

3. Set the lye water aside and melt grease or fats to a clear liquid. Pour the clear liquid through a kitchen strainer and allow to cool until the liquid begins to offer resistance to stirring.

4. When both the lye mixture and the grease reach the temperatures shown on the accompanying chart (according to type of tallow or lard), very carefully pour the lye mixture into the melted grease in a steady, thin stream. Stir constantly as you pour. Continue stirring until the mixture reaches the consistency of thick honey (about ten to fifteen minutes).

5. Pour the thickened soap into a wooden frame lined with a wet cotton sheet. Cover the frame with a clean board, then with newspapers or an old blanket, and allow the soap to very slowly cool. In a couple of weeks, remove the soap from the wooden frame and cut into cakes.

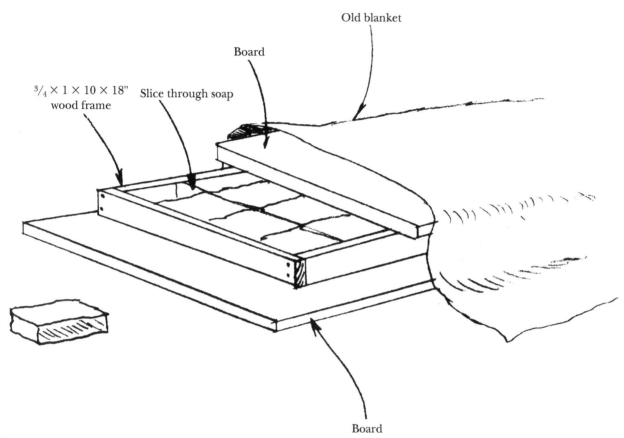

THE OLD-TIMERS MADE SOAP FROM ANIMAL FAT AND LYE. IT'S AN UNUSUAL, BUT INTERESTING OLD-TIME CRAFT.

The soap can be scented with a few drops of your favorite scent, or any scent that does not contain alcohol. The petals of your favorite fragrant flower or herb are also great additions.

Making Lye

You can also make your own lye from recycled wood ashes. You'll need a five-gallon can with a few drain holes punched in the center of the bottom of the can. Place a five-inch layer of straw in the bottom of the can, and then fill the can with ashes. Place the can on top of another five-gallon can and pour water on the ashes. Each day pour more water over the ashes as the water is absorbed. When the bottom can is full of "lye water," remove the solution. Boil this solution until a piece of soap or raw potato will float in it.

Caution: Be very careful in handling the lye water, as it is very caustic.

Temperature Chart

Fat

Lard or soft fat, 98° to 100°F	Lye 77° to 80°F
Tallow, 125° to 130°F	Lye 93° to 96°F
Half lard and half tallow, 105° to 110°F	Lye 83° to 86°F

Spinning, Dying, and Weaving

The settlers made their clothing from thread hand-spun from wool, which often came from their own sheep. Natural dyes taken from native plants or plants from their home gardens colored them. After that they were made into rugs, blankets, and clothing.

Spinning Wool

Numerous books and information sources are available on spinning, dying, and weaving wool for clothing or other items. There are many steps involved in spinning wool, and we can't cover all the details here, but we can cover the basics.

The first step is to wash the wool twice in warm water with detergent and then rinse in cold water. Do not over-wash or you will wash out all the oil, which makes the wool harder to spin.

The next step is to card the wool. Carding breaks it up and prepares the wool for spinning. Two sets of cards are used, breaking cards and fine cards. Rough-toothed breaking cards are used to separate the fibers. A handful of wool is placed on one card and the second card drawn across it with enough pressure to separate and fluff the wool. It may take two or three times to

fluff the wool properly. The wool is then rolled into "bats" or small rolls. Before spinning, the bats must be combed using a fine card. The same motion is used as before, separating the wool and placing it on one card, then drawing the other card across the wool to comb it until it is soft and silky. The final step is to roll the softened wool into rolls about one half to three quarters of an inch in diameter. These rolls are then ready for spinning.

In most instances, the wool was spun on a spinning wheel. These wooden works of art were a very important part of many homes in the olden days. The wool rolls were stretched, twisted, or "spun" into threads on the machines.

In most instances, the wool was spun in its natural color. A skein reeler was used to wind the threads into skeins. The skeins could then be hung or dipped in the hot dye.

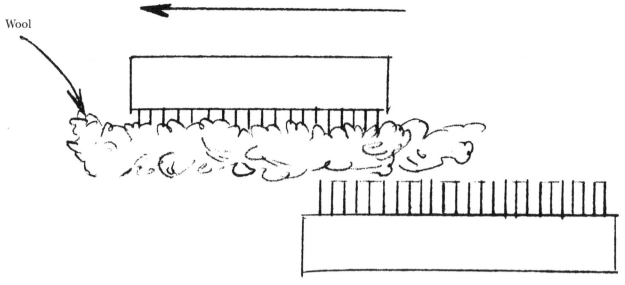

Wool

Stationary card

ANOTHER TRADITIONAL OLD-TIME SKILL WAS MAKING WOOL INTO CLOTHING. SEVERAL STEPS ARE REQUIRED; THE FIRST IS CARDING OR SEPARATING THE FIBERS.

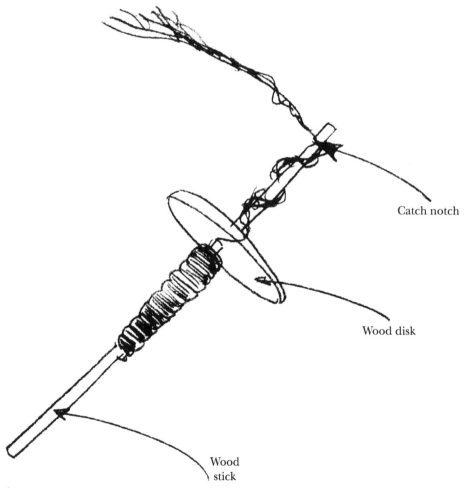

Catch notch

Wood disk

Wood stick

A DROP-SPINDLE IS THE SIMPLEST SPINNING DEVICE AND HAS BEEN AROUND FROM THE TIME HUMANKIND BEGAN USING FIBERS FOR CLOTHING. IT IS EASILY MADE AND USED.

94

NATURAL DYES, SUCH AS THOSE MADE FROM POKEWEED BERRIES, CAN BE USED TO DYE THE "YARN."

Natural Dyes

Natural plant dyes can be used to dye cloth or wool a wide variety of colors. The natural colors are softer and not as bright as today's manufactured dyes. Green dyes can come from staghorn sumac leaves, twigs, and seeds. Yellow can be made from dandelion flowers. Blue can be made from elderberries; brown comes from black walnut hulls; and red comes from pokeberries.

Gather the plants needed and crush them. Cover with water and boil for at least two hours. Strain through a clean cloth to remove the plant material. Wash the fabric or wool to be dyed in soft water or rainwater with plenty of soap and then rinse thoroughly to remove all soap. Place the wet fabric in a large pan. Cover completely with a dye bath that has been heated to lukewarm and then raise the temperature to 200°F. Maintain this temperature for at least thirty minutes or until you attain the desired color. Rinse the dye material once in hot water, then at least three times in warm water. To make the dyes colorfast, add alum to the dye bath.

Weaving

Weaving is one of man's oldest crafts. Weaving items of wool you've spun and dyed yourself is a traditional and satisfying experience. There are hundreds of methods and kinds of weaving, just as there are many different kinds of looms. Once you have the materials, such as spun wool or yarn, you can, however, weave simple items on a basic homemade loom to learn the craft of weaving.

One of the simplest looms to make is a cardboard loom. Place a piece of squared draftsman paper on a large piece of stiff cardboard. Cut notches in two opposite ends of the card, making sure the notches are spaced equally. Fasten the "warp" thread over the card by threading it through the notches. Weave by threading the weft threads through the warp threads using a long, heavy, blunt needle. This loom is great for making small items such as handbags. An alternate style, as used by many of our grandmothers, utilizes a simple wooden frame with small nails on two ends to hold the warp threads.

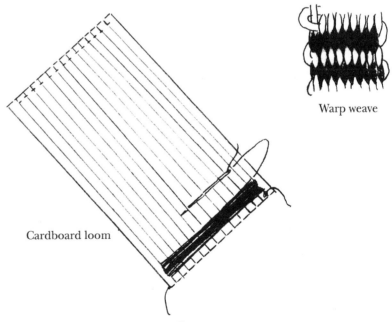

Warp weave

Cardboard loom

THE THREADS ARE THEN WOVEN. ONE SIMPLE LOOM TO EXPERIMENT WITH IS A CARDBOARD LOOM.

The simplest form of weaving is called plain weave. Both warp and weft threads are visible in this type of weave. Another type, warp weave, leaves only the warp threads showing, while weft weave leaves only the weft threads showing.

One of the earliest looms is the bow loom. It is still being used by many primitive peoples to weave thin ribbons and bands. A thin flexible branch of wood is used to hold two "shed rods" on each end. The warp threads are fastened to this and the bow keeps the loom taut while the weft threads are woven through the warp threads.

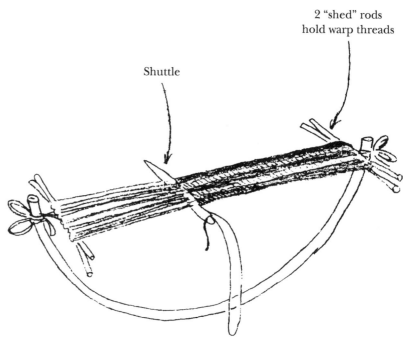

Shuttle

2 "shed" rods
hold warp threads

A PRIMITIVE BOW-LOOM CAN ALSO BE MADE AND USED TO TRY YOUR HAND AT THE AGE-OLD SKILL OF WEAVING.

Braided Rugs

Braided rugs are another old-time item that is still popular. Today, however, most braided rugs are commercially produced replicas. Authentic braided rugs can still be made, however, perhaps even better than the ones our grandmothers and great-grandmothers made. Out of necessity, our ancestors made braided rugs out of their worn-out wool clothing. These days, readily available materials make it easy to plan and create a braided rug in a specific color range and pattern to suit our needs.

Materials

Garage and rummage sales along with bolt-end sales are all good sources of new and used materials. You will need approximately three quarters to one pound of material for each square foot of braided rug. It is best if all the material for a rug is of a similar weight and texture. Wool is still the best braided rug material; however, some of the washable acrylics that look like wool can be used, too. The material must be non-stretch and always cut on the straight of the material, never on the bias. The material should also be heavy enough to produce a durable, long-lasting rug. All material should be clean and pressed before starting and any new material should be pre-shrunk and pressed. Use button or carpet thread and a large eye needle to stitch the braids together.

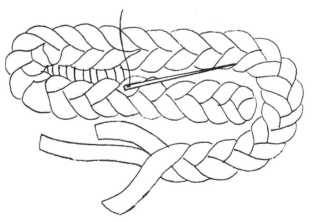

BRAIDED RUGS ARE JUST AS POPULAR AT CRAFT MARKETS THESE DAYS AS THEY WERE IN THE OLDEN DAYS. AND, THEY'RE EASY AND FUN TO MAKE.

Planning

Before starting on any rug, know the size and shape you wish it to be. The most common braided rug shape is oval, but round and square rugs can also be made. Cut a paper pattern and use this to make a color plan for your rug. No more than three colors should be used on any one rug; however, several shades of those colors can be incorporated. Another way to have color variation is to use a solid color and plaids within the same color range. Therefore, three solid colors and a variety of plaids or shades of those same colors would allow you to gradually move from one color to the next. Always change colors on the curve of the rug, adding one strip of the new color at a time to the braid until the entire braid is the new color.

Braiding strips can be cut anywhere from one and a half to four inches wide, depending on the thickness of the material. Cut sample strips of your material in different widths and braid to determine the best width for your material. When you have settled on a suitable width, measure the width of your braid, go back to your

paper pattern and measure and mark the number of braid rows that will be needed for your rug size on the pattern. From this determine the color pattern and exactly how many rows of each color will be needed. Always end the outside with the darkest solid color.

Preparing

After determining the desired width for each strip, cut all strips to the same width. The strips are folded with each outside edge folded to the center and then folded in the center again. All strips should be folded and pressed in place and then wound into balls or around a piece of cardboard. To join strips, press the material flat and sew with a bias seam. Trim the seam and press flat, then repress into the braid folds. Stagger all seams, even those seams where you are changing colors.

Braiding

To start a three-strand braid, begin by making a "T" with the end of one short strip inserted into the center of one long strip and stitched into

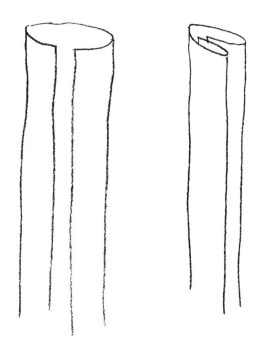

STRIPS ARE CUT TO A DESIRED WIDTH, FOLDED WITH EACH OUTSIDE TOWARD THE CENTER, AND THEN FOLDED IN THE CENTER AGAIN.

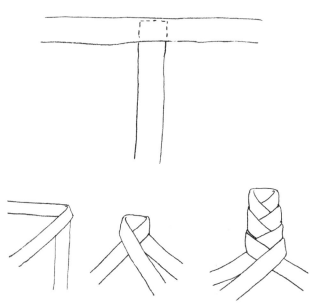

THE STRIPS ARE THEN SIMPLY BRAIDED USING EITHER A THREE-STRAND OR FOUR-STRAND BRAID, THEN STITCHED TOGETHER TO CREATE AN OVAL.

place. Fold over the two ends of the long strip and begin the three-strand braid.

To start a four-strand braid, begin by making an "E" with the ends of two short strips inserted into the center area of one long strip and both stitched in place. Fold over the two ends of the long strip and begin the four-strand braid.

The center braid for an oval rug will be slightly more than one-third the length of the finished rug. A forty-inch rug would need a starting braid of approximately fourteen inches. Stitch the braids together on a flat surface using the carpet thread and a large-eyed, blunt needle. Run the needle under the braid loops and stitch together loop to loop except on the rounded ends. Stitch two loops into one loop on the ends, but be sure that each round lays flat before and after stitching. If necessary take out the stitches and redo an end, just don't continue with the rug unless each rounded end lays flat.

Continue braiding and stitching together, following your color pattern for the rug. Again, stagger all joining strips, even the color changes. To end the rug, taper the last few inches of the last strips to make the braid smaller and then conceal the ends of each strip into the previous braid row. Tack the ends with thread if needed.

PART FIVE

From the Wild

Our ancestors took many of their foods from the wild. These days, a number of foods may still be collected from the wild. It's fun and a great reason for being outdoors. Wild forage includes such things as greens, berries, fruits, nuts, mushrooms, and even some "unusual" foods.

Wild Greens

My grandmother considered spring "spring-tonic" time. No, she didn't sip any kind of "sauce" in her tonic; she certainly didn't agree with that. She felt, along with many rural Missouri folks her age, that nothing healed the body better after a long winter than gathering a mess of wild greens.

Foraging for Edible Greens

I'm not certain about the healing properties of wild greens, but I do know they are just plain good tasting. They're easy to find and identify, but to the uninitiated, picking wild greens can be confusing. Some plants are quite a bit tastier than others; learning to find and identify the better ones is a challenge, though.

You can't take a stroll in the outdoors without being surrounded by edible wild greens. They're everywhere: roadsides, fields and meadows, undeveloped lots, abandoned homesteads, and old overgrown farm lots. Following are some of our favorites.

Dandelion *(Taraxacum officinale)*: The common dandelion is one of the easiest to identify and earliest of the greens. It covers yards across much of the country. Just as soon as the plant gets large enough to identify correctly, pop off the fresh young leaves. Shake off all dirt, rinse, and place in a pan of water. Boil for about seven minutes, drain, and serve with a pat of butter, and salt and pepper to taste. As the leaves get older, they become bitter. Changing the cooking water a couple of times will remove some of the bitterness.

WILD GREENS ARE GREAT TASTING AND NUTRITIOUS FOODS— EVEN THE COMMON DANDELION.

Dock *(Rumex)*: Several varieties of this very popular wild green are common. It is one of the earliest of greens to appear in the spring. My favorite was called "slick dock" by the old-timers.

103

Curly dock is a close relative and an easy plant to identify. It has dark green, crinkly, curly leaves. It is, however, one of the more bitter or strongly flavored wild greens, unless gathered very early.

SEVERAL FORMS OF DOCK ARE ALSO TASTY GREENS.

Lamb's-quarter *(Chenopodium)*: This is often called wild spinach, and is the mildest of greens. It is also easy to identify and, in fact, is grown in gardens in England under the name goosefoot as a substitute for spinach. Lamb's-quarter grows especially well in overgrown lots and pastures. Cook this one only until it becomes limp, and then serve with butter. It can also be eaten raw with vinegar-and-oil dressing.

LAMBS-QUARTER IS A POPULAR WILD GREEN THAT IS GROWN DOMESTICALLY IN ENGLISH GARDENS.

Plantain *(Plantago)*: Considered a broadleaf yard pest, it can also be eaten as a green. Only the tender young leaves should be gathered because the older leaves are quite bitter. Because of its astringent qualities, Native Americans and settlers also used it as a poultice.

Pokeweed *(Phytolacca americana)*: Pokeweed is probably the most well known of wild greens. It is even sold in grocery stores in the South under the name "poke sallet." Pokeweed is extremely tasty. Since it grows so abundantly, a lot can be gathered in a short amount of time. Poke is also one of the easiest plants to identify, and if you once locate a patch of poke, you can return to it for many years. There is one caution that must be remembered with pokeweed—only the tender young leaves or sprouts of early spring are edible. The rest of the plant, including old or full-grown leaves, stalk, berries and especially the roots are poisonous and must never be eaten.

POKEWEED, IN ITS EARLY STAGES, IS A FAVORITE GREEN, BUT THE ROOTS, BERRIES, STEMS, AND LARGE LEAVES ARE POISONOUS.

Since greens cook down greatly in volume, it takes a pretty fair collection to make up a "mess." Pokeweeds have the largest bulk; it is easy to gather enough to freeze a few batches for winter.

Watercress *(Nasturtium officinale)*: Another favorite spring green is watercress. It is found in just about every state in the union as well as across much of southern Canada. It grows in cool, clean streams or springs. It makes a great, but tart lettuce for sandwiches, added green in salads, or even as a garnish for culinary efforts. You can also make up a pure salad. You'll need a large bowl of cleaned, stemmed leaves. Wash thoroughly, drain, and place on a paper towel to cool in the refrigerator. Make up a dressing of one-half cup of mayonnaise with one tablespoon of horseradish. Add a dash of lemon pepper. Stir the dressing together and toss with the salad.

I have often wondered if the greens my grandmother gathered were the only ingredient in her spring tonic. It seems she was always a great deal happier, more cheerful, and sparkling after her midday wanderings for greens. After a long, cold winter, an easy walk in the warm spring sun with the excuse of gathering greens might just be the tonic for most of us today as well.

Other Wild Plants

A number of other wild plants can provide a wide variety of foods, from coffee and lemonade substitutes to fruits, vegetables, and nutty-tasting seeds.

Some Wild Favorites

Bulrush *(Scirpus validus)*: Bulrush was a favored food of the Native Americans. Found over most of North America in swampy or marshy areas, the leaves appear similar to cattails. Like cattails, much of the plant can be eaten. The roots can be gathered and eaten any time; merely wash and clean thoroughly, and then scrape to remove the tiny hairlike roots from the main roots. Wrap in damp leaves or aluminum foil and bake. They can also be peeled, diced, and added to stews. You can grind the roots to produce tasty flour or boil them to produce a starchy gruel. Allow water to evaporate from the gruel and grind into flour. The tender young shoots and the portion of the stalks at the base are an excellent vegetable. Gather the stalks and shoots, pull back the leaves, and then pull the shoots out from the roots. Wash thoroughly in running water and allow them to soak for a while in salt water. Prepare as you would asparagus.

Burdock *(Arctium minus)*: A member of the thistle family, burdock is an unusual plant. It is easily identified and provides several different foods. Very early in the spring, the young leaves can be cooked as a potherb. The young leafstalks can be cooked like asparagus. The long taproot of the plant is excellent and must be dug up, since it can't be pulled from the ground. Peel the rind from the root core, slice thinly crosswise, and cook for thirty minutes in water. A pinch of baking soda added to the water helps cut the bitterness. Drain off water and salt and pepper to taste.

Cattail *(Typha latifolia)*: One of the most easily recognized and versatile wild foods, cattails can provide vegetables, salad, and even "flour." Extremely early in the spring, when the new leaves start to sprout, the tiny stalks and leaves greatly resemble asparagus. In fact, they're often called "Cossack asparagus." They can be eaten fresh if the water they are taken from is not polluted or they can be prepared and cooked in the same manner as asparagus. In late spring, bloom spikes emerge on the stems. When they reach about four inches in length they are prepared and eaten just like ears of corn. Husk off the outer leaves and drop the spikes into boiling, salted water. Boil for about ten minutes, butter and season, and eat like corn-on-the-cob. A lump about the size of a potato is located where the stems join the roots. This is also a very tasty vegetable. Run your hand down into the water until you feel the lump, then pull out the plant. Peel and boil just like a potato; it even tastes some-

CATTAILS CAN PROVIDE A WIDE VARIETY OF FOODS. EAT THEM AS YOU WOULD ASPARAGUS, POTATOES, OR EVEN "CORN-ON-THE-COB."

what like a potato. Cattail pollen can be substituted for flour in many recipes, although it does have a more "buttery" taste. To gather, place a paper over the top of a clean bucket. Cut a slot in the paper, push the pollen-laden spikes into the bucket, and shake.

Chicory _(Cichorium intybus)_: A substitute for coffee in the South, chicory grows wild over much of the United States and Canada. Also

called "blue sailor" because of its delicate blue flowers, the leaves grow in tight rosettes much like dandelion leaves. The long taproots are used to make the "coffee." The taproots are dug up, scrubbed clean, and slowly roasted or dried

THE TAPROOTS OF THE COMMON CHICORY CAN BE GROUND INTO A COFFEE SUBSTITUTE.

in an oven set at its lowest temperature and with the door open. When the roots will break with a snap, they're done. The dried roots can then be used as a coffee substitute or mixed with coffee beans. Grind in a coffee grinder.

Mayapple or **American mandrake _(Podophyllum peltatum)_:** Found in damp, moist spots such as along stream banks or under heavy covering of deep woods, the mayapple has a shape like a miniature umbrella. The roots, stems, flowers, and leaves are poisonous because they contain podophyllum, which acts on the liver and can be fatal. In the fall, the plant produces a single edible fruit about the size of a small egg. It has a smooth yellow skin and is often called "wild lemon." The fruit is luscious, has a sweet musky smell, and has a flavor resembling several tropical fruits. It is delicious made into a marmalade.

Milkweed *(Asclepias)*: One of the most common weeds in North America, milkweed was once eaten heartily and provided four different types of vegetables. The young shoots are prepared and eaten like asparagus. The tender young top leaves were eaten as greens. The unopened flower heads were eaten like broccoli, and then the young seedpods were eaten like okra. Yet, the shoots, the top leaves, the flower heads, and the seedpods don't taste like those other garden plants. They taste like milkweed, and it takes a bit of getting used to.

Several poisonous plants have a milky sap like milkweed, so make sure you know how to identify the plant. All four parts of it are prepared in the same way. Place in boiling water for one minute, remove, and drain off water. Replace the water and boil again. Repeat at least four times, and then boil for at least fifteen minutes and serve.

Staghorn sumac *(Rhus typhina)*: A favorite of Native American children, pioneer children also called it the "lemonade tree" because the juice made from the berries resembles pink lemonade. The branches resemble the horns of deer or stag in velvet. The berries are covered with tiny hairs containing malic acid and produce a great sour drink. As a kid, I would gather handfuls of them and suck on them on the way home from school. To make sumac lemonade, place several cups of washed berries in a pan and crush slightly. Pour boiling water over them and allow to steep until the lemonade is well colored. Add honey to sweeten to taste and serve cold. The berries were also used by Native Americans to make a beautiful green dye.

Caution: There is a poisonous sumac plant, but it has loose, drooping clusters of white berries.

Sunflower *(Helianthus)*: The wild sunflower is a native of North America, ranging from California to Canada. It grows from three to six feet high and has rays of bright yellow surrounding a one- to four-inch dark brown or purple seed head. The Native Americans used the seeds to make a coarse meal, a snack, and to make oil. They also used the flowers to make a yellow dye and the stalks to produce a silky, hemplike fiber. Gather the flower heads when the first outside rows of seeds are dry. Hang them upside down in a warm, dry place. After drying thoroughly, rub the heads and the seeds will fall out. To remove the kernels from the seed shells for cooking, break them with a small hammer, rock, or food mill. Pour into a pan of water, where the shells will float to the surface and the kernels will fall to the bottom. The kernels can be dried, roasted in a slow oven, used as a snack, or ground into flour or meal.

Wild onions *(Allium)*: Wild onions grow over most of North America and greatly resemble domestic onions. The leaves are a bit more delicate and the slender shafts have white to light rose-colored flowers. Several wild plants resemble onions and a few are poisonous. They do not, however, smell like onions, as do wild onions. Wild onions may be used, just like their domestic cousins, in your favorite recipes.

Wild rice *(Zizania aquatica)*: One of the most delicious wild foods is wild rice. It is the very same food found in the supermarket, and in some parts of the country, you can gather your own wild rice. It is an easily recognized grass that is from four to six feet tall. It has small dark seeds enclosed in husks ending in a stiff, hairlike tip. Wild rice is commonly found in shallow water over mucky bottoms. The best method of gathering is the Native American method of paddling a canoe or boat through the rice. Lay a blanket or piece of clean plastic in the bottom of the boat or canoe. Bend the rice over the blanket and beat off the seed heads with the canoe paddle. Spread the gathered seeds out on a clean plastic or cloth in a warm, dry spot, such as the attic, and allow to dry thoroughly. Then rub the kernels through your hands to loosen and remove the husks. Pour the kernels back and forth between two buckets on a windy day to remove the chaff. Store the cleaned rice in jars in a cool, dry place. Use in the same way as you would purchased brown or wild rice.

Mushrooms

An old-time spring rite in many parts of the country was, and still is, the annual search for edible mushrooms, such as morels. Morels grow over most of the United States and parts of Canada. Sometimes they're also called "sponge" mushrooms because they greatly resemble miniature sponges. Growing from two to six inches tall, these mushrooms may be pale cream, brown, gray, or even black in color. They are the amateur's delight because they're easily identified and distinguished from poisonous mushrooms, including the false morel (*Helvella esculenta*). True mushrooms have a pitted-pocked surface. False morels have a convoluted surface that resembles brain tissue. Morel hunting is an art that turns into a passion for many. Morels can be found in the deepest woods as well as your backyard. They are commonly found where there is rich, aerated

MUSHROOMS, SUCH AS THE MORELS, PROVIDE TASTY FOODS AND HUNTING THEM IS AN ANNUAL SPRING RITE IN SOME PARTS OF THE COUNTRY.

soil with a high amount of humus. Morels may be fried, added to scrambled eggs, or used in gourmet delights such as stuffed mushrooms.

Some of the most overlooked foods are the fall mushrooms. One of the easiest to identify is the club fungi (*Claveria*). There are about 150 known species of this unusual-appearing mushroom. Since it resembles a piece of coral, it is often called "coral mushroom." Each body of the mushroom is a mass of upright branches coming off the main body. The color can vary from off-white to amber. Coral mushrooms are normally found in oak-hickory forests. They may be prepared and eaten just like spring mushrooms, but they must be eaten while young. As they get older, they lose their flavor and toughen up.

Wild Honey

One of the most popular wild foods of our grandfathers was wild honey from a "bee tree." In late spring, the old-timers would watch the woods and meadows for bees. If they didn't happen to locate bees, they would make up bait to attract them. The bait was a bit of sugar water or even honey placed on a stump. As soon as a bee visited the bait, the bee hunters would "line-out" the bee or follow it to a bee tree.

After locating the tree, the next task was to obtain the honey—and that was the hard part. In the very early days, the hunters simply cut down the tree and removed the honey and comb. In later years, the old-timers would bring a hive to the bee tree and set it near the tree. The bees were smoked out of the tree, the honey as well as the queen bee removed, and the queen bee placed in her new home. The other bees would follow and a new supply of honey was started if the bees were left in the tree. Most knowledgeable bee hunters robbed a bee tree only in the spring, because if they robbed it late in the summer or early fall, the bees wouldn't have enough honey to survive the winter.

Wild Nuts

Nutmeats provide some of nature's richest foods. A large variety of nuts are available to the astute forager. Many, such as the black walnut and pecan, are the same nuts as purchased commercially. Other nuts are found only in the wild.

Foraging for Wild Nuts

Acorns *(Quercus)*: A staple food of the Native Americans, acorns are not as sweet as other nuts, but they can provide a tasty food with a little effort. There are many different kinds of oak trees that produce acorns, but those from the white oak are the sweetest tasting. After gathering, shell out the nutmeats or kernels. Acorns are quite bitter due to the amount of tannin in them, which must be leached out by boiling the kernels in water. Change the water each time it becomes brown, pouring the nutmeats into fresh, boiling water. It takes about an hour and numerous water changes to remove the bitterness. Then remove the kernels and place in the sun to dry. You can also dry them in your oven set at the lowest temperature and with the door propped open. To make an acorn meal for cooking, grind the kernels in a food chopper or food mill. Regrinding the coarse meal with mill plates set as tight as possible can make a finer flour. This is an excellent-tasting flour that can be used in dark bread, muffin, or pancake recipes.

American hazelnut *(Corylus americana)*: Also called filberts, these are very sweet-tasting nuts that grow on a small shrub. The nuts are in clusters and encased in a paper husk. The best location to find them is along country roadsides or the occasional fence line that is not cleared. Hazelnuts are great as a snack and make a scrumptious pie.

IT'S FUN TO FORAGE FOR WILD NUTS, WHICH PROVIDE GREAT TASTING NUTMEATS FOR CAKES, COOKIES, AND EVEN PIES.

Beech *(Fagus grandifolia)*: Normally found in the deep forest, these nuts are small, but delicious.

Black walnuts *(Juglans nigra)*: Walnuts are one of the favorite nuts, and are often used in candies and cakes. Although there are many cultured walnut trees, they also grow in the wild. Good places to look for wild trees are in river bottom fields, public timberlands, and around abandoned farms. Walnuts are covered with greenish black outer husks, which first must be removed. One of the easiest methods to remove the husks is to pour them in a pile and drive over them several times with a car to loosen the husks.

BLACK WALNUT MEATS ARE PRIMARILY USED FOR FLAVORING COOKIES, CAKES, AND CANDIES.

Then pour the walnuts into a tub of water and roll around with a hoe. Discard those that float to the top. Remove the walnuts from the water and clean off all husks using leather gloves (the walnuts will stain your hands). Place in a burlap sack, hang up, and allow to dry for about a week. Then crack the walnut shells and pick out the meats.

Butternut *(Juglans cinerea)*: Butternuts are similar in appearance to black walnuts, although the leaves of the tree are longer. The outer husk of butternut is covered with a sticky surface and the husk is used to make a yellow or orange dye. Use butternuts just as you would walnuts.

Chinquapin *(Castanea)*: Chinquapins resemble the American chestnut, but are smaller. The nuts are also smaller and each single nut is encased in a prickly husk.

Hickory *(Carya)*: Hickory is used in much the same manner as walnuts.

HICKORY NUTS MAKE A SCRUMPTIOUS PIE—IF YOU CAN BEAT THE SQUIRRELS TO THEM.

Pecan *(Carya illinoensis)*: Pecans are possibly everyone's favorite nuts. In addition to being cultured in pecan groves, pecan trees also grow quite readily in the wild. Pecan trees prefer moist bottomland and are a common tree in many forested bottomlands. Pecans are picked up in the autumn when the nuts fall to the ground. As they dry, the outer husk breaks apart and is easily removed. The thin shells are cracked and the meats used for pies and candies.

Piñon nuts *(Pinus)*: Piñon nuts are said to be the oldest food of the southwest Native Americans. The tree pitch was used as a chewing gum to sooth sore throats and as a cure-all for everything from rheumatism to stomach discomforts. The inner bark was mashed, cooked, and smoked for a survival food. The Native Americans ground the nuts using grinding stones. While the nuts were still green, they were ground and shaped into balls that were eaten. When they were dried, the nuts were ground into a meal.

Wild Berries

Wild berries are plentiful, easily recognized, and provide lots of tasty sweets. All can be eaten fresh, made into jams and jellies or pies, or frozen for delicious treats throughout the winter.

Foraging for Berries

Blackberries (*Rubus pensilvanicus* and others) and **raspberries (*Rubus occidentalis*)**: Both blackberries and raspberries are found in abundance in the wild. The best blackberry spots are in overgrown fields in sandy or well-drained areas. Both berries are also often found around abandoned homesteads. Raspberries are primarily found in shady, deep woods locations. For easy picking, cut the tips off the fingers and thumbs of a pair of old leather gloves. Then use a belt to hold a small can or plastic ice-cream bucket to your waist. Both berries are excellent fresh. Pour cold water over them to force the bugs to float to the top. Then wash, drain, and refrigerate. The berries can be eaten fresh or frozen for later use, and made into pies, cobblers, jellies, jams, wines, and cordials. The berries are great in a custard-type dessert. Mix a quart of berries with a cup of water and a cup of honey. Bring to a boil and simmer until the berries are soft. Mix two tablespoons of cornstarch with a little water and add to thicken the juice. Pour into dessert cups and chill. Serve with whipped cream.

EVERYONE LIKES WILD BERRIES SUCH AS STRAWBERRIES, BLACKBERRIES, OR RASPBERRIES. THEY CAN BE EATEN FRESH, FROZEN, AND ADDED TO CEREALS, BAKED INTO PIES, AND MADE INTO JAMS AND JELLIES.

Elderberries (*Sambucus canadensis*): A small shrub often found along overgrown fences, stream banks, or roadsides, the plant has small white flowers, followed by small black-colored berries. Elderberries are often cultivated, but grow in the wild as well. They are great in pies as well as in wine and jellies and jams, or simply add a handful to your

ELDERBERRIES ARE VERY PROLIFIC. YOU CAN MAKE PLENTY OF GREAT-TASTING JELLY WITH A SMALL PATCH OF ELDERBERRIES.

GOOSEBERRIES CAN BE MADE INTO PIE OR JAM. GOOSEBERRIES ARE QUITE TART, BUT ARE EXCELLENT WHEN MIXED WITH MULBERRIES.

favorite muffin recipe. Elderberry fritters are made by dipping the blossoms in egg and flour and then frying.

For elderberry jelly, boil the washed berries over a high heat, then reduce heat and cook for about thirty minutes, stirring constantly. Strain the juice through a jelly cloth. Measure juice and add an equal amount of honey. Bring the mixture to a boil over a high heat. Boil until the juice reaches 220°F on a candy thermometer. Pour into sterilized jelly glasses, seal, and process in a boiling water bath.

Gooseberries and **currants** *(Ribes)*: A wide variety of gooseberries and currants are found in the wild. The most common currants are the American red currant, the wild black currant, and the golden or buffalo currant. The most common wild gooseberries are the prickly gooseberry and smooth-fruited or northern gooseberry. Both gooseberries and currants should be gathered when fully ripe in early summer. Currants make great jellies; gooseberries make great pies.

Gooseberry Pie

Pastry for a 2-crust pie
2 cups cleaned, stemmed gooseberries
1½ to 2 cups sugar
½ cup flour
2 tablespoons butter or margarine

Mix the flour and sugar together. Line a pie pan with a bottom pastry and pour in some of the gooseberries. Cover this with the flour/sugar mixture. Repeat layering gooseberries and flour mixture to fill the pan. Place 2 tablespoons butter or margarine on top of the mixture and add the top crust. Bake in a 425°F oven for 40 to 45 minutes or until golden brown and bubbly. Serve topped with homemade vanilla ice cream.

Juneberry *(Amelanchier arborea)*: Also called serviceberry, sarvice berry, or shadbush, this small tree grows over much of North America and is one of the first trees to bloom in the spring. In June, the berries ripen. They're small, round, and normally purple. They have a lovely aroma and can be made into delicious jellies.

Red mulberry *(Morus rubra)*: A mulberry tree laden with fruit will attract just about any species of bird and wildlife. The berries, however, are rather bland, although they can be made into jams and jellies. My grandmother's use of them was to mix them equally with gooseberries in a pie. The bland flavoring cuts the sour tartness of the gooseberries and it's a great combination.

YOU'LL HAVE TO BEAT THE SQUIRRELS TO THE MULBERRIES. THEY ARE VERY BLAND AND BEST BLENDED WITH OTHER FRUITS SUCH AS GOOSEBERRIES.

Wild strawberries *(Fragaria virginiana* and *F. vesca)*: Wild strawberries are found over most of North America and are easily recognized even by novice woodsmen because of their resemblance to domestic strawberries. Wild strawberries are, however, much sweeter and smaller.

They are great in jams and jellies or made into a pie.

Strawberry Pie

1 cup mashed wild strawberries
2 cups fresh whole wild strawberries
3 teaspoons cornstarch
1 cup sugar
1 tablespoon lemon juice
1 tablespoon melted butter
9-inch baked pastry shell

Stir the cornstarch into the sugar, along with the lemon juice and melted butter. Cook over medium heat, gradually stirring in crushed berries. Stir constantly until the mixture boils. Lower the heat and continue cooking and stirring for about 2 minutes. Allow the mixture to cool, and then stir 2 cups of fresh whole berries into the mixture. Pour into a baked, 9-inch pastry shell. Serve chilled with fresh whipped cream.

Wild Fruits

A number of wild fruits are available to the astute forager. Make note of the locations of your favorite trees and the general time of year when the fruits are ripe and you won't miss any of nature's harvest in the years to come.

Foraging for Wild Fruits

Black locust *(Robinia pseudoacacia)*: Also called honey locust or yellow locust, black locust is a fairly large tree with rough, scaly bark. The limbs have clusters of large thorns. Before they dry, the seedpods are filled with an unusual, sweet-tasting pulp that surrounds the seeds. In the olden days, the fleshy pods were eaten both green and dried. Native Americans used the seeds as food, cooked with meat, or dried for winter use.

Hawthorn *(Crataegus)*: Similar in appearance to a very small apple, the various species of hawthorns produce a fruit that makes great jellies and butters. Cook the fruits to soften and mash through a colander, or run through a juicer to remove the pulp. For two cups of pulp, add two cups sugar, a dash of cinnamon and cloves, and the juice of half a lemon. Slowly bring to a boil, stirring to prevent sticking. Turn down the heat and simmer until the butter bubbles and thickens. Pour into sterilized jars, seal, and process in a boiling water bath.

THE FRUIT OF THE HAWTHORN TREE IS SIMILAR TO A MINIATURE CRABAPPLE AND MAKES A DELICIOUS JELLY.

Pawpaw *(Asimina triloba)*: One of the most unusual fruits is the pawpaw. The short, soft fruits are about three to five inches long and greenish brown. Their taste is quite unusual—a tropical flavor that somewhat resembles a banana or a persimmon, as well as other sweet fruits. Pawpaws can be baked in foil, in the skin for about ten to fifteen minutes in a 350°F oven. One of the best

117

uses is to extract the pulp and substitute for bananas in nut breads.

Pawpaw Bread

1 cup pawpaw pulp
½ cup oil
2 eggs
½ cup French vanilla or banana-flavored
    yogurt
2 cups flour
1 teaspoon baking soda
½ teaspoon salt
1 teaspoon vanilla
½ cup hickory nuts or walnuts

Mix the pawpaw pulp with the oil, eggs, and yogurt. Sift together the flour, baking soda, and salt. Stir the flour mixture a little at a time into the pawpaw mixture just until blended. Stir in vanilla and nuts. Bake in a 350°F oven in a large loaf pan, 3 mini-loaves, or a muffin tin.

Persimmon (*Diospyros virginiana*): One of the most delicious wild fruits in North America, persimmons are often called "sugar plums" by those who have tasted their sweet flavor. But, to be edible, the fruit must be "mushy" ripe. A persimmon that is not quite ripe is so bitter it will

A VARIETY OF WILD FRUITS ARE ALSO AVAILABLE FOR THE SERIOUS FORAGER. PERSIMMONS WERE A FAVORITE WITH THE OLD-TIMERS.

leave you puckered up for a week. Ripe persimmons are soft and fragile enough to melt in your mouth. Ripe persimmons are a pinkish orange, the fruit about an inch to one and one-half inches in diameter, and filled with juicy orange pulp and two to six large seeds. The pulp can be used in fruit breads, puddings, or other recipes. To extract the pulp wash the fruits and then run through a juice extractor or colander or mash the fruit and pick out the seeds and skins. The pulp may be used fresh or frozen. Persimmon pudding is an old-time Ozark favorite.

Ozark Persimmon Pudding

2 cups persimmon pulp
2 cups sweet milk
2 eggs
2 cups sugar
2 teaspoons baking powder
1 teaspoon salt
2 cups all-purpose flour
1 cup melted margarine or butter
1 cup pecan meats

Add sweet milk, eggs, and sugar to persimmon pulp. Beat to a creamy mixture. Mix baking powder and salt into the flour. Stir in the pulp mixture; add the melted margarine or butter and pecan meats. Place the mixture in a greased and floured 9-by-13 pan. Bake in 350°F oven for 45 minutes. To serve, cut in squares and top with whipped cream.

Wild cherry (*Prunus serotina*): One of the most common wild fruits is wild cherry. Wild cherries range from small shrubs to large trees and are found from the Arctic regions to the deepest South. They are easily recognized by their simple alternate leaves and fruits. Several varieties exist, but the most common is chokecherry. Cherries are popular for a variety of homemade foods, including cordials, wine, and jelly. They're flavorful, but bitter, and it takes quite a bit of sweetening to make them edible.

Wild grape *(Vitis)*: Wild grapes are one of the most abundant late summer/early fall wild foods. Found over much of North America, they range from the fox grapes of the North to the mustangs of the Southwest, and the muscadines of the South. Wild grapes are normally found along river or creek bottoms or in thick woods. They are easily recognized by their tangled vines and fruits. Wild grapes can be used in wines as

WILD GRAPES CAN BE MADE INTO JELLIES AND JAMS OR EVEN WINE.

well as for jellies and jams. Moonseed somewhat resembles grapes, but has poisonous berries. Make sure you identify it correctly.

For wild grape jelly, wash, stem, and crush grapes. For each quart of grapes, add about one-half cup water and simmer for ten to fifteen minutes. Squeeze through a jelly bag. For each five cups of juice add five or six cups of sugar and one package of pectin, or follow directions on pectin package.

Wild plum *(Prunus)*: Wild plums grow in dense thickets and when you find a thicket you'll be able to pick enough of the delicious fruits for lots of pies, jellies, and even wine. They are easily recognized, with whitish to yellowish blossoms followed by fruits that may be either purple or dark orange. There are about ten varieties of plums in North America, but the most common are the Chickasaw and American. The Chickasaw has a dark orange fruit; the American has dark purple fruit. Plums have a tart, pleasant taste and can be cooked and made into preserves and jellies. They're also excellent wild fruits for drying. Remove the pits, allow to dry, and then store in tight jars.

Wild Spices and Teas

You can add to your spice shelf and tea jar with a foraging trip to the wilds.

Wild Spices

A few can be used fresh, but most are dried for use throughout the year.

Carolina vanilla *(Trilisa odoratissima)*: Also called the vanilla plant because the leaves smell like vanilla when crushed.

Coltsfoot *(Tussilago farfara)*: The Native Americans used the ground leaves as a substitute for salt.

Purple avens *(Geum rivale)*: This plant is sometimes called the chocolate root plant because the purplish root is used as a substitute for chocolate.

Spicebush *(Lindera benzoin)*: From five to fifteen feet high, this shrub has dark-brown bark and thin brittle twigs. The berries are about half an inch long, bright scarlet, and contain one seed. In early times, the berries were dried, powdered, and then used as a substitute for allspice.

Sweet bay *(Magnolia virginiana)*: Also called laurel or red bay tree, the dried leaves provide a flavoring that is used in Creole dishes and for flavoring gravies and roasts.

Wild garlic and wild onion *(Allium)*: Also called field garlic, wild garlic tastes somewhat like domestic garlic, but has only one bulb. Be sure the wild onion has an onion smell.

Wild ginger *(Asarum canadense)*: Found in damp woods, wild ginger is a creeping plant with two broad, heart- or kidney-shaped leaves. It has a single large flower on a short nodding stem. The roots can be dug, pulverized, and used as you would use purchased ginger.

Wild Teas

Wild teas can provide zesty beverages. These include:

Chia *(Salvia columbariae)*: A member of the sage family, chia is found in the Southwest, and is still popular today as a beverage plant. The tiny seeds are soaked in cold water. A bit of lemon and sugar is added and the beverage served chilled.

Oswego tea *(Monarda didyma)*: Also called bee balm, horse mint, and wild bergamot, this beautiful flowered plant is found on dry hilly lands over much of North America and was favored by Native Americans and settlers. To make the tea, add two teaspoons of fresh leaves to a cup of boiling water and sweeten to taste.

New Jersey tea *(Ceanothus americanus)*: This shrub, also called redroot, was used during the

American Revolution to brew tea as a substitute for the Oriental tea carried on British vessels. The leaves are dried to make tea.

Roses *(Rosa)*: Roses offer a very potent wild food that is loaded with vitamin C. Some folks like to nibble on the petals or use them to garnish salads. Candied petals were an old-time delicacy, which we still relish today. Rosehips can be gathered in the fall and are great in jellies, jams, syrups, or even wine, but they are most often used as tea.

WILD ROSEHIPS ARE FULL OF VITAMIN C AND MAKE A GREAT TEA.

Sassafras *(Sassafras albidum)*: The roots of the sassafras tree are used to steep a spring tonic tea, and their root beer odor is unmistakable. The roots are cut, washed, mashed, and boiled

to create the liquid. The liquid can be served sweetened or unsweetened. Do not overdo sassafras. Recent studies have shown safrole (from the sassafras root) to be a possible cause of liver cancer in laboratory rats; therefore, the FDA has banned the sale of sassafras tea. The Native American Choctaws dried and powdered the leaves to provide file powder for use in stews and gumbos.

Sweet goldenrod *(Solidago odora)*: This anise-scented goldenrod makes a fairly good tea, also called Blue Mountain tea. The leaves secrete an aroma and flavor somewhat like anise.

Wild Mints *(Mentha)*: In addition to being grown and cultivated in gardens, both spearmint and peppermint are found in the wild over much of North America. Peppermint is a perennial plant and found in wet places, such as along stream banks and springs. Their square stems and unmistakable odor when crushed are clear markers of the mint family. The mints make a flavorful tea, jelly, and sauce. To extract their essence, merely boil fresh leaves in water for a few minutes. Keep refrigerated. A mint sauce, perfect for lamb or venison, is made by stirring a tablespoon of honey into a combination of a quarter-cup vinegar and a quarter-cup water. Place a half cup of crushed mint leaves in a saucepan and pour

A VARIETY OF PLANTS CAN PROVIDE SPICES AND TEA FLAVORINGS. THE ROOTS OF THE SASSAFRAS TREE CAN BE STEEPED TO PRODUCE "ROOT BEER"-FLAVORED TEA. NOTE THE THREE-LEAF LOBES.

WILD MINTS CAN BE USED FOR TEAS, SAUCES, OR FLAVORFUL JELLY.

the water mixture over it. Allow to seep on low heat for about an hour.

Caution: Many plants look alike, and there are quite a few plants that are poisonous. Some may cause minor discomfort. Some can kill you. Make sure you positively identify a plant before eating any part of it. A number of helpful plant identification books are on the market.

PART SIX

Preserving Foods

Our ancestors had a number of different methods of preserving foods. Several of the oldest methods of preserving foods, such as root cellar (or basement) storage and smoking and drying are just as popular today. Other popular preserving methods include canning and freezing as well as salt curing, sugar curing, and making jams and jellies.

Before preserving any foods for your family, determine your family's needs. What fruits, vegetables, and meats does your family enjoy? How many people do you serve at a meal? Are they big eaters or small children? Do you entertain regularly? How often do you serve each of these meats, fruits, and vegetables? Determine what you and your family will use and enjoy. Concentrate on raising and preserving those foods first and then try a few new items each year. Some will be winners; others will be losers. Keep a written record each year of the foods you preserve, the recipes used, and so forth. Don't forget to also record how much of each your family eats each year and use this information to adjust amounts for the following year.

Cool Storage

A root cellar was a necessity to the early homesteaders. Not only did a root cellar keep fruits and vegetables cold but not frozen in the winter, but the root cellar was also the main source of cool storage in the summer. The only other cool summer storage available to early settlers was a spring or well. Many watermelons have been suspended in a spring or down a well to chill for a hot summer treat.

Root Cellar

The primary method of storing many fruits and vegetables throughout the winter was simply storing bushel baskets of fruits and vegetables on shelves in a root cellar or basement. My granddad's root cellar was a favorite place with us kids. Dug halfway into the ground, poured of concrete, and then covered with a mound of dirt, the cellar stayed about 50°F year-round. It had a pleasant, faintly vegetable and earthy smell. We loved to play with the ventilator in the top. Someone would stand over the ventilator and when anyone in the cellar talked, it had a deep, mysterious sound. Granddad kept vegetables, milk products, eggs, and fruit in the cellar, and when tornadoes swept the country, we ended up in the cellar as well. A basement cellar will also work, as long as it's not open to a furnace or other heating system. One of the keys to a good cellar is to provide ventilation. Opening and closing the cellar door and ventilator

A ROOT CELLAR WAS A TRADITIONAL STORAGE AREA FOR A VARIETY OF FOODS, INCLUDING VEGETABLES, FRUITS, EGGS, AND EVEN FOR SEPARATING MILK FROM CREAM.

controls air circulation, temperature, and humidity. Granddad's cellar had two doors, one sloping to access the steps and one at the bottom to close off the cellar proper. The best fruits and vegetables for root cellar storage are the root crops and the fruits that are bred for storage. They should be of a late-season variety so they won't be overripe at the time of harvest. Never store fruits and vegetables together; store each as far away from the other as possible. You'll also need plenty of racks and bins to hold all the food products.

Apple Barrel

The old-fashioned apple barrel was one of the storage methods of the old-timers. This old, energy-free method will still work today. Fruits such as apples need a cool, but dry place for storage and in many parts of the country, the buried apple barrel fits the bill.

In the traditional method, drain holes are drilled in a wooden barrel that is then sunk into the ground. Tack screen wire over the drain holes to prevent rodents from entering. Dig a hole large enough for the barrel to fit in, with a layer of gravel all around the barrel. Leave about a fourth of the barrel protruding. Mound dirt around the barrel up to the top edge and then place a ten-inch layer of straw, hay, or sawdust over the dirt and another layer of soil over this. Cover the top of the barrel with a layer of screen wire, then straw, and, finally, a board weighted in place with rocks. In areas where the temperature may drop lower than 20°F, lay the board directly over the barrel instead of the screen wire.

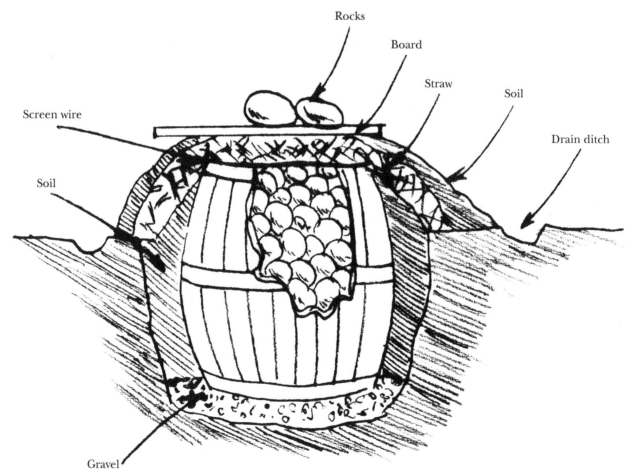

AN APPLE BARREL IS A SIMPLE, OLD-TIME COUNTRY METHOD OF PRESERVING APPLES.

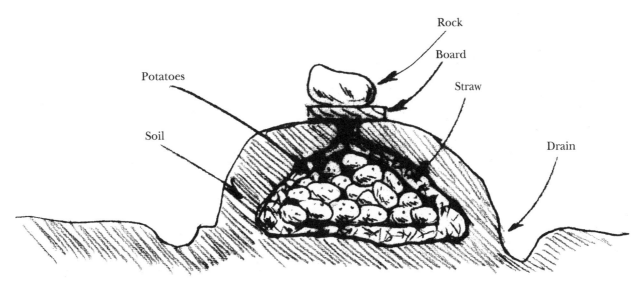

A PIT DUG IN THE GARDEN CAN STORE VEGETABLES.

Storage Pit

Fruits and vegetables can also be stored in dirt mounds or pits. Store each fruit or vegetable in a separate pit. The cone-shaped pit is nothing more than a flat area of dirt that is slightly above ground level and with a straw covering. Make a pyramid of the fruit or vegetable on the straw, add a layer of straw around the fruit or vegetable, and then a heavy dirt covering over the straw. Leave a cone of straw up through the center top of the outside dirt for ventilation and cover this with a stone that will keep out rainwater. Dig a shallow trench around the outside of the pit to allow rainwater to run around the pit, not through it. All the contents of a pit must be removed once it is opened, so several small pits are a better idea than one large pit. Also, the pit may be hard to open in the late winter if the ground is frozen.

Curing, Drying, Smoking, and Salting Foods

Whether sugar curing a ham, drying apples, or salt curing cabbage into sauerkraut, all these old-time preserving methods are as effective today as they were for our ancestors. Meats can be preserved in a number of methods including freezing, canning, corning, making into sausage or jerky, drying, or smoking. Back in the old days, before freezing and canning, meat was often made into a smoke-dried jerky. Techniques for making jerky are evident from many of the earliest cultures, including the Egyptians.

Sugar Curing

Sugar curing is an old-fashioned country method of preparing pork ham sides and shoulders for home storage. It provides great tasting meat with a flavor all its own. Chill the meat and keep it cold, but not frozen. Trim off excess fat. Weigh the trimmed meat to determine the amount of curing material needed. For every 100 pounds of ham or shoulder, you should use a mixture of eight pounds salt, two pounds brown sugar, and two ounces of saltpeter. We also like to add ground black pepper and ground red pepper. Blend the mixture together with your hands (with rubber gloves) until the brown sugar and spices are evenly distributed.

Divide the appropriate amount of sugar cure mix in half and rub half on the meat. Make sure to get a layer about one-eighth-inch thick and make sure the cure is worked in and around all bones and all crevices. Some old-timers placed the meat in a clean wooden barrel and stored the meat at 36° to 40°F. The old timers figured the meat should cure about two days per pound of meat. After about eight days, the meat is covered with the other half of the cure. The meat is removed from the barrel, wrapped in papers, and placed in a soft bag, tying the end and hanging the meat butt down in a cool, dark place.

Here's how my grandfather did it and the method we still use. We prefer to coat the meat with the entire cure, wrap in sheets of newspaper, and then place in a clean cloth bag and

SUGAR CURING OF HAMS AND OTHER MEATS IS A TRADITIONAL COUNTRY SKILL. IT'S ALSO FAIRLY EASY, IF YOU'VE DONE YOUR OWN BUTCHERING.

meat in the cooled crock, and pour the thoroughly mixed solution over the meat to completely cover it. Place a large, clean plate and weight it down to keep the meat covered in the solution. Make sure the meat stays at the proper temperature. Remove the meat on the seventh day and pour the curing mixture into another container. Repack the meat, stir up the solution, and pour it back over the meat. Repeat this "overhauling" procedure on the fourteenth and twenty-ninth days. It will normally take about four days per pound for a ham and a minimum of twenty-eight days for bacon. Then remove the meat from the brine, soak in cold water, and hang in a cold place to dry. You can then loosely wrap in paper, then in muslin, and hang in a cold place until the weather warms. You can also smoke the meat. If at any time the pickling mixture becomes sour or syrupy, remove the meat, scrub in hot water, discard the mixture, scald the container, make up a new mixture, and continue the cure.

hang butt down immediately in a cool, dark place to cure. We normally hang the hams from butchering day in late January or early February for about eight weeks. Before the weather warms in the spring, we take down the hams and place them in the freezer for further storage.

Sweet-Pickle Cure

Another preserving method is applying a sweet-pickle cure. Although this method requires more work, many people prefer it. Trim chilled meat cuts to remove all excess fat, gristle, and blood. Make up a cold pickle solution by dissolving eight pounds of salt, three pounds of sugar, and two ounces of saltpeter into four and a half gallons of water at 36° to 40°F. Place in a clean crock or barrel in a cold-storage area of 36° to 40°F and allow it to cool thoroughly. Place the

Smoke Curing

Smoke curing also adds to the flavor and preservation of the hams. A number of commercial smokers, along with all the necessary supplies and specific instructions for the various meats are available. You can also build a small smokehouse for hams and shoulders from a clean, fifty-gallon drum with both ends removed. Place the barrel over a shallow trench with a small fire in the trench. Build a fire of hardwood such as hickory or oak. Bring the heat in the smokehouse to 100° or 120°F. Hang the meat from wooden strips across the barrel top and then place cheesecloth over the top. Place a lid over the top, but keep the lid open to let moisture escape. Then close the top and smoke for one to two days.

A better smoker is made from an old discarded refrigerator. The refrigerator should be placed up on concrete blocks and an opening cut in the top. A metal flue with a flue cap can be used to direct the smoke out the top. A fire pit is dug a short distance away and a metal stovepipe run underground from the fire pit to an opening cut in the bottom of the refrigerator/smoker for safety.

The meat should first be cured as described earlier. After curing, soak in cold fresh water for about half an hour to soak off some of the surface brine. Use heavy string to make loops for hanging the meat in the smokehouse. Hams and shoulders can be supported with strings tied through the shank. Wooden or metal skewers can be used to hang bacon. Then scrub the meat with hot water and a sharp brush. The water should be between 110° and 125°F. Hang the meat in a cool place and allow it to dry overnight. If the meat isn't properly scrubbed, the smoke coloring will be streaked. When you're ready to smoke, hang the pieces in the smokehouse or smoker so no pieces are touching. Build a fire of hardwood and allow the smokehouse to heat up to 100° or 120°F or just hot enough to melt the surface fat on the pork. Once it reaches that temperature, open the top "damper" just a little bit to let out any moisture. On the second day, close the ventilator and continue to smoke for at least one more

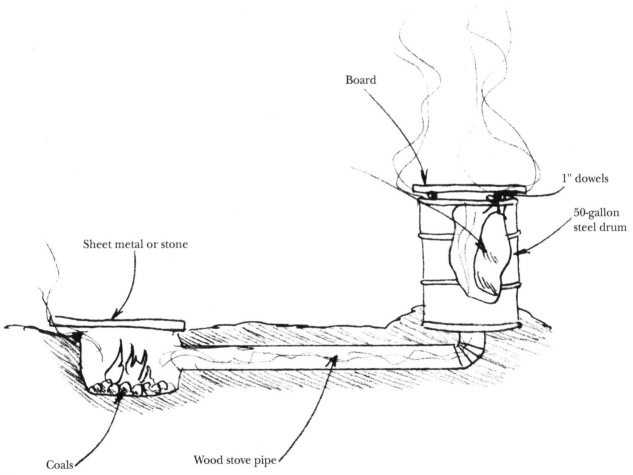

SMOKING ADDS TO THE FLAVOR AND PRESERVATION OF SUGAR-CURED MEATS.

day, or until the meat surfaces reach the desired color. Do not overheat the meat after the first day, and never scorch or cook the meat. Maintain the 100° to 120°F temperature to cold smoke the meat. One of the biggest problems with smoking is inattention to the fire; the fire should produce a slight haze of smoke. Use green twigs or sawdust to maintain the smoke. Once smoked, the warm meat should be tested with a ham trier or a clean, stiff wire run into the meat. It should be run in along the bone to the center of the ham and then withdrawn. If it has a sour odor, the meat is tainted. Cut open the meat and examine for spoilage. If the meat gives off a smell of putrification, it should be destroyed.

After you have smoked the meat to satisfaction and tested for quality, it should be wrapped and bagged for storage. Wrap the meat in heavy paper. Some people also like to rub on a bit of black and red pepper to discourage insects. Place in a muslin bag and hang in a cool, dark place that is well ventilated. Hams properly prepared in this manner will often keep a year or so and eventually develop the flavor characteristic of country-cured ham.

Even with the best of storage of cured and/or smoked hams, you'll probably end up with a bit of surface mold and this can easily be trimmed off before use. Sugar/brine cured and smoked hams should first be parboiled to remove some of the salty flavoring and then cooked.

Smoke Cooking

Smoke cooking with indirect heat or hot smoking (barbecuing) with direct heat are both excellent methods for cooking meats. Smoke cooking is a southern tradition. Parked behind many a barn or shed in my part of the Ozarks is a homemade smoker. Today, however, a variety of manufactured cookers and smokers make smoking and smoke cooking easy and reliable.

Three types of smoke cookers are available. The first type is the simple barbecue grill, either charcoal or gas. You either pile on the charcoal briquettes or light the gas and cook with the heat. Charcoal adds some smoke flavor and wood

chips can be added to the ignited charcoal as well as to most gas grills for added smoke flavoring. The second type of smoke cooker is a moist-heat smoker that utilizes a high dome with a lid and a separate pan to hold a marinade. Moistened wood chips are added for smoking. A number of these smoke cookers are available, including models from Cabela's, Brinkman, Coleman, and Bass Pro. Both of these smokers cook by direct heat.

True smokers, however, use indirect heat, with the coals in one area of the smoker and the meat in another. They are quite often larger models of welded metal to maintain more consistent heat, and are capable of handling bigger fires as well as greater amounts of meat at one loading. A number of these smokers are available, but the best I've tested is the Good-One Grill and Smoker from Ron Goodwin Enterprises. The Good-One Grill is available in several sizes from small to large commercial models. All are built with the same basic design. The front lower compartment is the firebox and grill. You can grill just as you would with any charcoal grill. The upper back compartment, however, is for smoking or cooking meats with lower, indirect heat. On the lower front of the firebox are the air control dampers to control the heat in the firebox and grill area. On the top of the smoker lid is an exhaust vent. The dampers control the heat in the smoker. The smokers are constructed with a clean-out pan located under the firebox grate.

To smoke, the top grate is removed from the bottom compartment and charcoal placed on the bottom grate. You'll need about ten pounds of charcoal for several hours of smoking. After the coals are burning, add the wood chunks to provide the smoke flavor and close the bottom lid. Just as in any smoking, the type of wood chunks used provides the flavoring. These types of smokers do not use water pans. "Water pans make steam heat, which can cause smoke to disappear rapidly and tends to make meat soggy," says Ron Goodwin. "We don't recommend water pans for true, old-fashioned pit barbecue flavor." Ron also suggests using pure charcoal chunks rather than briquettes, although the former are a little harder to obtain. "Another secret to good barbecue smoked meat is a smoker that will hold an even temperature and the right amount and kind of wood," Ron adds. "Hickory, mesquite, oak, pecan, alder, and fruits woods: cherry, peach, apple, or grape vine are recommended. Poultry requires much less wood than other meats and game birds and waterfowl are very good if smoked using fruit woods. The best result for smoke flavor is to use chunks of wood, two or three chunks, about three to four inches in size usually give a nice smoked flavor."

Maintaining an even temperature over a long period of time is important for ease in smoke cooking. The Good-One smoker has a temperature gauge and a variety of means of regulating the heat. By simply opening and closing the dampers you can control the heat precisely. You will also need a meat thermometer to check the internal temperature of your meat.

Smoke cooking is an excellent method for cooking a roast or ham (hind quarter) because it keeps the moisture in the meat rather than drying it out. Even the relatively dry meats like venison come out moist and for the most part tender.

For a roast, ham, or hind quarter cook at 275° to 300°F for two hours, and then cut the smoker temperature back with the damper to 225°F. Finish cooking at that temperature for one hour for each pound of meat. Use a meat thermometer and cook until the internal temperature reaches 180° to 190°F. Wrapping drier meats such as venison in bacon strips will add some flavoring and also keep the meat from drying out.

I've also discovered that, regardless of the meat being smoked, I prefer to smoke for about an hour or two, and then wrap the meat in foil for the remainder of the cooking process. This tends to hold in even more moisture. The meat can be basted with barbecue sauce, left natural, or basted in your favorite sauce.

Drying

Drying is one of humankind's oldest forms of food preservation. It is also one of the simplest.

Sun drying requires only something to hold the food, something to cover it to keep away insects, and plenty of hot, dry weather. Many of the old-timers learned to dry food for storage during World War II, when canning supplies and sugar were short. Dried foods offer several advantages: the first is simplicity of storage. Second, dried foods can be carried or transported easily, one of the reasons for their popularity as "trail foods."

Many foods, including fruits, berries, vegetables, and meats can be dried fairly easily. Drying can be simple sun drying, drying in an oven, or with an electric dehydrator. The latter offers the easiest and most consistent drying of most foods. We have dried everything from tomatoes to apples to jerky in our Excalibur Dehydrator. All that's needed is to set the temperature and turn it on. And, both temperature and moisture control are the two most important elements in successfully drying foods. The temperature should be a constant source, and there should be plenty of good air circulation. If food is dried at too low a temperature, there is a chance it will spoil before it dries properly. If you dry it too fast and at too high a temperature, it will lose nutrients and vitamins. The temperature and amount of time required depends on the food, the size and thickness of the pieces to be dried, and your particular drying equipment. You'll simply have to experiment to determine the best method for specific foods.

DRYING IS ONE OF THE OLDEST FORMS OF PRESERVATION. MODERN DEHYDRATORS MAKE THE CHORE EASY.

Make sure you use only good produce and it is well cleaned of all dirt and debris. Use an easily cleanable cutting surface and cut the pieces to approximately uniform size. This makes drying easier and provides more evenly textured foods.

Fruits and Vegetables

Most vegetables, except for peppers, onions, tomatoes, and herbs should be blanched before drying. This stops enzyme action. Blanching is simply placing the produce in boiling water for a few minutes, removing it, and plunging it into cold water to chill immediately.

Many fruits will discolor quickly once they have been cut. This doesn't hurt the taste, but the food doesn't have an appealing appearance. Dipping the fruit slices or pieces in ascorbic acid or lemon juice will prevent darkening.

Sun Drying

An extremely, hot, dry climate is required for good sun drying. Most fruits and vegetables will dry within two to three days under these conditions. An old window screen makes an excellent drying platform. Wash it thoroughly, then place it up on some sawhorses or other raised form to allow for circulation. Place the produce on the screen and cover with cheesecloth. Take the screen inside each night to prevent the pieces from picking up moisture from dew. As the pieces dry, stir them around and turn them over so they dry evenly throughout. After a couple of days of drying, cut into a piece to test. If it is dark and moist in the center, it must be dried further. Another test is to place a piece in a glass jar and seal it tightly. Place the jar in a dark, cool place, and then check it in a couple of days for condensation.

Oven Drying

Produce should not be placed on metal cooking trays. The best trays for oven drying are wooden frames covered with a thin cotton material or you can apply a light coating of salad oil to metal trays to prevent the produce from sticking. Set the oven at 150°F and allow it to preheat. Place the trays in the oven and leave the door ajar.

About every half hour, switch the trays around, placing the bottom on the top and the top on the bottom. If using a gas oven, watch carefully that the burner does not go out.

Dehydrators

Commercial dryers have a heat source and fan to provide constant circulation. They also have easily cleaned trays, making it easier to consistently dry items from produce to meats. Temperature controls on most dehydrators will range from 95° to 150°F. Follow the directions with your particular dehydrator for specific foods.

Jerky

Jerky is still a great way of preserving meat, and provides a tasty, healthy snack food. One of my favorite pastimes is to sit in a deer stand waiting for a deer to come by all the while chewing on a piece of jerky from the previous season. Jerky is made by removing moisture from the meat, thereby preventing enzymes from contacting or reacting with it. In the past, jerky making consisted of soaking meat in a marinade, and then simply drying it in an oven or dehydrator. Yet, most dehydrators only achieve a temperature of 140°F, and recent outbreaks of illnesses caused by salmonella and E. coli in homemade jerky have raised some questions about the safety of the traditional jerky-making methods.

According to the United States Department of Agriculture's Food Safety and Inspection Service (FSIS), "When raw meat or poultry is dehydrated at home—either in a warm oven or a food dehydrator—to make jerky which will be stored on the shelf, pathogenic bacteria are likely to survive the dry heat of a warm oven and especially the 130° to 140°F of a food dehydrator." Following is their recommended methods of properly drying jerky.

Due to the possibility of illness from salmonella and E. coli 0157:H7 from homemade jerky, the USDA current recommendation for making jerky safely is to *heat meat to 160°F before the dehydrating process.* This step assures that any bacteria present will be destroyed by wet heat. But most

MEATS CAN ALSO BE DRIED INTO JERKY IN SMOKER/
DRYERS, SUCH AS THE BRADLEY SMOKER SHOWN.

- Use clean equipment and utensils.
- Keep meat and poultry refrigerated at 40°F or slightly below; use or freeze ground meats and poultry within two days; whole red meats, within three to five days.
- Defrost frozen meat in the refrigerator, not on the kitchen counter.
- Marinate meat in the refrigerator. Don't save marinade to re-use. Marinades are used to tenderize and flavor the jerky before dehydrating it.
- Steam or roast meat and poultry to 160°F as measured with a meat thermometer before dehydrating it.
- Dry meats in a food dehydrator that has an adjustable temperature dial and will maintain a temperature of at least 130° to 140°F throughout the drying process.

Following is a quite simple method for making jerky. I like to partially freeze the meat to make slicing easier. An electric slicer can also make the chore easier. Trim away all fat, which can create off flavors, and as much connective tissue as possible from the meat. Then cut the meat into strips about one quarter inch thick with the grain, rather than across the grain. Combine the meat with marinade in a glass bowl or zippered plastic bag and refrigerate for at least two hours.

dehydrator instructions do not include this step, and a dehydrator may not reach temperatures high enough to heat meat to 160°F. After heating to 160°F, maintaining a constant dehydrator temperature of 130° to 140°F during the drying process is important because (1) the process must be fast enough to dry food before it spoils; and (2) it must remove enough water that microorganisms are unable to grow.

The USDA recommends the following safe handling and preparation methods:

- Always wash hands thoroughly with soap and water before and after working with meat products.

Jerky

Use the following ingredients to make marinade:

1 tablespoon garlic salt
1 tablespoon lemon pepper
1 tablespoon onion powder
Tabasco Sauce (from a few drops to 1 or more tablespoons, depending on taste)
1 cup soy sauce and water to cover.

Combine marinade and meat in a glass bowl or zippered plastic bag and refrigerate 12 hours or overnight.

Remove, shake excess marinade from the strips, pat dry, and sprinkle with seasoned salt and garlic pepper. For spicier jerky, use the seasoned salt plus seasoned pepper or Cajun seasoning.

The jerky can then be dried in the oven or dehydrator following the USDA temperature recommendations.

Oven Drying Jerky

Place a sheet of aluminum foil in the bottom of your stove's oven to catch any drippings and drape the meat over the oven racks, leaving enough space between pieces for the air to circulate. Spraying the oven racks with a cooking spray keeps the jerky strips from sticking. The oven should be set to 350°F and the meat baked until the internal temperature reaches 160°F. Then set the oven to 170°F and prop the door open from two to six inches.

Most jerky will take five or six hours to dry but times vary, depending on the heat of your individual oven and the thickness of the meat. Check for doneness after three hours and remove pieces as they become dry. Jerky is done when you can still bend it—overdone when it snaps. Store the finished product in a cool, dry place. Vacuum sealing works well for storing jerky as well.

Marinade Cooked Jerky

Another method is simmering jerky in marinade before drying, as suggested by the Penn State College of Agricultural Sciences.

Prepare two to three cups of your favorite marinade and bring it to a rolling boil over medium heat. Add a few meat strips, making sure the marinade covers them. Reheat to a full boil. Remove the pan from the heat source. Remove the strips from the hot marinade and place them in a single, non-overlapping layer on drying racks.

Dry the strips at 140° to 150°F in a dehydrator, oven, or smoker.

Note: It is not advised to presoak the strips in marinade. Putting un-marinated strips into boiling marinade minimizes any cooked flavors and maintains the safety of the marinade.

Ground Jerky

Although jerky is traditionally made by slicing meat into strips, jerky can also be made from ground meat using a jerky-making machine. This is actually a better way of using the tougher cuts of meat. Once ground and made back into strips, the jerky is easy to chew. Grinders and jerky-making machines are available from Cabela's and Bass Pro.

The first step is to grind the meat either by hand or with an electric grinder. Then place in a plastic or stainless steel bowl and add dry jerky flavoring. A number of mixes are available for this, or you can make up your own.

Ground Jerky

5 pounds ground meat (domestic or wild)
5 heaping teaspoons Morton Tender Quick Salt or 1½ level teaspoons per pound of ground meat
¼ cup brown sugar
1 teaspoon garlic powder
1 teaspoon onion powder
¼ to ½ teaspoon ground red pepper or ½ teaspoon dried red pepper flakes

Mix the spices together and then sprinkle over the ground meat. Use your hands to mix together, sprinkling a little of the spice mixture, mixing that in and adding more spices. Another mixing method is to dissolve the dry mixed spices in ¼ to ½ cup water. Stir until dissolved, and then pour over the ground meat and mix in with hands or a large spoon. More or less of the garlic, onion, and red pepper can be added to suit. Always mix in an enameled, stainless steel or plastic container and wear disposable gloves if mixing by hand.

The meat is allowed to marinate with the mix in the refrigerator for 12 hours or overnight. Then place the ground and marinated meat in the jerky machine and extrude the meat into strips or sticks onto aluminum foil or a baking pan. Or roll the meat between two sheets of waxed paper to a thin,

¼-inch sheet. Remove the top sheet of waxed paper and cut into even-sized bars. Bake in the oven at 350°F to the recommended internal temperature and then continue drying in the oven or dehydrator as described previously.

Storing Jerky

Jerky should be stored in clean plastic bags or jars or wrapped in freezer paper and frozen. If not allowed to pick up moisture, jerky will keep indefinitely, but the quality and taste starts to deteriorate within a few months. Vacuum packing and freezing offers the best long-term storage method.

Sausage

Next to jerky, sausage in one form or another is also a very popular method of preserving meat. Sausages are made of ground meat and are a good way of using the tougher cuts. The most common sausages are the cooked/smoked varieties and a number of different kinds can be made depending on the spices and flavorings added. Flavorings and sausage stuffers are available from Luhr-Jensen, as well as The SausageMaker and other companies. Following are recipes for three of the most popular sausages.

Note: If making sausage from venison, for a moister sausage, you can mix ground pork with the ground venison in proportions of one-fourth to one-half ground pork or grind a little beef suet with the venison.

Pepperoni

For each pound of ground meat, add the following:

1½ level teaspoons Morton Tender Quick or Morton Sugar Cure
½ teaspoon ground black pepper
½ teaspoon mustard seed
½ teaspoon fennel seed
½ teaspoon garlic powder
¼ teaspoon crushed red pepper flakes
¼ teaspoon anise seed

Combine ingredients and mix until well blended. Refrigerate 12 hours or overnight. Stuff sausages and smoke or bake until a meat thermometer inserted in the center reaches 160°F.

Summer Sausage

For each pound of ground meat, add the following:

1½ level teaspoons Morton Tender Quick or Morton Sugar Cure
½ teaspoon ground black pepper
½ teaspoon garlic powder
½ teaspoon whole mustard seed
⅛ teaspoon ground ginger
⅛ teaspoon ground coriander

Combine ingredients and mix until well blended. Refrigerate 12 hours or overnight. Stuff sausages and smoke or bake until a meat thermometer inserted in the center reaches 160°F.

Bologna

For each pound of ground meat, add the following:

1½ level teaspoons Morton Tender Quick or Morton Sugar Cure
½ teaspoon ground black or white pepper
¼ teaspoon paprika
¼ teaspoon onion powder
⅛ teaspoon ground nutmeg
⅛ teaspoon allspice

Combine ingredients and mix until well blended. Refrigerate 12 hours or overnight. Stuff sausages and smoke or bake until a meat thermometer inserted in the center reaches 160°F.

Grinding Sausage

The first step is to grind the meat. If using frozen meat, thaw in a refrigerator, not at room temperature. Keep the meat as cold as possible during the grinding and mixing processes. The meat should never be warmer than 40°F. Make sure you use only good quality products including sodium nitrite (contained in the Morton Tender Quick meat cure). The sodium nitrite improves flavor, inhibits growth of *Clostridium botulinum,* and gives the characteristic pink coloring.

If you have dual grinding plates, grind the meat first with a coarse grind plate and then with a finer plate. Some recipes call for 75 percent of the meat to be ground with a coarse plate and 25 percent ground with a finer plate. Developing your own style is what sausage making is all about. I would suggest keeping copious notes while sausage making until you develop a few favorites.

Add the curing ingredients to the ground meat. It's a good idea to mix the ingredients in a bit of water to allow them to dissolve completely before adding to the sausage. Mix the curing ingredients thoroughly throughout the sausage. Allow the sausage and cure to set the required amount of time as per the mix instructions in a refrigerator, typically twelve hours or overnight.

Stuffing Sausage
The sausage is then stuffed into casings. The casings may be hog casings or synthetic casings. Hog casings must first be soaked in clean water before using and then rinsed completely. They're a bit more difficult to work with than synthetic casings. Synthetic casings must also be soaked, but do not need the cleaning step. Sausage casings are available from The SausageMaker and others. The Luhr-Jensen kit comes complete with the casings needed.

Sausage may be stuffed in three ways. Luhr-Jensen has a Sausage Making Kit that includes a variety of sausage mixes as well as a hand stuffer. The latter is a plastic tube over which the casings are fitted. The ground meat is then spooned into the stuffer and a hand-held plunger pushes the sausage through the tube into the casing.

The SausageMaker has a tabletop-mounted cast-iron stuffer that increases the volume of sausage that can be stuffed and reduces the time involved in stuffing casings. The unit is made to be fastened to a table or work surface. I fastened the stuffer to a board and the board can then be clamped to the table top with a wooden or C-clamp. This allows the unit to be removed for cleaning and storage when not in use.

Most of today's electric meat grinders also come with sausage stuffers. Some may allow the use of grinding plates so you can regrind with smaller openings as well. This is the quickest and easiest method of stuffing sausages.

Smoking Sausages
If you have a commercial smoker with the capability of reaching 180°F you can smoke the sausages in it. Smoke at 140°F for one hour. Raise the temperature to 160°F and smoke for another hour. Then raise the temperature to 180°F and smoke until the internal temperature of the meat reaches 160°F. Use a meat thermometer inserted into the center of the sausage to test for the internal temperature. Test several sausages in different locations of the smokehouse to assure the correct temperature has been reached.

Remove the sausages from the smoker and shower with hot water for a minute. Then spray with cold water or place in ice water to cool down the sausages quickly. Sausages should be stored in a refrigerator at 40°F or cooler. We like to vacuum pack the sausages and freeze them, taking out only one or two as needed. This way we have fresh sausages throughout the year for instant hors d'oeuvres anytime.

If using a cold smoker or homemade smoker that doesn't have the capability to regulate or reach the temperatures needed, smoke at the hottest temperature available for a couple of hours. Then place the sausages in your oven set at 350°F. The sausages can be placed on a cookie sheet. Bake until the internal temperature reaches 160°F.

Corning or Salt Preserving
Meats can also be corned or immersed in brine as preserving methods. Corning definitely changes the taste of wild and domestic meats and also acts

as a tenderizer. You might want to try corning some venison the next time you're deciding what to do with the meat from that trophy buck.

The USDA recommends the following recipe:

Corned Meat

3 pounds (6¾ cup) salt
10 ounces (1⅜ cup) sugar
2 ounces sodium nitrate
½ ounce sodium nitrite
3 level teaspoons black pepper
3 level teaspoons ground cloves
6 bay leaves
12 level teaspoons mixed pickling spice

For onion flavor, add 1 medium-sized onion, minced. For garlic flavor, add 4 garlic cloves, minced. Put the ingredients into a pickle crock or glass jar and add enough water to make a total of 6 gallons, including the ingredients.

The container should be covered. A good piece of round is wonderful corned, but less desirable cuts of meat such as brisket can be corned. The ideal temperature for corning meat is about 38°F.

Place meat into the liquid. Put a heavy plate on meat; weight plate, if necessary, to keep meat below pickle brine.

Leave the meat in corning liquid for fifteen days. On the fifth and tenth days, stir the liquid well, remove the meat and put it back so the bottom piece is on top. After the fifteenth day, remove the meat. Use what you want immediately and store the balance in a cool place refrigerated at 38°F. It is recommended that after meat is removed from the corning liquid it should be cooked and consumed within one week or frozen for up to one month.

The meat at this stage has a grayish pink color. When cooked, corned meat changes to the characteristic pink color associated with a cured product. Cook the corned meat as you would a corned beef brisket from the market by simmering in water until tender.

Easy Corned Meat

Morton Salt has a simpler corned meat recipe. Mix Morton Tender Quick at the rate of two pounds Tender Quick per gallon of water needed to cover the meat. The water should have been boiled and cooled before using. Stir to dissolve the Tender Quick in the water and then pour over the meat packed in a clean crock or glass container. Spices may be added if desired. Morton suggests corning uniform pieces of meat so the curing time will be the same. The meat should stay in the cure about two days per pound with smaller pieces ready to use in about a week. Again, weight down the meat in the cure and refrigerate at temperatures between 36°F and 40°F while curing. After five days, take the meat from the brine, stir the brine, and place the meat back in the brine with the top meat now on the bottom.

Corned Roast

This is a quick corned meat recipe that you can prepare any time of the year with a fresh boneless roast. Even a roast from the freezer is simple to brine in the refrigerator.

3 to 3½ pounds boneless roast
2½ tablespoons Morton Tender Quick or
   Morton Sugar Cure
1 tablespoon brown sugar
1½ teaspoons black pepper
½ teaspoon paprika
½ teaspoon ground bay leaves
½ teaspoon allspice
¼ teaspoon garlic powder

Blend the spices into the Tender Quick or Sugar Cure. Rub this mixture into all sides of the roast. Place the meat in a plastic food bag and tie securely or place meat in a tightly sealed plastic food container. Refrigerate and allow to cure 5 days per inch of meat thickness. At the end of the curing time, cover with water and simmer until tender.

Sauerkraut

One simple method of preserving a food was making sauerkraut from cabbage. In the old days, kraut was made in huge stone jars, which were covered with a cloth and/or board and kept in a cool, dry place, such as a root cellar. When you wanted kraut for dinner, you simply spooned it out and heated it on the stove. I can well remember the kraut barrel in my dad's cellar. It wasn't my favorite smell.

You can make this old-time food quite easily, and then process it in a pressure canner for longer-lasting and better flavor—and without the kraut smell drifting up from your basement.

1. Remove the outer leaves and any other unwanted, insect-chewed, or discolored portions from firm, ripe cabbage heads. Wash well and drain.
2. Cut the heads into quarters and then shred. The old-time method was to use a "kraut cutter." You can also shred with a food processor.
3. Sprinkle three tablespoons of pure granulated salt over each five pounds of shredded cabbage. Allow the salted cabbage to continue to drain for fifteen to twenty minutes.
4. Place the salted cabbage in a large crock and "bruise" or squeeze it with your hands. Squeeze and mash until you have enough juice to cover the shredded cabbage.
5. Place a large plate on top of the cabbage and put a clean (washed) rock on top of the plate to keep the cabbage down in the liquid. A heavy-duty plastic bag filled with water will also work, as will a clean jar filled with water. Cover the top of the crock

with a clean cloth to keep out insects. The crock should be kept in a cool place while fermenting.

6. Fermentation should stop in two to three weeks. Remove the kraut from the crock and pack in jars. Process in a pressure canner according to the instructions that came with your canner.

Sauerkraut can spoil or develop off colors or odors for several reasons. If the kraut is too soft, either there was not enough salt, fermentation temperature was too high, there was an uneven distribution of salt, or there were air pockets. If the kraut is rotted, the cabbage wasn't kept under the liquid. If the kraut is dark, there was not enough juice to cover the cabbage, the storage period was too long, or there was uneven distribution of salt or exposure to air. In any of these cases, discard the kraut.

Apple Cider

Apples were a favorite of our pioneering grandparents. They ate apples fresh off the tree, stored apples for winter use, dried them, and made them into sweet cider, hard cider, or vine-

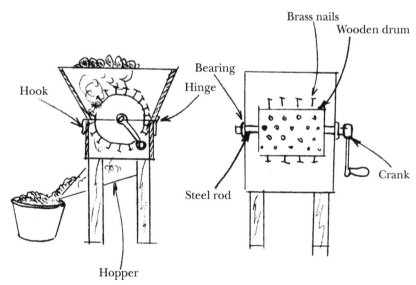

CIDER CAN BE MADE USING A HOMEMADE CRUSHER.

gar. Hard cider is sweet cider to which yeast and sugar is added and allowed to ferment. Vinegar is made by allowing unpasteurized sweet cider to sour. You can easily make your own sweet cider, and you can use the small, bruised, or imperfect apples that would otherwise be discarded.

The first step is to wash all the apples thoroughly and then mince or crush them. One way is to place a few in an old tub and crush them with the end of a baseball bat. Or to quickly pulp the apples, you can make your own homemade wooden apple crusher. To get the most from your apples, you'll also need an apple or fruit press. Place a heavy muslin bag in the apple press. Pour in the crushed apples and turn down the press to squeeze out the juice. To keep the cider from turning into vinegar, it must be kept refrigerated. Cider can be kept longer by pasteurizing it and canning or freezing.

AN OLD-FASHIONED APPLE PRESS IS USED TO SQUEEZE THE PULP.

Canning Foods

Most foods, including meats, fruits, and vegetables, can be preserved by canning. Although canning is more time consuming than quickly freezing your meat and produce, canned foods require no electric power while stored and you don't have to wait for them to thaw before preparing a meal. Canning is also a good way to prepare many ready-to-eat treats such as homemade vegetable soup, your own recipe for spaghetti, pizza, chili sauce, or our favorites, taco sauce and salsa. If in doubt about the processing time of any mixture, always process for the longest time recommended for any one ingredient.

Pressure Canning Meats

Pressure canning easily preserves meats. It saves space if the meat is deboned and sliced or diced before canning. The meat can be precooked before canning or it can be packed raw. Whichever method you choose, process only quality chilled meat with all fat and connective tissue removed. Soak the meat for an hour or so in a brine of one tablespoon salt for each quart of water needed to cover the meat. Rinse the brine from the meat before proceeding.

Hot-Packed Meat

Precook the meat. Pack the chunks or cubes of meat into canning jars, adding one teaspoon salt per quart. Fill the jars leaving one inch of headspace. Add boiling broth, water, or tomato juice to the jars, again leaving one inch of headspace.

Ground meat can also be pressure canned. Brown the meat and pack into jars. Add boiling bouillon, water, or tomato juice. Add salt, adjust-

BONELESS CUTS OF MEAT ARE PRESSURE CANNED. ALTHOUGH NOT THE MOST POPULAR WAY OF PRESERVING MEATS, THEY ARE READY TO EAT, NO THAWING REQUIRED.

ing the amount if adding bouillon. Leave one inch of headspace. The ground meat can be loose packed, made into patties, or shaped into balls. Ground meat can only be hot packed.

Raw Packed Meats

Fill jars with raw meat chunks or cubes, leaving one inch of headspace. Add one teaspoon salt per quart jar. Do not add any liquid.

Processing Meats

Follow all the steps for pressure canning meats as given in the recipe book that came with your pressure canner. If it's an older model, check with your local county extension office to see if the time and pressure recommended in your booklet are the current standards. Follow the current standard time and pressure recommendations for the type of meat being canned.

If you haven't previously canned any meat, try at least a portion of this year's bounty. Not only does the finished product have a different taste, but added convenience as well. Canned meat is ready to use in any recipes calling for boned, diced meat, and most of the ground meat recipes.

Canning Fruits and Vegetables

Most vegetables and fruits can be canned, but some are better canned than others. Our family loves home-canned green beans and will not touch them frozen. Corn, however, we prefer frozen. Many fruits have more of a "fresh-picked" taste when frozen rather than canned. Peaches, however, are equally good canned and frozen, just different. Apples are very good canned whether sliced for pies or made into applesauce. Pears also can well. Most of the berries are better frozen; however, pie filling can be made with the berries and canned or frozen. If you haven't canned fruits and vegetables in the past, you will soon learn which ones your family enjoys. Our family loves canned tomato products.

We can a lot of tomatoes and tomato products such as whole tomatoes, tomato juice, salsa,

A TRADITIONAL OLD-TIME COUNTRY WAY OF PRESERVING FOODS IS BY HOME CANNING. USE A PRESSURE CANNER AND CAREFULLY FOLLOW YOUR CANNER'S DIRECTIONS FOR SPECIFIC FOODS.

taco sauce, chili sauce, pizza, or spaghetti sauce and in bumper years even barbeque sauce. To make any product from tomato juice, the tomatoes are washed and cut into chunks with all bad spots removed. In order not to lose any tomatoes, we wash and cut up tomatoes daily and freeze them in zippered bags. When bags of tomatoes fill the freezer, we do a big canning. The tomatoes are cooked in large pots until cooked down to the desired consistency. We cook the tomatoes in the pressure canner pans and also in an electric roaster. The electric roaster is especially convenient since it can be used outside and not heat up the kitchen. Tomatoes to be canned as juice are cooked very little. If we plan to make tomato, taco, chili, or pizza sauce from the tomatoes, then the tomatoes are cooked down until fairly thick. It is much easier to cook the excess liquid from the tomatoes than to cook the sauce until thick. When the tomatoes are cooked to the desired consistency, we take the mess outside and hand-crank the tomatoes through a Victorio Strainer. The tomato juice is then reheated and canned or made into the sauce of choice and then canned.

Use only approved canning jars, lids, and rings. Prepare the jars according to manufacturer's instructions and process all products according to USDA recommendations. Various recipes are available from Kerr and Ball and www.homecanning.com, the home canning Web site. Home-canned products store best in a cool place; a food cellar is the perfect spot for canned foods.

Freezing Foods

One of the most common methods of preserving fruits, vegetables, and meats these days is by freezing and storing in a freezer. While simple and effective, there are limits to freezing's ability to maintain quality. Freezing protects from immediate spoilage, but affects quality and flavor by drying out the foods. This is especially true in "frost-free" freezers, where moisture is pulled from the refrigerated air to prevent frost build-up.

It's important to handle foods correctly before packaging. Boneless meat such as the loins should be frozen intact, rather than sliced ready to fry. Moisture escapes from each cut surface, speeding deterioration. Cut the meat as desired after it has partially thawed, but is still firm enough to slice easily. Vegetables should be blanched before freezing. Blanching should be done for the recommended time in boiling water. The vegetables are immediately immersed in cold water to chill as quickly as possible, then drained and packaged.

Freezing is also a traditional preservation method, and it's quick and easy. Many vegetables must first be "blanched," or dipped in boiling water to kill surface germs.

Packaging

Wrap foods carefully to maintain quality for as long as possible. Heavy-duty freezer paper or heavy-duty aluminum foil should be used. Both are equally effective, although foil is easier to use on odd-shaped pieces. Plastic zippered freezer bags are a very convenient way of freezing small or large portions of meats, vegetables, and fruits. A better method, however, is to double wrap where possible. First, use transparent freezer wrap, followed by freezer paper, aluminum foil, or a zippered freezer bag. If using freezer paper, use freezer tape to seal the package.

149

THE BLANCHED VEGETABLES ARE THEN COOLED QUICKLY BY PLUNGING IN COLD WATER.

And, above all else, mark the packages with their contents and the month and year you wrapped them. You might also want to denote the specific crop such as early corn, fall broccoli, stewing hen, and so forth. Regardless of how careful we are about labeling, it seems that once or twice a year we pull out a mystery package with no label. When wrapping or sealing bags, squeeze as much air from around the food as possible.

Storage Times

You should plan to use all foods within a year of freezing. Not only does this provide the best quality, but it also indicates that you are growing

THE COOL, DRAINED VEGETABLES ARE THEN PLACED IN FREEZER CONTAINERS OR BAGS.

and butchering the correct amounts for your family. Depending on how the food is wrapped and what type of freezer is used, quality may remain constant for longer periods. Freezing for longer periods affects taste and quality, but poses no other risks. The following chart gives an approximate storage guide for various cuts of meat, fruits, and vegetables.

Food Type	Maximum storage
Hamburger	Up to 3 months
Roasts	10 months
Steaks	8 months
Potatoes, cut-up	2 to 3 months
Apples, peaches, pears, and plums	8 to 12 months
Citrus fruits	4 to 6 months
Whole chickens and turkeys	12 months
Chicken and turkey pieces	9 months
Most vegetables	8 to 12 months
Wild game	6 to 12 months

As you can see, the larger cuts of meats keep the longest. Rather than slicing into steaks, freeze a whole "steak section" and slice after the meat has been thawed. Also, only properly blanched fruits and vegetables will keep the recommended times.

Vacuum Packing

The ultimate method of preserving by freezing is using a vacuum packing machine to remove oxygen from the container. Oxidation (exposure to oxygen in the air) is the main cause of food spoilage. When foods absorb oxygen, they begin a process of irreversible chemical change. Contact with oxygen causes foods to lose nutritional value, texture, flavor, and overall quality.

When oxygen is removed from the storage environment, foods can be stored three to five times longer than with conventional storage methods. In the absence of oxygen, dried foods, frozen foods, and perishable foods requiring refrigeration will retain their "just-bought" freshness and flavor much longer—resulting in less food waste.

Oxygen enables microorganisms such as bacteria, mold, and yeast to grow. These microorganisms cause rapid deterioration of food. Exposure to freezing cold air also causes "freezer burn" in frozen foods. (Freezer burn is localized dehydration.) Oxygen causes foods that are moderately high in fats and oils to yield a rancid odor and flavor. Air carries moisture and moisture causes the food to become soggy and lose its texture. Moisture causes "caking" in dry solids, making them difficult to handle. Oxygen also allows insects to survive and hatch.

Preventing air from coming in contact with stored food is a two-step process:

1. Remove all the air currently in the container.
2. Prevent air from re-entering the container. This requires that two conditions be met:
   a. The container needs to be made of a material that provides a barrier to oxygen.
   b. The seal on the container needs to be airtight.

Vacuum packaging is the process of removing the air from a container so that a vacuum is created, and then sealing the container so that air cannot re-enter.

Vacuum-packaging systems are able to create a vacuum in storage bags, canisters, jars, cans, and bottles. Storage bags used for freezing are especially designed to provide an oxygen and moisture barrier and to maintain an airtight seal. To provide an effective barrier, the bags should be constructed of plastic or a nylon layer. The bags should have a pattern of small "air channels" to ensure that air pockets don't form as the air is being removed.

It's important to choose the proper vacuum packaging system. Bag sealers, sometimes thought of as vacuum-packaging systems, utilize a heated wire that welds the bag closed. They do not have any mechanism for removing air from the bag before sealing. Bag sealers utilizing a fan have a small rotary fan to extract some of the air out of the plastic bags before they are sealed. Some systems utilize polyethylene bags. Others provide sheets of plastic from which bags of different lengths can be made by "welding" the seams with a heated wire bag-sealing mechanism. The fans in these models don't have enough suction to create a vacuum. The amount of air removed is comparable to using a straw to suck air out of the bag. The plastic will shape itself loosely to the contours of the food in the bag, but it will be obvious that air remains inside. The type of bag material and the strength of the seal, will determine whether oxygen is able to re-enter the bag.

A VACUUM PACKER SUCH AS THE TILIA FOODSAVER II SHOWN INCREASES FREEZER STORAGE TIME AND PREVENTS FREEZER BURN.

Electric-powered vacuum packaging systems, such as the FoodSaver Professional II, eliminate exposure to oxygen. These systems extract the existing air in a variety of containers including bags. The FoodSaver Professional II stores game in patented bags that keep food fresh three to five times longer and eliminate freezer burn.

Once a small package is vacuum packed, it stays fresh in the freezer for up to two years—large cuts of meat stay fresh in the freezer for up to three years. Plus, vacuum-packaged foods take up less space in the freezer because they don't have to be packed in water. Space the packages out in the freezer until they freeze completely. They can then be restacked to save space. Do not refreeze thawed raw meat. Thaw any meat in a refrigerator instead of at room temperature.

Meat to be frozen should be kept refrigerated at 40°F or slightly below before freezing. Ground meats should be frozen within two days, whole cuts of meat within three to five days.

Making Jellies, Jams, and Fruit Butters

Making jellies, jams, and fruit butters from fruits and some vegetables is another form of preserving that might be called "sugaring." Little more than fruits and lots of sugar are needed to preserve in this way. You will need jars, preferably with large openings so the jelly can be unmolded into a serving dish or scooped directly from the jar.

The Basics

All jelly must be processed in a boiling water bath, so pint and half-pint fruit jars are the best "jelly jars." Decorative jars, just for jelly making, are also available. To make jelly you will also need a jelly bag or cloth. A Victorio Strainer with a fruit or berry screen will make the process easier, but for truly clear jelly, the juice will still need to be poured through a jelly cloth.

Jelly, jam, and fruit butters are delicious spread over hot biscuits, but you can also use them in a number of other ways, including flavoring desserts and glazing meats.

It is easiest to make jelly and jam with powdered pectin; however, powdered pectin wasn't available to our ancestors. They used natural fruit pectin or the pectin from under-ripe fruits such

MAKING JAMS AND JELLIES IS A TRADITIONAL WAY OF PRESERVING MANY FRUITS, BERRIES, AND EVEN SOME VEGETABLES. THESE FRESH-PICKED BLACKBERRIES WILL MAKE DELICIOUS JAM OR JELLY.

as apples. Make the following pectin test on your fruit to determine the pectin content before proceeding with jam or jelly:

Cook eight tablespoons juice and five tablespoons sugar until thickened. If this mixture is jelled when cooled, go ahead and prepare your jam or jelly without adding any powdered pectin.

If the juice doesn't have enough pectin, mix with another fruit high in pectin or make it into a softer jam, preserve, or butter.

The amount of acid in the fruit is also important. To test for acid, mix one teaspoon lemon juice with three tablespoons water and two teaspoons sugar. If your fruit juice tastes less tart than the lemon juice mixture, one tablespoon lemon juice should be added to each cup of fruit juice.

The amount of sugar is dependent on the amount of pectin and acid in the fruit. Juice that is high in pectin usually requires equal cups of sugar and juice. Juice that has less pectin requires less sugar or about three quarters of a cup of sugar to each cup of fruit juice.

To test the jelly for doneness, use a candy or deep-fat thermometer and cook the jelly to eight degrees over the boiling point at your elevation and your humidity that day. It is best to check the boiling point each day before cooking jelly, as this will change daily. An easier, but less reliable test is the refrigerator test. Remove the cooked jelly from the stove, drop a circle of jelly about the size of a quarter onto a small plate, and place in the refrigerator or freezer. Leave a few minutes or until cool. If the jelly holds its shape, it will probably be sufficiently jelled when cool. The oldest test for doneness is the spoon test. Dip a large, metal spoon into the boiling jelly. Lift the spoon away from the steam of the jelly and turn sideways to let the jelly run from the spoon. When the jelly thickens and pours off the spoon in a sheet, it has probably reached the jelling point.

PEACHES ARE TRADITIONALLY MADE INTO JAM.

To make jams or jellies with purchased powdered pectin, follow the cooking directions on the package.

After cooking the jam or jelly, let sit for approximately five minutes, stirring and skimming the foam from the top as you stir. When making jam this will also help keep the fruit from floating to the top.

Pour the jam or jelly into hot, sterilized jars, seal with sterilized lids and process in a boiling water bath.

Easy Spicy Apple Butter

10 quarts thick apple pulp
3 tablespoons cinnamon
1 teaspoon cloves
1 teaspoon allspice
2 cups each brown sugar and white sugar,
   or to taste

Cook washed, quartered apple chunks with as little water as possible. I cook these in an electric roaster until thick. Crank through a Victorio Strainer or press through a colander. Pour 10 quarts thick pulp back into the cleaned electric roaster, stir in the spices and sugars, and cook to desired consistency. Stir occasionally, especially around the edges of the pan. Pack into hot, sterilized jars, seal with sterilized lids and process in boiling water bath for 15 minutes.

PART SEVEN

Woodcrafting

Handcrafting items from the woodlot, including furniture and home accessories such as baskets and tools was a very important activity of the early settlers. Many of these crafts and skills have continued to be popular today. For instance, white-oak baskets are not only fashionable today but also just as useful as in years past. Rustic furniture has also become extremely popular.

Slab and Rustic Furniture

In the olden days, of necessity, many furniture items were made of slabs and saplings. It's also a great way these days to utilize sawmill slabs as well as saplings taken during woodlot thinning operations to build camp- or lodge-style furniture. The furniture created is extremely sturdy in addition to adding a "rustic" flavor to home décor. And, construction is easy.

Materials

If you have a woodlot, you probably have plenty of materials for rustic furniture. Most woodlots benefit from thinning trees, removing dead trees, and other timber management practices. With a chainsaw and portable band saw mill, such as the TimberKing, you can acquire all types of building materials. In fact, you might even end up with a small at-home business. If you don't have a woodlot, you can often still acquire the materials. Slabs are often free for the asking at sawmills, and tree trimmings or branches may be available from dealers in cordwood.

The type of woods will vary with availability and locality and may range from oak to cedar to pine to redwood, birch, and cypress. Furniture that is to be left outdoors should be made of pine, cedar, oak, or cypress. Furniture to be used indoors can be made of almost any wood, but the lighter woods, such as cypress and cedar are best because you can use thicker slabs, yet still create furniture that is reasonably lightweight.

OF NECESSITY, MANY FURNITURE ITEMS AND ACCESSORIES IN THE OLDEN DAYS WERE MADE FROM WOOD SLABS AND SAPLINGS. FURNITURE SUCH AS THIS BENCH CAN CREATE A RUSTIC FEEL IN TODAY'S CAMP OR LODGE.

For most construction, you'll need slabs at least four feet long and twelve to eighteen inches wide. These slabs should be from three to six inches thick at their thickest part. With some species the bark may be left on, especially when building outdoor furniture. Some species tend to shed their bark and it's best to remove it, especially for indoor furniture. Pine and cedar are good examples of woods that look best with the bark removed.

You will also need saplings for the legs, arms, and stretchers. Again, you'll have to use wood that is readily available locally. The saplings should range from one to three inches in diameter for chairs and tables. For beds, the saplings should range from four to six inches in diameter. Just about any sapling wood will do, but again the lighter weight woods make lighter furniture for indoor use. The saplings also don't have to match the wood used for the slabs and the bark can be left on or removed from the saplings as well.

Slabs, or the waste from sawmills, are used to create the furniture.

Tools

You really don't need many tools for this type of project; the furniture can be constructed with simple hand tools. A chain saw for cutting trees and saplings, as well as for faster cutting of pieces to length also comes in handy. A hand crosscut or bucksaw can also be used for cutting the pieces to length. A brace and bits (including an expansive bit), drawknife, spokeshave, hammer or mallet, and plane will build most projects. You may also wish to use a hand adz for scooping out chair seats and other hollow areas. If you get into large-scale furniture production there are also pow-

ered tenoning tools, from woodcraft supply, that can be used to cut the round tenons quickly and easily on the ends of the legs as well as various other power tools to make the jobs easier.

Slab Preparation

The sawn surface of the slabs may be quite rough, especially if sawn on large circular saw mills. Band saw mills, on the other hand, leave a smoother surface. Rough surfaces may need to be smoothed. The amount of smoothness depends on your desires. The surfaces can be smoothed with the jackplane or a powered belt sander can be used for initial smoothing, followed by finish sanders if you prefer an extremely smooth surface. The ends should also be smoothed up. The edges and corners should be smoothed and rounded. Then inspect the entire piece for any splinters or sharp edges. Some extremely rough bark may also need to be smoothed slightly with a drawknife or spokeshave. Try to use sapling sections without knots or bumps. If they do have knots or bumps, cut them flush or smooth them. Inspect the saplings to make sure there are no sharp bumps or knots.

Constructing a Simple Bench or Stool

At this point, you're ready to begin construction of the furniture. Determine the length of the legs. Remember in this type of furniture, the legs are usually placed at an angle and this requires slightly longer lengths. The next step is to determine the diameter of the tenons. This will usually be just slightly smaller than the outside diameter or bark if it is left on. A one-inch diameter is a good starting point. Once you've decided on the diameter, set the expansive bit to the correct size and bore the holes for the legs. Make sure to keep the angles the same for all four legs. The easiest way of doing this is with an angle-boring jig. This allows you to assure correct and consistent angles on all holes. The angle should be between 80 and 85 degrees in two directions. Using the drawknife, and with the leg clamped in a vise or other type of clamp, shape the end of the leg into a round tenon that

THE LEGS ARE CUT TO LENGTH FROM SAPLINGS AND THEN TENONS CUT ON THE LEGS USING A TENONING MACHINE IN A PORTABLE ELECTRIC DRILL.

A better method is the open tenon. In this case, the hole for the tenon is bored all the way through the slab. The tenon is cut long enough so about one-half inch protrudes through the top of the slab. A slot is cut in the top of the tenon, and the tenon driven in place in the hole. A wedge is then driven in from the top of the slab. Once the leg is wedged tightly in place, the end of the tenon and wedge are cut off flush with the top of the slab. The slab is then sanded or planed to smooth the joints. As most of this type of furniture is made of green wood, it will eventually shrink and the legs become loose. To retighten, simply drive in another wedge or a larger wedge. On thick slabs, a pin can be used to hold the tenons in place.

will fit snugly into the hole. Tenons may be fastened in place in one of three ways. If the wood is seasoned, which it rarely is in this type of construction, you can glue the tenons in place. Or you can drive a nail in at an angle to hold the tenons. The more traditional and best method, however, is to anchor the tenons in place with a wedge. This can be with a concealed or blind wedge, or the wedge can be exposed. The exposed method also allows you to retighten the tenons should they come loose.

To create a blind wedge, try-fit the tenon in place. It should be snug, but not too tight. Saw a slot in the top of the tenon and start a thin and short wedge in place. Insert the tenon with wedge in place and use the mallet or hammer to drive it securely in place.

HOLES ARE BORED AT AN ANGLE WITH A FORSTNER BIT AND PORTABLE ELECTRIC DRILL OR BRACE AND BIT.

On a simple bench or stool, you may wish to stop at this point. Stretchers, or rungs, however, can strengthen the furniture piece greatly and also help prevent undue warping as the wood dries. The stretchers should be slightly smaller than the legs.

Try-fit the legs in place and make a mark on each leg corresponding to a mark on the bottom side of the slab. This allows you to relocate the legs precisely during assembly. Then measure the distance up from the bottom of the legs you wish to install the stretchers. Mark the

ROUND THE EDGES OF THE BENCH WITH A DRAWKNIFE.

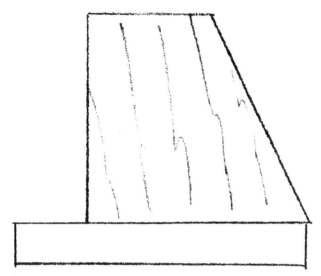

AN ANGLE GUIDE CAN HELP KEEP THE ANGLES CONSISTENT.

SLOTS ARE CUT IN THE TOP OF THE TENONS AND THE TENONS DRIVEN INTO THE HOLES. WEDGES ARE THEN CUT TO FIT INTO THE SLOTS AND DRIVEN IN PLACE.

center of the tenon location on each leg. Note you will have to stagger the stretchers from side to side and front to back. Measure the length for the stretchers, leaving enough extra length for each tenon end. Cut the stretchers to length. Bore the holes in the legs for the tenons and then shape the tenons on the stretchers. Try-fit all pieces to assure everything fits and then assemble the stretchers to the legs first, and finally drive the tenons of the assembled legs and stretchers into the slab top. The stretchers should be pinned to the legs. This can be done with nails, wooden pins, or by boring holes in the ends of the stretchers and wrapping wet rawhide around the legs. The wet rawhide is a crude, but definitely rustic method that will hold forever.

Once the bench or stool is assembled, place it on a flat, smooth surface. You'll discover it probably doesn't sit flat. Use small pieces of wood to wedge the shorter legs until the furniture piece sits flat and level. Mark the amount needed to be removed from a leg or legs to create a level surface. Mark all around the leg so you can cut the leg flat or you'll end up continually cutting. With the piece on its side, saw the legs to the correct length.

THE TENON-WEDGE ASSEMBLY IS CUT FLUSH WITH THE TOP.

THE TOP SANDED SMOOTH.

Once you construct a simple bench or stool, you'll probably wish to tackle some more complicated projects. These can include benches and chairs with backs and arms. The same basic construction methods are used. Backs are usually held in place with wooden pins or nails.

One of the most common outdoor benches is the "half-log" bench. It is often made from storm blown trees or logs that are not particularly good saw logs, but you don't wish to waste. These are quite sturdy and long-lasting pieces of furniture.

You can also make tables in the same manner. It usually requires several slabs for the top or

THE BARK CAN BE REMOVED FROM SOME WOODS, SUCH AS THE RED CEDAR SHOWN, TO PRODUCE A BEAUTIFUL BENCH SUITABLE FOR INTERIOR USE.

THE FURNITURE PIECES CAN BE LEFT AS IS OR FINISHED.

you may be able to acquire some planks. If you have a portable sawmill, you can make the plank tables quite easily.

Camp Bed

One of the most common projects, and one I've seen in numerous hunting camps, is a bed. Tenon-jointed sapling beds are quite easy to make and can be extremely sturdy if constructed properly. You can even make great bunk beds for your hunting camp in this manner. The pole or saplings must be at least four inches in diameter. The old-timers used rope to hold the mattress in place. Three-eighths-inch rope spaced four inches apart in both directions is the traditional method of assembling a "rope" bed. A heavy cloth or canvas is then placed over the rope and the old-timers topped it off with a goose down feather mattress. If you intend to use a bedspring and mattress set, make sure you measure the bedspring first and assemble the bed to the proper size. The bedspring should sit inside the side and end support pieces. Cutting a lip on the inside of the saplings can do this. You can also nail a straight two by two to the inside of the sides. Bed slats are then used on the supports to hold the bedsprings in place.

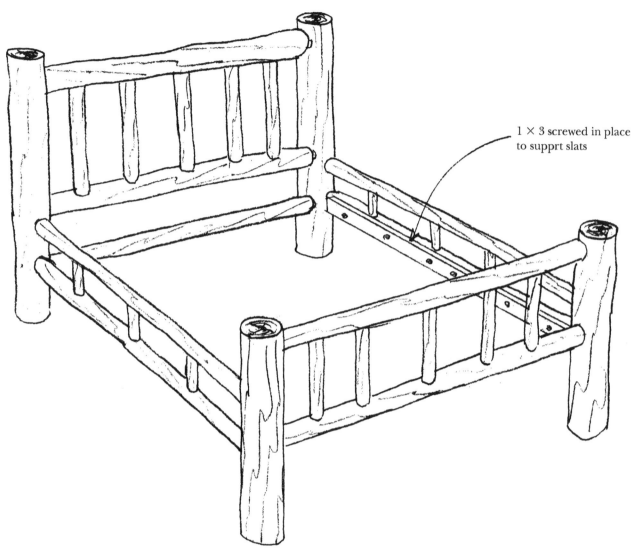

1 × 3 screwed in place
to supprt slats

A TENON-SAPLING BED IS A VERY COMMON HUNTING CAMP PROJECT, AND EASY TO MAKE.

Bentwood Furniture

Furniture that is even more elaborate can be constructed utilizing the bentwood technique. By scrounging, you can often find bent pieces that are ready to be used. Or, you can bend small diameter green saplings of pliable woods such as hickory or willow to the shape desired, and then anchor in place with tenons or fasteners.

Finishing

Outside furniture can be left as is, or you can lengthen the life of the furniture by coating with protective wood oil such as that used for wood decks. You can also make up your own protective coating of three parts linseed oil to one part turpentine. Another method is to use a spar or marine varnish over the exposed wood portions. You can oil the bark portions or leave them unprotected. Interior pieces can be treated in the same way, but peeled furniture pieces look best with several coats of a good polyurethane varnish. You can also stain and varnish the pieces for an even more unusual look.

Split Bottom Chair Seats

You can also make rustic sapling chairs with split bottom seats, a traditional eastern mountain-style chair. The splits are actually thin strips or splints of wood woven in place on the seat frame. The wood most often used was white oak, although sometimes hickory was used. A sapling about five inches in diameter and straight without any limbs or imperfections for eight to nine feet is required. The first step is to split the sapling into quarters and then split it again into eighths. Remove the heartwood cen-

ter section, as this is too soft to create splints. Using a sharp knife, remove the bark from the sections. Once the sections are prepared, insert a sharp knife into the center of the end of one section and parallel to the "flat" sides of the section. Tap on the knife blade to start the split. Once the split begins, you can force your fingers into the crack and very carefully pull the two pieces apart. Continue splitting the sections until you have the desired thickness. Splits for chair bottoms are normally one-sixteenth to one-eighth inch thick. If a split is too thick in spots, the bumps can be shaved off with a very sharp pocketknife or drawknife.

The best tactic is to use the splits the day they are created, but they can be kept wet in a large tub or a stream until they're to be used. Before using them on a chair, soak them overnight. This will cause them to shrink as they

WHITE OAK SPLITS CAN BE USED TO COVER THE BOTTOMS OF TRADITIONAL SPLIT-BOTTOM CHAIRS.

THE SPLITS ARE SOAKED OVERNIGHT AND THE STARTING SPLIT IS STAPLED IN PLACE.

THE SPLITS ARE THEN INTERWOVEN TO CREATE THE SEAT.

dry on the chair, making a tight-fitting chair bottom.

The first step in weaving a chair bottom of wood splits is to tack one end of one split to the chair on the back and then weave it around the chair bottom. When you run out of a split, fasten a second split in place by wrapping with string and tying the two pieces together. To finish the chair, weave across the splits over and under the other splits, tacking the last split in place on the underside of the chair. Weave on both top and bottom for a strong chair.

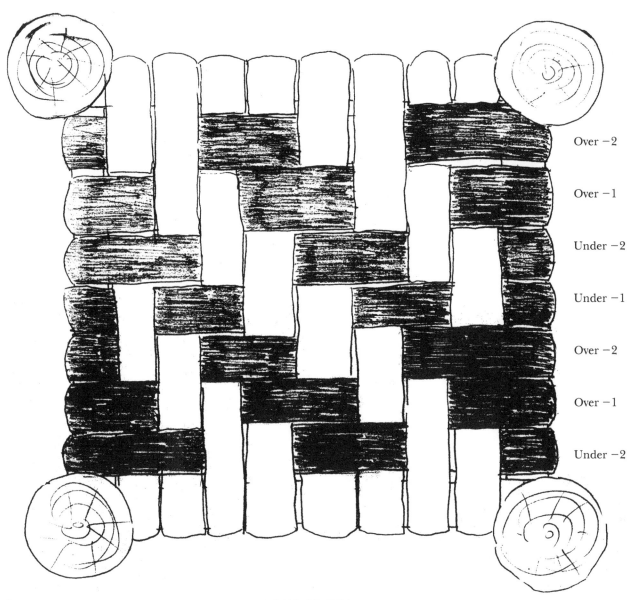

Over −2

Over −1

Under −2

Under −1

Over −2

Over −1

Under −2

A TYPICAL HERRINGBONE WOVEN, WHITE OAK SPLIT CHAIR BOTTOM.

Rustic Accessories

You are limited only by your imagination in what you can craft from branches, saplings, and other natural materials gathered from the woodlands. Candlesticks, coat and hat racks, shelves, lamps, are even lampshades from white birch bark are just a few examples. Look for interesting shapes or branches with curves—any feature that will provide interest and variety in design.

Whistle

When I was a child my dad made me a wooden whistle. The whistle was fun, but part of my enjoyment was watching him whittle it. To make one of your own, you'll need a six-inch twig from a smooth barked tree, such as maple. The twig should be about three eighths of an inch in diameter and from the outer green branches of the tree. The best whistles are actually made from sprouts that often come off the bottom of maple trees. The twig must be free of buds and knots and the bark should be smooth. The only other thing you'll need is a sharp pocketknife.

1. Cut one end of the twig straight across to square off one end. Next, make a slanting cut, leaving about a third of the square end. This creates the "mouthpiece."
2. About three quarters of an inch from the straight cut end, cut a notch in the twig. This is made on top of the twig, opposite the slanting cut.

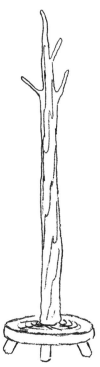

A VARIETY OF RUSTIC ACCESSORIES, SUCH AS THIS HALL TREE, CAN BE MADE TO MATCH THE SLAB FURNITURE.

167

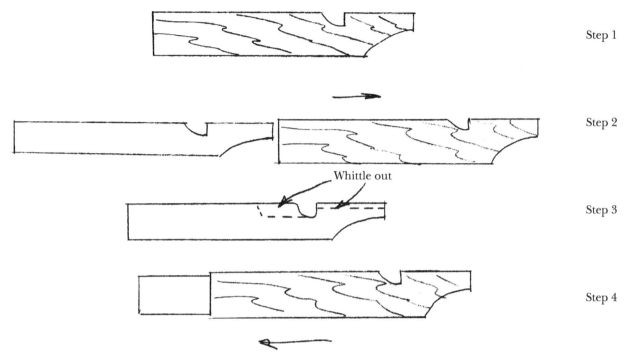

Step 1

Step 2

Whittle out

Step 3

Step 4

A WHISTLE MADE FROM A TREE TWIG IS FUN TO MAKE.

3. Cut through the bark only, encircling the twig about three inches from the slanting end.

4. Gently pound on the bark to loosen it. Turn the twig continually so you loosen all sides. The bark needs to come off as a tube or shell. Sometimes soaking in hot water can help in loosening the bark shell. Once the bark shell is loose, pull it off, being careful to keep it intact.

5. Cut a sliver of wood off the top of the twig from the notch to the end of the straight cut.

6. Then make a straight cut down about an inch and a half back from the notch. Cut about halfway through the twig and then cut the notch down to match. Remove the wood between these two cuts.

7. Slip the bark shell back over the twig. Align the notch on the shell with the inside edge of the notch on the twig. Blow through the whistle. You may have to whittle the top of the twig in the mouth-

piece area to achieve a clear, ringing tone.

White Oak Gathering Basket

White oak splits were also used to make all types of baskets, from gathering baskets to pack baskets for trappers. The same basic methods are used to create the splits for baskets as was used for chair bottoms, however, you will need two framing pieces and several weaving pieces. The framing pieces should be about a quarter of an inch thick and about one inch wide. The weaving splits should be about one-sixteenth of an inch thick and from a half inch to one inch wide. A gathering basket approximately seventeen inches in diameter requires framing splits fifty-four inches in length. These consist of a rim and handle framing piece and both should be about the same length.

1. Start construction of the basket by bending the framing splits into loops and fastening the loops together using waxed string to tie them together. Soaking the pieces in

WHITE OAK SPLITS CAN ALSO BE MADE INTO BEAUTIFUL LONG-LASTING STURDY BASKETS. THE SPLITS ARE FIRST CUT FROM QUARTERED SAPLINGS USING A FROE AND PEELING THEM AWAY.

BEFORE BEING WOVEN INTO BASKETS, THE SPLITS MUST BE SOAKED OVERNIGHT IN WATER.

hot water prior to working with them will make them easier to bend and work.

2. Begin the weaving at the point where the handle and rim frame pieces cross. Use your narrowest and thinnest splits for this area. Weave with a simple over-under pattern as you go around the joint created by the framing piece.

3. After about a dozen splits have been woven on one end, do the same on the opposite end.

4. Using heavier framing splits, add eight rib splits to the bottom, weaving them in place with the splits crisscrossed over and under. These framing ribs should have their ends tapered to a point for easier insertion and weaving. Begin the rib place-

ment by inserting one end of one rib into the weaving on each side of the handle.

5. Once the ribs are in place, all other weaving is done in the basket proper by weaving splits over and under the rib framing pieces and around the rim framing. If you need to introduce a new split, simply tuck it under a couple of ribs back. As you can guess, the longer splits will make a neater basket. Weave from each end of the basket to the center. When you come to the center make sure there is no wide crack between the center splits. If necessary, overlap the splits in the row to create a tight center area. Fasten the first split by tucking it under a rib.

6. You can finish off the basket by going around the rim with a thin, narrow split. This not only provides a more finished look, but also adds strength to the basket.

Wood Tools

Wood pieces can also be whittled or shaped into a wide arrange of tools and even storage boxes. The old timers cut thin sheets of basswood, scored it like cardboard, and then bent it to shape around forms to create lightweight wooden boxes. Thin pieces of steamed elm, beech, or ash were also bent into circles to create the traditional "Shaker" boxes. These boxes were often held together with a wood hoop.

MANY WOODEN TOOLS, SUCH AS THIS APPLE-BUTTER STIRRER, WERE ALSO MADE BY THE OLD-TIMERS.

Wood pieces were also used to create apple butter paddles, pie crust crimpers, butter molds, grain shovels, piggins, plates, spoons, scoops, dippers, tankards, meat-pounding mallets, hay forks, sap pails, grain winnowers, rakes, and many other items. Re-creating some of the old-time tools is a lot of fun and produces great decorative items.

Christmas Wreaths and Garland

If you have access to evergreens, you can easily create your own Christmas wreaths and decorations. Wreaths can be made of almost any evergreen material, including the various species of pines, juniper, spruce, fir, hemlock, cypress, holly, and cedar. When trimming your yard or woodlot trees, keep the trimmings for wreaths and centerpieces.

To make a wreath, gather the materials and store them in a cool place so the needles won't fall off. Bend a length of No. 11 wire into a circle and wire it together with fine gauge wire. Make several wraps of the 24-gauge wire around the larger wire circle. Holding several bunches of needles against the wire circle, wrap with the smaller gauge wire to fasten in place. Overlap another bunch of branches over the first, and wrap it in place. Continue wrapping until the entire wreath is formed, clip off any straggly branches, and tie a large red bow at the top. Add any additional adornment as desired.

Evergreen material can also be made into natural swags and garland. Simply start with two evergreen boughs with the stick ends overlapped so that no stick shows. Wrap these with a light gauge wire in a looping wrap. Add one bough at a time, wrapping as you go until the garland or swag is the length needed. Decorate as desired.

Pinecones make a great natural embellishment to wreaths or garland. Pinecones can also be made into wreaths. Start with a heavy gauge wire frame and, using a light gauge wire, wire pinecones in place. Pinecones can also be spray painted in almost any color for more colorful "natural" wreaths or when added to wreaths, swags, or garland.

Grapevine Wreaths

You can also create unusual wreaths from wild grapevines. And, in many instances, trimming back the smaller-diameter vines will help the tree they grow on, as grape vines will smother many trees. Simply create a circle of a section of grape vine and tie it together. Continue to wrap and twist additional grape vines around the circle to complete the "wreath." Grapevine wreaths can be decorated for any season of the year and can be used inside or out.

CHRISTMAS WREATHS AND GARLAND CAN BE MADE FROM EVERGREEN TRIMMINGS. GRAPEVINES MAKE UNUSUAL WREATHS.

PART EIGHT

Around the Farm

Out of necessity, farmers and ranchers the world over are "jacks-of-all-trades." In many instances, they don't have time to go to town to have something fixed or to buy something. Or, they simply can't afford a manufactured item, so they make it or fix it themselves. Oftentimes that project is made from materials scrounged from the area.

Sharpening Tools

One of the most important jobs around the house or farm is sharpening tools, from knives to scissors to axes to farm and garden implements. To many people, getting a good edge on a knife or axe is a skill that disappeared with Daniel Boone. Many years ago I sat on my Uncle Mike's back step and watched him hone his belt knife until he could take a hair and shave slivers from it. All it took was patience, time, and several good stories. The problem today is most of us don't take the time to get a good edge on a blade, let alone pass along invaluable stories.

Tools

My granddad had a foot-powered sharpening hone in his backyard. It had a small pan with a control to drip water onto the wheel as it was turned by your foot. Honing with it took a bit of practice, as you had to keep it running by pumping with your feet and at the same time hold the knife properly in place on the hone. Any number of modern-day products makes this age-old chore much easier. A steel, such as used by professional butchers, is a handy tool for a quick touch-up. A number of diamond-coated or ceramic sharpening stones and hones are also available.

Knives

An extremely battered knife will require filing to even up the blade and remove nicks and dents. Do not use an electric grinder on a good knife be-cause you stand the chance of overgrinding and even overheating, which ruins the temper. Use a good bastard-cut mill file to even up the blade. For restoring keenness to a sharp blade, however, use only a hone or steel, or diamond sharpeners. For quick touch-ups the Hewlett Jewelstik Diamond Sharpening Steels are available in several sizes, including models small enough for a pocket or fanny pack.

Handheld hones are some of the most popular sharpening devices and include those from Chef'sChoice, Gatco DMT Diamond Stones, Smith's, and Norton. These simple tools are used by placing them on a solid work surface and drawing the knife blade across the hone. It is important to first determine the angle desired for the finished edge. The angle can vary from 5 to 10 degrees. The sharper the angle, the thinner and sharper the blade. The thinner edges,

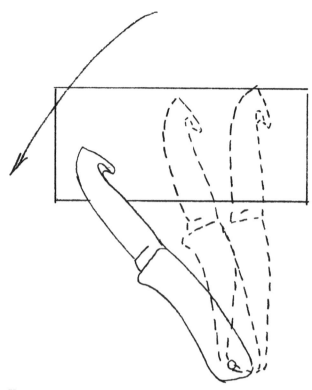

KEEPING KNIVES SHARP IS EASY IF YOU FOLLOW A FEW BASIC RULES. USE A GOOD SHARPENING STONE AND LIGHT OIL. STROKE IN THE PATTERN SHOWN.

smaller knives. The knife blade can also be moved in a circular or figure eight pattern as well.

The most important factor is removing the same amount of metal from both sides of the blade. Count your strokes on one side, then turn the blade over and hone the other side with an equal number of strokes. The pressure applied is also important. Start with a moderate to heavy pressure and finish with lighter strokes. If the blade is really dull, use the coarse side of the stone to develop a good angle on the edge before going to the finer grit.

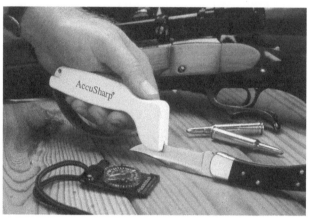

ONE OF THE EASIEST SHARPENING SYSTEMS IS THE ACCUSHARP. MERELY HOLD THE KNIFE IN POSITION AND DRAW THE ACCUSHARP AGAINST THE BLADE. (PHOTO COURTESY ACCUSHARP)

however, are less durable than the thicker ones. Try to stay with the existing blade angle, which is 7 to 8 degrees on most knives.

Gatco Sharpening Systems utilize a rod-hone handle, a permanently affixed rod that maintains a fixed and constant sharpening angle. Combined with the knife-clamp angle guide, it assures consistent, correct angle sharpening every time.

In most instances, honing is made faster and easier by using oil, or even spittle, on the stone to lubricate it. Some companies sell the lubricant with their hones or stones.

Depending on the size and shape of the sharpener and the knife, you can move either one and hold the other steady. In most instances, it's easier to keep the hone steady and move the knife. Any number of honing patterns may be used, depending on the size of the knife. Simply stroking the blade down and outward is good for

The main ingredient is patience. Wipe the stone clean after each use. If the stone becomes filled with grit, clean it with lacquer thinner and a brush, then re-oil. At the beginning of the honing, you'll see a burred or "white" edge along the blade when you sight down it. Whet the blade until you remove all this white area. Don't test the keen of the blade with your thumb. If the blade is properly sharpened, you'll get a nasty cut. Instead, hold a piece of newspaper in one hand and slice with the knife. The blade should slice smoothly without catching on the paper. For a truly keen blade, finish by stropping it on a leather strop. This can be your hunting belt, or make up a leather strop to keep at your bench.

Since I come from a big hunting family, I usually end up butchering a lot of game and I keep a number of skinning, butchering, and hunting knives extremely sharp for the chore. I've found nothing beats the EdgeCraft Chef'sChoice 120V Select Diamond Hone Sharpener. I can sharpen even a fairly dull knife within seconds with the tool, without the possibility of ruining the knife blade. The electric sharpener utilizes a three-stage sharpening system. Stage 1 is for excessively dull or damaged knives. Stage 2 is used for routine sharpening. Stage 3 is a Strop Polishing stage that utilizes a patented material to create micro and polished microflute cutters on the blade edge for a super sharp edge.

AN AXE SHOULD ALSO BE KEPT SHARP. USE A GOOD MEDIUM-CUT BASTARD-CUT MILL FILE TO KEEP THE EDGE PROPERLY SHAPED AND SHARP.

EDGECRAFT CHEF'SCHOICE DIAMOND HONE SHARPENER MAKES SHARPENING KNIVES QUICK AND EASY.

Axes

The first step in sharpening an axe is to file the edge to even it up and remove the inevitable nicks. Place the axe head in a vise or, if you're in camp, extend the edge of the blade over the end of a stump or log. Use a good medium-cut eight- to ten-inch bastard-cut mill file and holding it flat, stroke from the eye of the head out toward the edge. File only on the going away stroke and keep turning the blade to file both edges evenly. Continue filing until you completely reshape and sharpen the edge. The main thing is to produce a round edge, not a "wedge." The latter has a tendency to do just that, wedge tight on a good hard swing, whereas a rounded shoulder will throw the chips outward from the blade. To provide support, keep the cutting edge convex. An axe should never be thinned any more than when it comes from the factory, or the edge will break and chip easily. File the axe in a fan shape, leaving a bit more metal at the corners for reinforcement. You should be able to sight down the edge and not see any bright or white spots. These indicate a dull or unsharpened area. Finally, use a fine, round hand stone or hone in a circular pattern to hone the edge to final sharpness.

Fencing

First-rate fencing is essential on a farm or ranch. It encloses pastures for animals, from sheep to cattle, and forms pens and corrals for sorting or holding livestock.

Choosing Materials

Choose a fencing material appropriate to the livestock you are enclosing. Poultry will need poultry fencing or netting which consists of a light-gauge galvanized wire with one- to two-inch hexagonal mesh openings. It's available in rolls from one to six feet in height. Pigs root and lift upward. Fencing for hogs should be of hog-wire from three to four feet high. A strand of barbed

GOOD FENCING IS A NECESSARY PART OF ANY COUNTRY HOMESTEAD. A WIDE VARIETY OF FENCING MATERIALS EXIST FOR DIFFERENT APPLICATIONS.

wire should be stretched across the bottom to deter pigs from rooting under the fence. Cows reach over and reach through a fence. The best permanent fencing for cattle consists of six strands of barbed wire. For small calves, the cattle fencing can consist of hog-wire for the bottom and barbed wire for the top. A strand of barbed wire must also fit down on the top of the hog wire or cattle will push through and push down the woven wire. Sheep and goats should be contained with woven wire to prevent snagging their wool. A strand of barbed wire above and below can be used to help keep out predators. Horses reach over and push a fence down. The best horse fencing consists of wooden boards or a fence with a welded pipe top section.

In addition to the different wires and fencing materials, you'll need posts. Posts may be untreated wood, pressure-treated wood, metal, fiberglass, or plastic. If using untreated wood posts, choose long-lasting materials such as cypress, red cedar, locust, or hedge (Osage orange). Posts of the latter will oftentimes last longer than the builder. Steel posts from five to eight feet in length are common for creating many livestock fences. They are driven in place with a hand posthole driver, or with a machine. Tapered or pointed, pressure-treated wooden posts are also available with the ends shaped for driving with a maul or power equipment.

Building Fences

Building long-lasting and effective fences is a craft, but also extremely hard work. The fence is only as good as the posts that support it and proper post installation and spacing is extremely important. The posts must be of the proper size

to match the fencing and animals to control and they must be set to the proper depth and anchored solidly.

For the most part, posts should be set at least three feet in the ground with corner posts set four feet deep. Fences should be kept as straight as possible. Any time you must change directions or elevations, a corner or "stretcher" post must be installed. Curved fences will eventually loosen, as will areas with changes in elevation. A corner post usually consists of the actual corner post and a brace post placed at each direction of the fence. It's a good idea to place the corner

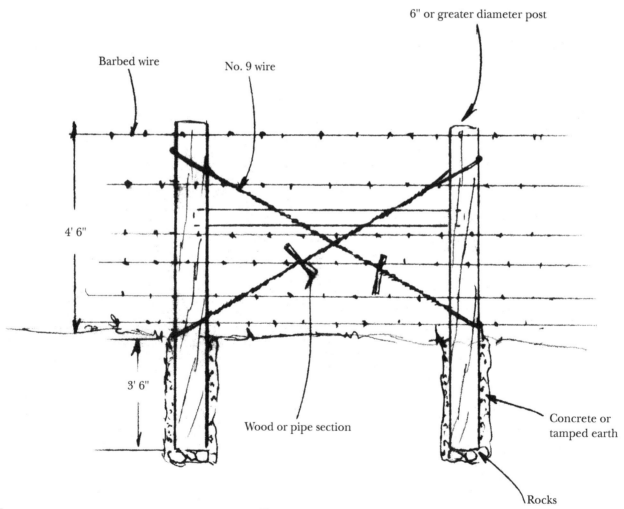

INSTALLATION OF POSTS IS EXTREMELY IMPORTANT. THEY SHOULD BE WELL ANCHORED AND CORNER AND STRETCHER POSTS SHOULD BE WELL BRACED.

posts in place, and then temporarily install a strand of fencing wire between the two corner posts. This makes it easy to position the brace posts in line with the fence. If they're even slightly out of line, they can cause the fence to become loosened. The posts should be sturdy, at least six inches or larger in diameter and set solidly in place at least four feet in the ground. They should be plumbed and the best side of crooked posts set to the fence side. The posts can be set in tamped earth or concrete. If using tamped earth, place several rocks in the bottom of the hole and around the post first. Tamp these solidly in place, add a layer of soil and tamp it, and continue adding rocks and soil to secure the posts in place. The corner posts and brace posts should be notched and a cross-brace inserted in both directions. Loop four strands of No. 9 gauge wire around the bottom of the corner post and up to the top of the brace posts. Twist the wire taut to "guy" the corner and brace posts together. Repeat for the top of the corner post and the bottom of the two brace posts. Corner posts can be further anchored in place, especially in sandy soil, by using a "deadman" or log buried in the ground and the post guyed to the log. When changing directions in the fence, use the three-post corner system. When changing fence elevation, use two posts with a brace and double wire guy. Once the corner posts have been set, and the brace posts aligned, temporarily stretch a wire to act as a line post guide. The line posts are then driven or set in holes bored in the ground and aligned with the temporary guide wire. They should also be installed plumb. Line posts are typically set two to three feet in the ground if wood, about a foot to a foot and half if driven steel. They may be spaced as far apart as sixteen feet, but twelve feet provides a much sturdier fence. Braced line posts should be installed every 100 yards or so. They are positioned eight feet apart and braced as for corner or elevation change posts. Do not set posts in gullies or streams where they can be washed out by floodwaters. For most purposes, the wire should be on the inside or livestock side of the fence to pre-

vent the animals from popping out staples or loosening fasteners when they push against it. Whether you use woven wire or individual strands of barbed wire, first wrap one end around an anchored post and fasten it solidly in place. Then stretch the wire to the next line brace or corner post using a wire stretcher and solid object. A dummy post temporarily anchored in place, or even your pickup or tractor can act as an anchor for the fence stretcher. A homemade, woven wire fence clamp makes it easier to stretch woven wire. Be extremely careful when working with barbed wire. If the fence stretcher happens to let go of the wire, it can quickly curl up on you causing serious injury.

CORRALS OF METAL OR WOOD SHOULD BE STURDY AND SUITED TO THE LIVESTOCK.

Depending on the livestock to be worked, sorting pens can be made of woven wire, wood, or welded steel pipe. Corrals for heavy-duty use by large animals should be made of sturdy pressure-treated wood or welded metal pipe. Corral fencing should be at least six feet tall for larger livestock such as cattle or horses. A less permanent alternative is to use galvanized welded, metal cattle or pig panels. These can be wired to steel posts driven in the ground. This is an especially effective method to create a pigpen. You can simply step over the panel for getting in and out of the pen to feed and water. To make it even stronger, fasten a metal pipe rail to the top.

GATES CAN BE HANDMADE WOODEN OR STEEL.

Gates can be simple wire, handmade wooden, or welded steel. Make sure they're fastened to posts well secured in the ground to prevent sagging.

Electric Fencing

These days we utilize electric fencing a great deal on our farm. This is especially so with our intensive grazing program for beef cattle. The new electric fencing consists of permanent, offset, or portable systems. The permanent system is faster and easier to erect and requires less material and labor than other, non-electric types. The offset system utilizes special fasteners that allow you to install an electric wire or wires on old fencing. This is especially effective on rented land or for temporary purposes. High-tensile wire in this system can also be used for predator control on existing fences. The portable system features lightweight "step-in" plastic or steel posts and highly visible polywire or polytape. The system can be moved in a short amount of time. We utilize permanent fencing for the borders of our fields and the portable system for creating paddocks for grazing. The portable fencing can also be used to create wildlife-proof fencing for gardens and flowers. The energizers for these types of fences have high output and low impedance. The energizers are available for up to 100 miles of fencing or from 5- to 1,500-acre farms and ranches. Energizers are available for 110-volt, AC; 12-volt DC, battery powered; or 12-volt, solar powered. A wide range of poles, fasteners, and fencing is available. Permanent electric fencing should be installed with posts set in the same manner as for other types of fencing, although using primarily wooden posts. Semi-permanent, or "border" fencing as I call it, is installed with a combination of wood posts set in concrete for corners and direction or elevation changes. Metal posts are then installed every fifty feet. Temporary fencing is installed on push-in posts. The great part about the latter is you can fence off an area, utilize or graze it, and then remove the fencing for mowing or other purposes as you see fit.

ELECTRIC FENCING IS ONE VERY GOOD ALTERNATIVE THESE DAYS, REGARDLESS OF THE LIVESTOCK, OR EVEN WILDLIFE, YOU WISH TO CONTAIN OR KEEP OUT.

MODERN ENERGIZERS PROVIDE MORE POWER AND ARE EASIER TO WORK WITH.

Laying Stone

The age-old craft of stonework is very satisfying. A stone project has a sense of immortality. Many stone buildings, walls, walks, and fences are centuries old. You can use stone around your homestead to build long-lasting and beautiful projects such as patios, walks, steps, retaining walls, flowerbeds, or even buildings, if you have the patience and desire. Stone also blends in with almost any decor, from traditional to formal to rustic.

Getting Started

Although the basic stonework used for these types of projects is fairly simple, working with stone can be backbreaking. It's important not to lift too much, and to use your entire body, not just your back. It's also important to not try to do too much in a day's time. Not only is this hard on you, but also the stonework needs to be laid one layer at a time and then allowed to dry.

Many old-time stone projects were made from stone picked up from fields, hillsides, or creek beds by the builder or property owner because they were so readily available. We've built many projects around our "homestead" with stone from our Ozark Mountains fields. But many property owners these days have to purchase stone for their projects. Several different types of stone are available including granite, limestone, marble, slate, flagstone, sandstone, gneiss, and tap rock.

Stone is also available as either fieldstone, quarried stone, rubble stone, or ashlar. Field-

ONE OF THE OLDEST BUILDING MATERIALS IS STONE, WHICH CAN BE USED TO CONSTRUCT FENCES, BUILDINGS, WALLS, AND PATIOS.

stone consists of rocks in their natural shape, and the wide variety of shapes and colors can add to informal stone projects. Quarried stone is cut and shaped and is used in more formal projects. Cut stone is slabbed at the quarry, but the face is left natural. A good example is slate or flagstone for patios or walks. Rubble stone are the pieces left over from blasting and cutting the cut stone. Ashlar stone pieces are cut on all four sides to create a formal pattern. The face of ashlar is also cut or faceted in a decorative manner. This is the type of stone seen on churches and many commercial buildings. Naturally, the most expensive stone is ashlar, quarried stone is next, and fieldstone and rubble are the most economical.

Because of the cost of shipping, the choice of stone may be limited in some areas. It's wise to visit local stone yards and determine the kinds available before planning a project. Stone is sold by the cubic yard. To calculate the amount of stone you will need, figure the cubic volume in feet by multiplying the length times the width times the height. Then divide the cubic feet in the project by 27 to determine the cubic yards needed. If purchasing cut stone add 10 percent for breakage and waste. With rubble stone, which is not graded, but purchased in bulk, you will need 25 percent more for waste. In most instances, you will have the stones delivered. If transporting the stones yourself, do not overload your vehicle.

Whether you build a wall, patio, or walk, try to pick stones that have flat, fairly square sides. Round or cannon ball stones are hard to use. They don't stay in place when dry laid and are difficult to secure with mortar. Once you have the stones delivered, sort them into piles according to size, shape, and color. This will make designing your project easier.

Stonework requires only a few tools. You'll need heavy leather gloves, goggles, a tape measure, a sharp bladed trowel, and a brick or stonemason's hammer and chisel. For mortared projects, a wheelbarrow, mortar shovel and hoe, or powered mixer are required. For flat projects, such as walks and patios, you'll need stakes and string. For walls, you'll need stakes, string, a level, and a plumb bob.

Stone is laid dry or mortared. Following are a few sample projects.

Dry-laid Garden Walk

This is one of the easiest projects. The walk can be created with cut stones for a formal pattern or with fieldstone for an informal one. Two methods are used. The first is to cut the turf to the shape of individual stones, digging the soil down to level the stones, and positioning them level with each other. The second is to outline the walk with stakes and string, cut away the sod, place pressure-treated two-by-fours or landscaping timbers on either side and place the stones down flat with the side timbers. Fill in and around the stones with sand.

Dry-laid Patio

A dry-laid patio is created in the same manor as a walk. In this case, the patio is outlined with stakes and string, the turf removed, and the area excavated to the depth of the stones, plus two inches. Again, wooden sides are used to outline the patio. Place a two-inch layer of sand in the bottom and rake it flat and smooth. A raking board can be used to even out the sand and prevent any high or low spots. The sand should be somewhat higher in the middle or next to a building, to create water drainage. After the sand has been leveled, sprinkle it with water to pack it down and provide a more solid surface.

Position the stones in place, with about one-inch spacing around the stones. Make sure they

STONE CAN BE DRY-LAID OR MORTARED. (PHOTO COURTESY CULTURED STONE CORP.)

are set level, don't wobble, and are of an even height. Once all stones have been positioned, sprinkle sand in between the joints. Make sure all joints are well filled. Spray the patio lightly to dampen the sand. Wait a bit and add more sand to areas that are low. Spray again to settle the sand and then lightly sweep away any excess.

Mortared Patio

A formal, mortared patio consists of first a concrete pad to support the stone. The flagstone or slate pieces are then placed in a bed of mortar, mortar placed in the cracks, and then the excess mortar cleaned away before the mortar has a chance to set. This is a more complicated project requiring concrete and stonework skills.

Dry-laid Stone Wall or Fence

Another fairly simple project is a dry-laid stone wall or fence. A dry-laid stone wall also makes a fairly good, low-height retaining wall because the open areas allow water to run through without building up pressure behind it. A dry-laid wall can be laid out to follow the contours of a garden, in a straight line, a squared shape, or curved. The number one rule is to build a wall that's not top-heavy. A good mason's rule of

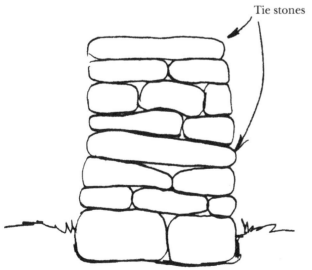

Tie stones

STONE CAN BE LAID DRY TO CREATE LOW WALLS OR FENCES. SHOWN IS A CROSS SECTION.

thumb is a wall up to three feet in height should be at least two feet in thickness. For each additional six inches of height, the wall width must be increased four inches. Low-height walls are usually created with plumb faces. Higher walls must be constructed with a taper to the top. Generally, this taper is about one-fifth narrower than the width of the wall base. Walls above three feet must have a footing that extends below the frost line in your area. Even with low walls, you should remove the turf; good stonemasons usually lay the bottom course below ground level. Because dry-laid walls are simply held in place by the weight of the stones, it's important to choose fairly flat, thin stones. Avoid round stones.

The first step is to outline the wall using stakes and a string line. A bottom string line should be placed on the stakes and a top string line as well. This provides a means of keeping the wall face plumb if desired. Lay the bottom layer of stones against the inside and outside string line. Normally a stone wall or fence consists of two outer stones with filler stones in between. Continue laying the next course, making sure to overlap the face sides of the wall. About every four to six horizontal feet, install a "bond" stone. This bond stone should overlap from front to back of both faces and tie the front and back face together. Close off the open end of the wall with three large stones to create a U shape. The most important factor is to make sure the stones overlap and all are stable, with no rocking or loose-fitting stones.

Mortared Stone Wall

A mortared stone wall has a more formal look, even when fieldstones are used. It is also considerably more work—and the work goes slowly since you can only mortar one course at a time. A mortared wall can also utilize fewer selected stones. The appearance of the wall can be varied with different shapes, types, and colors and even colored mortar. With a mortared wall, however, you do have a permanent structure. If you don't like it, you'll need a sledgehammer to take it apart.

A WALL IS BEGUN BY LAYING OUT THE OUTLINE WITH STAKES AND STRING. MORTAR IS THEN LAID FOR A MORTARED WALL AND STONES PLACED IN POSITION.

MORTAR IS FLUNG IN AROUND THE STONES, ANOTHER LAYER OF STONES ADDED, AND MORE MORTAR UNTIL THE WALL IS FINISHED. WORK ONE LAYER AT A TIME AND ALLOW THE MORTAR TO SET UP.

Construction is quite similar to a dry-laid wall. The main difference is the mortared wall must have a footing that is four to six inches wider than the wall and extending below the frost line in your area. The footing should be placed a couple of inches below the turf and then the soil graded back up to the wall.

Again, stakes and string lines are used. One method is to place a bottom string line just about an inch below the approximate height of the first course. Simply move the string line up as you lay additional courses.

The next step is to mix the mortar. Use a mortar mix of one part Portland cement to about four parts sand, plus a little water. Add a little bit of lime to make the batch stickier. Don't get the mortar too wet or it will not support the weight of the stones. Add water gradually. Stick your trowel down into the mixed mortar. The trowel should stand upright and not slump down. If it slumps, add more cement. Too dry mortar, on the other hand, sets too quickly to allow for easy masonry. Do not mix too much mortar at one time. Laying stonework is slow work and a large batch of mortar may dry before you can use all of it.

Place a layer of mortar under the string line and extending into the wall the approximate thickness of your largest stones. Place the first course in the mortar, scraping away the excess mortar squeezed out. Place a first course on the back side of the wall in the same manner. Place rubble rocks between the two courses, flinging mortar in and around the rubble rocks to hold them in place. Allow this course to set about an hour, and then remove excess mortar in the joints between the rocks. The mortar should be somewhat set, but not solid. Use the end of a round-headed bolt to scrape the mortar out of the joints and create a "sculpted" look to the wall. Use a hand broom to whisk away loose mortar. Then use a steel brush to remove mortar from the rock faces. Allow the first course to set overnight.

Now you're ready to lay the second course and it is done in the exact same manner. Place a layer of mortar and add the inner and outer face stones. Fill with rubble and add mortar in the center of the wall. Like a dry-laid wall, bonding stones reaching from front to back should also be placed about every four to six feet. It's a good idea to build up each corner or end first, then build between the two ends. Use the old mason's rule of overlapping stones for strength: two stones go over one; one stone goes over two. There should never be a vertical joint of masonry between the stones. In some instances, you may need to prop up stones with wooden sticks until the mortar sets.

A partially mortared wall has the appearance of a dry-laid wall, but is held more securely with

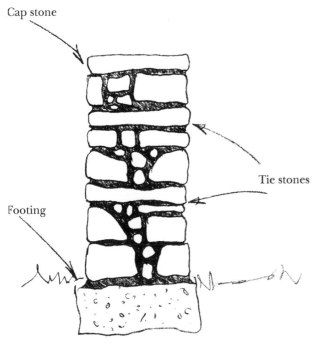

Cap stone

Tie stones

Footing

MORTARED STONE WALLS ARE MORE STURDY THEN DRY-LAID WALLS. SHOWN IS A CROSS-PART.

mortar on the inside. The mortar is kept at least four to six inches away from the face of the stones.

Terrace or retaining walls are constructed in much the same manner as for dry-laid or mortared walls. But because of the problem of water and ground pressure, many municipalities strictly govern this type of wall. You will probably have to get a building permit and show the inspector what type of wall you intend to build. Unless you are experienced, this is best left up to the experts. In both instances, the wall should be sloped backward and allowances made to drain water away from behind the wall.

Stone Veneering

Stones can also be veneered onto other surfaces such as brick or poured concrete. These must be thin veneer-type stones and they are adhered in place with a bed or mortar and metal wall anchors fastened to the wall. The courses are laid in the same manner as for laying a wall.

Artificial Stone

Artificial stone, such as that from Cultured Stone Corporation is a blend of Portland cement, lightweight aggregates, and iron oxide pigments cast in molds to resemble natural stone. These products require no additional footings, foundations, or wall ties and can be installed on a variety of surfaces, including wood framing, rigid foam, and masonry or concrete. A wide variety of shapes, sizes, and colors is available including stones for walls, patios, driveways, and walks and even shaped stone lintels and window moldings. The stones are very consistent in coloring and shape.

Each piece of Cultured Stone is applied individually with Type N mortar and attaches permanently to the wall. Then a mortar joint is grouted between the stones. Certain products are also designed to be installed without grouting to create a dry-laid look. Cultured Stone veneers are durable, maintenance-free, noncombustible, and are covered by a thirty-year limited warranty.

Using an Axe

The one single hand tool most often used on the farm in the olden days was an axe. It was used for everything from cutting down trees, clearing brush, chopping wood, making shingles, and other projects to even cutting ice on the pond for watering livestock in the wintertime. Knowing how to wield an axe properly is important not only from a safety standpoint, but also for ease in use. Even with experience and practice, however, using an axe is hard work.

The Basics

The first step is choosing an axe. Axes are available as both double- or single-bitted. A double-bit axe has a blade on both sides. This allows you to keep both sides sharp and simply turn the axe over if you happen to dull one side. Or, you may prefer to keep one side with a thinner sharp edge for wood slicing chores and the other with less of an angle for splitting wood. A double-bit axe is more dangerous. Never leave it sticking in a block of wood with the second blade upwards. A single-bit axe is safer, and normally has a fatter angle for more versatility. It can usually be used for both slicing and splitting chores.

The first rule of axemanship is to keep the blade sharp. A dull blade can cause the axe head to glance, possibly causing an accident. Take a good mill file to the woods with you and occasionally use it to touch up the blade as needed. The second rule is to make sure the area around you is clear before using the axe. Make sure there are no overhanging tree limbs for the axe

AN AXE IS A VERY IMPORTANT OLD-TIME TOOL. IT MUST BE KEPT SHARP AND USED PROPERLY. "LET THE AXE WORK FOR YOU," AS ONE OF MY UNCLES USED TO SAY.

189

FOLLOWING THROUGH WITH YOUR SWING IS EXTREMELY IMPORTANT.

to catch on. Make sure there is nothing on the ground that may cause you to stumble.

The third rule is to set a rhythm. My uncle always said to let the axe work for you rather than you working for it. Swing the axe down on the wood, pull it back off, swing it back up and behind you, then allow it to fall of it's own accord, guiding it and applying only light pressure. Always try to make cuts at a fairly sharp angle into the wood, but not too sharp as to cause a glancing blow. Coming straight down on the wood is not effective.

When felling trees, make a wide V cut about a third of the way through the tree on the side you wish it to fall. Make a second V cut from the opposite side. The tree should fall in the direction of the first cut.

When bucking or cutting limbs off a tree, stand to one side and chop on the opposite side of the tree. Lop off the branches from the butt end of the tree toward the top, making cuts from the bottom side of the limbs toward the top. Do not attempt to cut from the crotch side. Watch that the tree doesn't roll over on you when you

cut off the bottom branches or those supported on their ends on the ground.

When chopping larger branches and logs into sections, spread your feet wide apart for balance. Stand on the opposite side from which you're chopping. To cut small sticks into lengths, place them on a chopping block. Do not cut on the ground, as the ends may fly up and hit you.

To split logs, lay them in the crotch of a tree or stand them on one end. Don't attempt to split them while they are lying on the ground. They can roll, causing the axe to glance. Splitting firewood from logs should be done with a fat, wedge-shaped axe head and metal wedges and a maul. A heavy splitting maul is the best choice. Some woods won't split very easily, even with a maul, especially wide-diameter logs. These must be split using a pair of metal wedges. Position the log to be split on end. Drive the first wedge in following the grain or radial lines of the wood. Once the first wedge in place, usually about a half to two-thirds the length of the wedge, drive in the second wedge on the same grain or radial line. Drive it in far enough to loosen the first wedge. Usually it will drive in at least three quarters of its length. If the log is large, move the first wedge to another position on the radial line and drive it in place again. On some twisty, gnarly types of wood you may have to drive a wedge in from the side to finish the split or you may have to turn the log over and split from the opposite end.

ALWAYS CUT ON THE OPPOSITE SIDE FROM WHERE YOU ARE STANDING.

PART NINE

From the Kitchen

Skills in the kitchen were very important in the olden days. Most foods were made from "scratch," including many of the foods we take for granted these days. Butter, cheese, and even such things as peanut butter, wines, and beer were all made at home. Although we can readily purchase these items, some homesteaders may enjoy trying their hand at these age-old kitchen skills.

Dairy Products

One of the most important farm commodities was and still is the dairy foods. In the olden days, country folks made any number of food items from milk.

Milk

When I was a kid, we consumed raw milk. For safety, however, raw milk should be pasteurized. This can be done by heating the milk to 142°F and holding it at that temperature for thirty minutes or heating it to 161°F and holding it for fifteen seconds. Electric pasteurizers are available that do the chore quite easily.

The freshly drawn milk should be immediately strained through a clean cloth to remove debris or dirt that might have accidentally gotten into it. We had a milk strainer that held a paper strainer that made the chore easy. The strainer paper was discarded after each use. If you reuse cloths for straining, make sure to wash and boil them after each use. After straining, the milk should immediately be pasteurized and then cooled as rapidly as possible to 50°F or colder. Whole milk can be kept in a springhouse, cool cellar, or the refrigerator. We normally, however, first separated the cream from the milk. We used the cream for cooking or making into butter. The skim milk was then used for drinking, cooking, or making into cheese. Milk separators were a common item on many dairy farms in the old days, but for personal use, the easiest method is to simply store the milk in a cool place. After about twenty-four hours, the cream will rise to the top. The cream is then skimmed off with a ladle or spoon.

Keeping everything sanitary is extremely important in handling dairy products. All containers should be seamless so there are no cracks for dirt and milk to be caught in. Immediately after using, rinse all containers and utensils in cold water and then wash in extremely hot water with dairy-washing powder or detergent. Scrub with a brush to remove the butterfat, rinse in extremely hot water, and finally, scald them in boiling water.

My first off-the-farm job was working in a creamery. Each Saturday the farmers brought their skimmed cream in to be sold, along with the eggs they had collected. I had to candle the eggs, but another of my jobs was to "test" the cream for butterfat content and for sweetness. The sweetness was basically a taste test. After one taste test, I poured the cream into a large collecting vat only to have a dead rat float out as well. I quickly learned to pour first, then taste! The best

193

part was that the creamery made the cream and eggs into ice cream, a job I really enjoyed.

Cottage Cheese

My mother made cottage cheese once a week. You can make it from fresh-skimmed milk off the farm or from store-bought milk, although the latter won't be as rich. It takes about a gallon of milk to produce one quart of cottage cheese.

MILK CAN BE MADE INTO A WIDE VARIETY OF DAIRY PRODUCTS. MY MOM USED TO MAKE COTTAGE CHEESE, AND IT'S FAIRLY EASY TO DO.

1. Coagulate pasteurized skim milk by raising its temperature to 75°F in a double boiler. Stir in one-half cup fresh buttermilk for each gallon of milk.
2. Place the milk in a crock, glass, or enameled container. Cover and wait until the milk "sets up" similar to the consistency of custard.
3. Once the milk has solidified, cut it into curds by slicing through it with a knife into one-half to one-inch cubes. Continue dicing into smaller curds.
4. Set the curds aside for about fifteen minutes. Meanwhile, bring a container of water to 115° to 120°F. Place the curds in this using a double-boiler arrangement.
5. Bring the curds to a temperature of 120°F and then hold the heat steady and cook until the curds are firm and somewhat dry. Stir occasionally during cooking. This should take about twenty-four minutes.
6. Pour the curds into a cloth laid over a strainer and drain. Rinse the curds thoroughly, first with cool water, then with cold. Drain and squeeze dry. My mom hung the bag of curds over her clothesline to dry. Add salt and fresh cream to taste if desired.

Hard Cheese

Making hard cheese is a bit more work. Not that it's particularly complicated; it just requires more time and effort. You will need a few special tools including a cheese form and a cheese press. You can purchase both from specialty supply houses or you can make up your own. You will also need two large hot-water bath canners or similar pots to create a double-boiler system. A twenty-four-quart pot will hold about four gallons of milk and fits inside a thirty-six-gallon pot. You'll also need a few other items including a thermometer, strainer, cheesecloth, a large butcher knife, and a pound of paraffin.

Hard cheese is best made from whole milk. Goat's milk makes a very rich cheese. You will need a starter, which can be buttermilk, yogurt, or a powdered cheese starter available commercially. You will also need rennet, a commercial product that causes milk to curdle very quickly, and salt. Flake salt is the best choice.

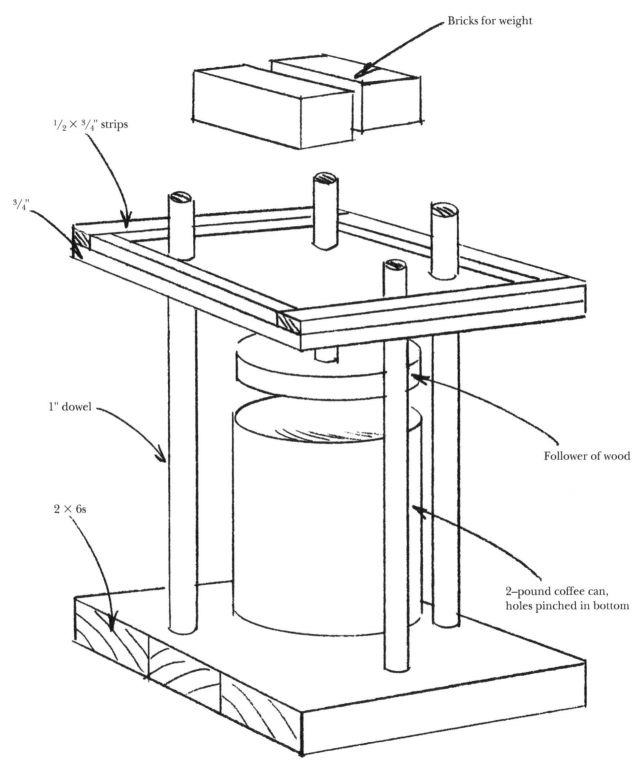

Bricks for weight

1/2 × 3/4" strips

3/4"

1" dowel

2 × 6s

Follower of wood

2–pound coffee can, holes pinched in bottom

MAKING HARD CHEESE REQUIRES A BIT MORE WORK, BUT IT'S NOT PARTICULARLY COMPLICATED. YOU WILL NEED A FEW SUPPLIES, INCLUDING A CHEESE PRESS.

The Basic Steps

1. Measure out four gallons of milk and pour into a large metal pot or canner. Heat the milk to 86°F and then add two cups of starter. Cover the container and allow the milk to sit overnight in a warm, but not hot place.

2. The next morning add one rennet tablet that has been dissolved in one-half cup of cool water. Stir the rennet mix thoroughly into the milk. Cover the container and allow the rennet to work, which should take about forty-five minutes.

3. Cut through the coagulated cheese, or curd, with a long knife with a rounded tip, such as a cake knife. Cut into one-half-inch cubes. Once you have made initial cuts, stir the curds and make sure they are evenly cut into cubes.

4. Place the curds in the smaller container. Place the small container inside the larger container and add water to the large container. Very slowly, heat the curds. Gradually bring the temperature up to 100°F. This should take about forty to forty-five minutes. Maintain this temperature until the curds become firm. Stir gently to prevent the curds from lumping or sticking. The curds are done when they are firm, but do not stick together if gently squeezed.

5. Place a cheese cloth in a strainer and pour the curds and whey into the cheese cloth to drain off the whey. As the whey drains, stir the curds gently to prevent them from sticking together.

6. Once the curds have cooled to 90°F, sprinkle two tablespoons of salt over the curds. Stir gently to mix the salt well into the curds.

7. After the curds have cooled to 85°F and the salt has been well dissolved, place the curds into a cheese form that has been lined with clean cheesecloth. Place the form in the cheese press. Use the instructions with the press to create the pressure

needed. A wine press or lard press will also work. Begin with light pressure and gradually increase it over an hour's time as the whey is squeezed out and the cheese compressed.

8. After about an hour, remove the cheese and dip the cheese wheel into warm water. Wipe away any fat that may have accumulated on the outside and smooth the surface with your fingers. Allow to dry or wipe dry with a clean soft cloth.

9. Place the cheese wheel back in the cheese form, using a circle of cheesecloth on both top and bottom, as well as one around the sides and slightly covering the top and bottom. Add pressure to compress and allow the cheese to stay in the press for about twenty-four hours.

10. Remove the cheese from the press and remove the cheesecloth covering. Wash in hot water. Use your fingers or a table knife dipped in hot water to seal off any holes. Wipe dry with a clean soft cloth and place in a cool, dry place where pets or rodents can't get to it. An old-fashioned pie-safe was used for more than one purpose at my grandmother's house including curing cheese. Remove the wheel and wipe it dry each day. A rind should begin to form within about four to five days.

11. Heat paraffin in a double boiler, not over direct heat. As soon as it is melted, dip the wheel into the paraffin. You will probably have to dip portions at a time. Make sure the entire wheel is covered.

12. The last step is to cure the cheese. Place it in a safe, cool, dry place to cure (40° to 60°F). Turn it over once each day and clean the storage area each day to prevent mold from forming. By the end of six to eight weeks the cheese should have firmed and aged to a mild flavor. For sharper cheese, cure from three to six months, depending on the desired flavor.

Making Butter

One of the chores I hated as a youngster was making butter. It just took so dad-burned long. It was nothing to sit on the kitchen floor, a glass butter churn between my legs and crank for a couple of hours while mom went about her other kitchen chores. When it came time to butter mom's homemade rolls, however, the delicious yellow butter made me forget the drudgery.

Other than the time involved, making butter is fairly easy. Butter, of course, is made from cream. Once the cream has been separated from the milk, it should be aged in the refrigerator for a couple of days. It takes about a quart of heavy cream to make up one pound of butter. This also usually results in about one pint of buttermilk.

1. Before churning, allow the cream to come to room temperature and then place in a churn and crank until the cream separates into butter and buttermilk. A modern method is to use a kitchen mixer. Begin at high speed until the cream turns into whipped cream. It will then gradually separate into butter and buttermilk. As it begins to separate, switch to low speed. Regardless of the method used, pour off the buttermilk. The buttermilk is often used for cooking, but some old-timers also liked to drink it.

2. The next step is to "paddle" the butter using wooden spatulas to force out all the buttermilk. Do this with the butter placed in a pan of ice water. Pour off the milk-clouded water, repeating several times until the water remains clear. Any milk that remains in the butter can turn it rancid. Mom used to add a pinch of salt for flavoring. The butter is then formed in tubs, or for more elegance, use an old-fashioned butter mold to mold the butter into squares or other shapes.

Homemade Ice Cream

If I hated butter making, I loved ice-cream making. It meant a celebration, often on the Fourth of July. As a small kid, I sat on the freezer while mom or dad cranked away. But first we had to go to town and buy block ice from the ice plant. This was broken up into chunks with a large mallet and ice picks. You can easily make up your own homemade ice cream and use either an old-fashioned hand-cranked machine or, these days, an electric model. Ice cream flavors are only limited by your imagination. Start by adding your family's favorite fruit or broken pieces of your favorite candy or candy bar to basic vanilla.

Vanilla Ice Cream

5½ cups milk
2 cups sugar
⅓ cup flour
½ teaspoon salt
4 eggs
4 teaspoons vanilla
1 quart whipping cream or light cream

In one bowl, use a wire whip to blend the flour, sugar, and salt together. In another bowl, slightly beat the 4 eggs. In a large, heavy pan, heat the 6 cups milk to scalding. Blend a small amount of the warm milk into the flour-sugar mixture with the wire whip. Stir this back into the pan of milk and continue cooking and stirring until the mixture thickens slightly. Blend a small amount of this hot mixture into the beaten eggs to gradually warm them and then stir this mixture back into the pan and cook for about 2 minutes. Do not overcook or the eggs could curdle. Cool in the refrigerator. Pour the cooled mixture into the freezer can, add vanilla and cream to the fill line. Makes 1 gallon.

Chocolate Ice Cream

Add ⅝ to ¾ cup cocoa sifted with the flour in the above recipe. Increase the sugar by ½ to ¾ cup. Stir 4 tablespoons butter until melted in the hot mixture before cooling or use an extra heavy cream to fill the freezer can.

Peanut Butter Ice Cream

Stir 1 cup smooth or crunchy peanut butter into the hot vanilla ice cream mixture before cooling. Use a lighter cream to finish filling the freezer can.

Fruit-Flavored Ice Creams

Crush 4 cups fresh or frozen fruit with ½ to 1 cup additional sugar. Use this mixture to finish filling the freezer can in place of the cream.

Banana Ice Cream

Mash 5 or 6 large bananas, enough to make at least 2 cups, and add to the cooled vanilla mixture. Fill freezer can with cream. No additional sugar is added.

Turning it into Ice Cream

1. Thoroughly wash the can, cover, and paddle in hot soapy water, then rinse in hot water and dry. Allow the can to cool, and then add in the mixture. Fill the freezer can to the fill line, normally about two-thirds full.
2. Place the paddle in the pan and cover, and then fasten the assembled can in the freezer.
3. Place crushed ice mixed with rock salt around the can and start turning the crank (use approximately one pound of salt per eight pounds of crushed ice).
4. Turn the crank slowly, adding ice and salt as needed to maintain a level around the can. Continue turning until you feel a slight resistance and then speed up the cranking. Continue turning until it becomes too hard to turn. Remove the paddle and lick it clean.
5. You can then pour the ice cream into freezer trays and freeze in your refrigerator. If you plan to eat it fairly quickly, however, the best method is to replace the pan cover with the cork in the paddle hole. Pour off the water and add more ice and salt around and over the pan. Cover the entire affair with blankets. In a couple of hours, the ice cream should be hard and delicious.

Country Cream Pie

Back in the days when most farms had a milk cow, excess cream was put to many uses. Cream pie was a favorite with many and it's still one of mine. The recipe makes up two pies.

Country Cream Pie

½ cup sugar
4 teaspoons flour
3 cups cream (4 cups for full or larger pies)
Pinch of salt
2 teaspoons vanilla
½ teaspoon lemon juice
4 egg whites, beaten until stiff

Mix the first six ingredients together, fold in the egg whites, and pour into unbaked pie shells. Bake for 15 minutes at 425°F then turn down the heat and bake for approximately 35 minutes at 275°F or until set.

Grains and Grain Products

Wheat is not called the staff of life for nothing. Grains provide over half the world's proteins. Everything from breakfast cereals to pastry is made from grains.

Grinding Your Own Grain

If you have the space, you can grow your own grains and harvest them by cutting with a scythe. The stalks with seed heads are then spread out on clean cloths on a smooth floor and threshed by beating or walking on them. The stems and chaff are then removed and the grain poured on a winnowing screen. Shake the screen to remove the dust and chaff. Remove any heavy particles by hand. Do this on a windy day and most of the chaff will fly away. A winnowing screen is nothing more than a frame of one-by-twos and a piece of window screen wire.

You can also buy cleaned or uncleaned grain from farmers, feed and grain stores, or health-food stores. Be sure the grain is fresh, has not been chemically treated, and is meant for human consumption. If you buy uncleaned grain, you will have to clean it by winnowing, or pouring the grains from one container to another on a windy day or in front of a fan.

Wheat, millet, rye, oats, rice, barley, and soybeans are some of the grains that can be ground easily at home using a coffee mill, hand mill, or electric mill. Some blenders will even grind grain.

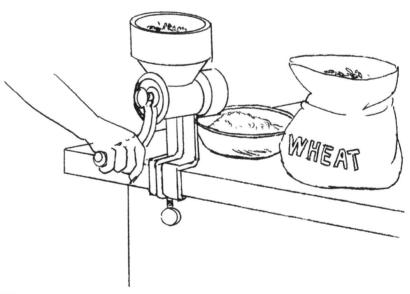

WITH A HOME GRINDER YOU CAN GRIND WHOLE GRAINS FOR ANY NUMBER OF FOOD PRODUCTS.

Grain may be ground to almost any form from rough "cracked" grain to superfine flour. Grinding to make fine flour will usually take two to three grindings. Keep the ground grain in well-sealed glass jars to prevent insect and weevil infestations. It's best to keep it in the refrigerator. After the grain has been ground, it keeps for about a month, and then begins to lose flavor. Grain that has not yet been ground can be stored in closed glass jars and kept in a cool, dry place. The grains may be used in all sorts of ways, both whole and ground, for cereals or baking all kinds of goodies.

Making Sourdough

The word sourdough brings to mind the gold prospectors, but sourdough is just as easy to make and tasty today as it was back in 1849. Thousands of sourdough recipes exist, but basically, it is made either with or without yeast. To make without yeast, place four cups of flour, two tablespoons of sugar, and a tablespoon of vinegar in a crock or plastic bowl. Add enough water to make a creamy batter. Cover this loosely with cheesecloth and leave in a warm spot. The mixture will bubble and ferment and should be ready to use in seven to ten days. If properly working, the mixture will give off a pleasant, but slightly sour smell.

You can make a modern version a bit more quickly. Simply dissolve one package of dry yeast in two cups of warm water. Mix in two cups of flour, cover with a cloth, and leave overnight in a warm spot.

Always reserve about a cup of sourdough starter to continue the strain. To this cup of starter, add enough flour and water to bring it back to the original level. Keep the starter refrigerated.

Sourdough Bread

Place all the sourdough, except the cup to maintain the strain, in a large mixing bowl. Add enough flour to make a bouncy slick dough. The secret of sourdough bread is to knead it very little. Shape into loaves and place in a warm spot until they rise. Bake in a 375°F oven for about forty-five minutes or until the crust browns and the loaves sound hollow when thumped.

Sourdough Biscuits

Use the same basic ingredients for biscuits as for bread, but add enough flour to make a stiffer dough. Don't let the dough rise. Quickly roll it out and pop into a hot (425°F) oven for ten to fifteen minutes.

Cornmeal Mush

One of my dad's favorite breakfast treats was cornmeal mush. Add two cups of cornmeal mixed with one pint of cold water to two and a half pints of boiling water and one tablespoon of salt. Pour into a square cake pan and allow to cool and harden. Slice off what you need and fry it. Serve with plenty of butter and honey or syrup.

Wines and Beer

Making wine and beer was another homestead skill that many old-timers enjoyed. You can still make your own wine and beer for home consumption quite easily from a variety of materials.

You'll need five to ten gallon stone crocks or heavy plastic buckets. Open containers must be lightly covered during fermentation to avoid

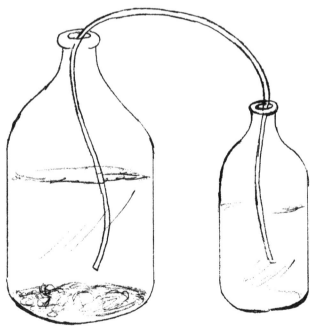

MAKING HOMEMADE WINE AND BEER IS ALSO A FUN HOBBY. ANY NUMBER OF RECIPES CAN BE USED.

"vinegar" flies. Cheesecloth with several layers of newspaper will work fine as a covering. You will also need brewer's yeast, which is often available at natural food stores. Active dry or cake yeast may be substituted, but it doesn't work quite as well. Spring water, boiled and with the minerals skimmed off the top, is better than tap water. Following are some basic old-time recipes:

Dandelion Wine

1 quart dandelion blossoms, packed down
1 gallon water
1 cake yeast
3 pounds sugar
3 very ripe bananas

Make sure dandelions are cleaned of all greenery. Boil in water for 20 minutes. Drain thoroughly and discard the blossoms. Cool the liquid to lukewarm and place in a stone crock. Add yeast, sugar, and thinly sliced bananas. Cover loosely. Let stand in a warm place and allow it to ferment for 9 to 10 days. Stir occasionally. When completely through working, strain with a clean cloth a time or two for clarity. Bottle and cork.

Rice Wine (sake)

2¼ pounds raw rice
4 pounds sugar
1 pound seeded raisins
1 pound seedless raisins
2 oranges cut into eighths (including peel)
6 quarts lukewarm water
1½ cake yeast

Combine all ingredients in a large container. Cover loosely. Let stand for 3 weeks, stirring every 5 days and then strain, bottle, and seal. Sake is best served warm.

Corncob Wine

Cut the corn from 6 fresh cobs. Combine cobs and the corn from 1 cob only with 1 gallon of warm water. Let stand 24 hours, strain.

Add 3 ounces of sugar and 1 quart unsweetened grape juice. Let stand 9 days. Strain again and bottle.

Elderberry Wine

12 quarts boiling water
4 quarts stemmed elderberries
6¾ cups sugar
3 teaspoons ground ginger
8 whole cloves
1 pound seeded or seedless raisins
1 package active dry yeast or compressed yeast

Pour boiling water on berries and let stand for 24 hours. Strain through coarse bag or cloth, breaking berries to extract all the juice. Add sugar, ginger, cloves, and raisins. Bring to boil and simmer 1 hour, skimming often. Cool to lukewarm. Measure the liquid and add 1 package of active dry yeast to each 16 quarts of mixture. Let stand for 2 weeks. Strain, bottle, and store for several months in a cool place before using. Yields approximately 8 quarts.

Grape Wine

Pick grapes from bunches to provide 20 pounds of grapes. Place in a large stone crock. Pour 6 quarts of boiling water over the grapes. Allow to cool, then use your hands to squeeze and break the grapes, or you can "stomp" on them if you desire. Stir the mixture, then cover loosely and allow to ferment for 3 days. Strain off the juice and discard the pomace. Clean the crock well, pour the strained juice back in, and add 10 pounds of sugar. Allow to ferment for a week, again loosely covered and in a warm place. At the end of the week, skim off the scum, strain, and pour into bottles. Do not cork tightly. Use cotton balls to loosely cork the bottles. Once fermentation has stopped, pour the wine into clean bottles. Throw away the sediment collected in the bottom of the bottles. Tightly cork and lay on their sides in a cool place (from 40° to 50°F). You can taste wine a few months after bottling, but it's best aged at least a year or longer.

Making Beer

Following is a simple old-time molasses beer recipe.

Molasses Beer

1 pound of dark molasses (about 10 liquid ounces)
2 gallons of water
2 bay leaves
1 cake active yeast
1 ounce of dried hops

Bring 4 quarts of water to a boil and add the hops. Boil for an hour to create a strong hop tea. Pour 4 quarts of lukewarm water into a crock. Stir in the molasses, strain the hop tea, and add it to the mixture. Allow the mixture to cool to room temperature. Dissolve the cake yeast in a cup of warm water and pour into the mixture. Cover with a plastic wrap held in place with a large rubber band. Place the crock in a warm place, but where the tem-perature won't exceed 75°F. The mixture will begin working by the next day and you'll hear it bubbling. Once the bubbling stops, usually in 4 to 5 days, siphon off the beer with a siphon tube, being careful not to stir up the sediment on the bottom. Bottle using new, strong bottles. Regardless, don't siphon off the beer before it stops working or you may explode the bottles. You can drink it in a few days, but it's also best aged.

Easy-Does-It Beer

10 gallons lukewarm water
1 can (3-pound) hop-flavored malt syrup
10 pounds sugar
¼ cup brewers yeast or 1 package yeast

Place the lukewarm water in a 12-gallon crock or plastic bucket. Pour in the dissolved yeast, sugar, and malt syrup. Cover with a cheesecloth and place in a warm place. Keep the foam skimmed off the top. Allow to work for 4 to 6 days, or until only about 10 tiny bubbles per minute can be seen in the center. Siphon off into heavy glass bottles. Add a pinch of sugar to each bottle and cap the bottles. Allow to age for at least 2 weeks.

PART TEN

Woodsmanship

Hunting, fishing, trapping, and understanding nature were all major factors of survival in the old days. Called woodsmanship, these skills can also be important today. In many instances these days, these same skills are enjoyed as recreation.

Reading the Weather

An understanding of weather is very important for planning farm work such as planting and harvesting. Being able to predict weather can also make any outing more pleasant—and it may also save your life.

AN UNDERSTANDING OF WEATHER IS IMPORTANT FOR MANY REASONS. CLOUD FORMATIONS CAN INDICATE COMING WEATHER TO KNOWLEDGEABLE WOODSMEN.

Clues from Clouds

One of the most reliable ways of forecasting weather is by observing cloud formations. There are four basic types of clouds based on their altitude. These include: high, middle, low, and vertical or stacking clouds. The latter may exist in more than one level at the same time.

High clouds are the cirrus types. They usually range well above 20,000 feet and are made up of ice crystals. If the clouds are thin and wispy, look for fair weather. If the clouds are rippled like sand dunes (cirrocumulus) and the wind is from NE to S, expect precipitation in fifteen to twenty hours. Sometimes these clouds create a hazy white layer that covers the sky (cirrostratus), creating a dim sun or moon. If you see these clouds on a summer morning, you may have rain in the late afternoon. Nimbus clouds are high wispy clouds that indicate fair weather. If the clouds begin to thicken, watch for precipitation.

Middle clouds are found from around 6,000 feet up to about 20,000 and they're good indicators of day-to-day weather. One of the most common is the altocumulus, with its light gray color and flattened shape. It also sometimes appears in layers (called "mare's tails" by the old-timers). If the wind is steady from the NE to S, expect precipitation within fifteen to twenty hours. Wind from other directions usually indicates an overcast sky with little or no precipitation. If the clouds begin to build in height, with flattened dark bottoms (cumulus congestus), and the winds are from SW to NW, you can expect precipitation and gusty winds, along with possible thunderstorms within five to ten hours. These can also bring about "wind squalls" without precipitation. Altostratus clouds create the thick, gray "blanket" that covers the sky and makes the sun or moon appear as a dim disc. These overcast conditions indicate possible precipitation such as rain, sleet, or snow.

The low clouds fall below 6,500 feet. They consist of stratus, which is a foggy overcast cloud covering the entire sky; nimbostratus, gray, diffused, layered clouds; and stratocumulus, which are lumpy, fairly dark gray clouds that are seen in patches or rows. Rain or snow is possible shortly with all of these clouds.

Vertical clouds include the cumulus, which resemble giant cotton balls. They usually mean fair weather. If their bottoms being to darken and the clouds grow taller, it indicates a coming storm within fifteen to twenty hours. Cumulonimbus clouds are the familiar thunderheads with their huge size and swirling dark gray colors with anvil-shaped tops. They mean a storm is in progress.

Cloud Watching

By watching the clouds you can determine if a particular weather system is approaching, and the approximate timing of it. During warm weather warm fronts, this usually begins with cirrus followed by cirrostratus, altostratus, nimbostratus, and stratus. The cumulonimbus thunderheads may also form last. Fog may also develop. As the warm front passes through, the stratus-type clouds will stay. Once the front has passed, relatively clear skies should occur. A few scattered stratocumulus clouds may be seen and, in the summer months, another cumulonimbus may form. Cold fronts usually begin with cirrus clouds, followed by cirrostratus and sometimes huge cumulus or cumulonimbus. As the cold front passes the towering cumulus and cumulonimbus will continue. Once

the cold front passes, the puffy white cumulus clouds will reform.

In mountainous country and on large bodies of water, the weather can turn for the worst in a few minutes, so keep a close watch on the changing weather conditions.

"MARE'S TAILS AND MACKEREL SCALES, MAKE LOFTY SHIPS LOWER THEIR SAILS."

You'll also need a couple of old-time tools for more precise weather prediction: a weather vane and barometer. The weather vane indicates the direction the wind blows from. If you're east of the Rocky Mountains, winds from the northeast, east, and south normally bring in bad weather. Easterly winds normally indicate a system developing to the south. This creates a warm front that brings rain or freezing rain or snow, depending on the timing of the season. Winds from the northwest, west, and southwest usually indicate fair weather. As a general rule, a strong, steady northwest wind usually indicates a high pressure and fair weather. If you're on the west side of the Rocky Mountains, winds from the west usually bring clouds and precipitation. Winds from the east usually mean only dry air. Wind direction changes can also be an indicator. An old-time saying is "Veering wind, fair weather—backing wind, foul weather." When a warm front approaches, winds shifting in clockwise fashion is called "veering." When winds change at different altitudes in a counterclockwise direction, it's called "backing." This occurs behind a cold front that has slowed or stalled and creates cloudy skies and precipitation.

The barometer refines your predictions. It's not the actual reading at any given moment, however, but a history of pressure readings. If pressure rises quite rapidly over a short period of time, watch for good weather. If the pressure stays fairly high, there will be good weather, too. A rapidly dropping barometer indicates air is rising, creating instability in the atmosphere and a storm may be on the way.

Watch the temperature, too. On a normal day, temperatures usually rise in the morning and fall slightly in the evening. On the other hand, a rising temperature in the evening indicates a warm front, which may bring on light precipitation. A falling morning temperature can indicate the approach of a cold front and thunderstorms or other violent weather patterns.

Old-time Weather Sayings

Many old-time weather sayings are reliable for short-term daily predictions. "When leaves show their undersides, rain betides." Leaves of plants seem to turn over and show their undersides—sometimes it's just wind, but coming storms usually generate downdrafts, which can cause leaves to turn over. This indicates a storm may hit within less than an hour.

"Halo around the sun or moon, rain or snow very soon." In the fall, winter, and early spring or cooler times of the year, a halo around the sun or moon can indicate weather changes within twenty-four hours. The halo is created when the light from the moon or sun is refracted by ice crystals held by the cirrus clouds. "Turrets and towers, will water the flowers." The high, puffy altocumulus clouds growing upwards often resemble castles with high turrets. These indicate possible severe thunderstorms. Other old sayings and proverbs were also based on cloud configuration and include:

MANY OLD-TIME WEATHER FORECAST PREDICTIONS WERE BASED ON SKY PATTERNS. FOR INSTANCE, RED SKY IN THE MORNING, SAILORS TAKE WARNING; RED SKY AT NIGHT, SAILORS DELIGHT.

Mare's tails and mackerel scales, make lofty ships lower their sails.

The higher the cloud, the finer the weather.

Rain before seven, stops before eleven.

A sunshiny shower won't last an hour.

Red sky at morning, sailors take warning. Red sky at night, sailors delight.

When the wind is in the east, 'tis neither good for man nor beast.

When the wind is from the south, has rain in her mouth.

When the wind is in the west, then the wind is at its best.

Woolly fleeces strewing the heavenly way; no
  rain disturbs a fine summer day.
When clouds appear like rocks and towers,
  the earth's refreshed by frequent showers.

The old-time woodsmen watched for other
natural signs as well when predicting the weather.
Smoke that rises up from the campfire indicates
clear weather. Smoke hanging low to the ground
indicates a gathering storm. The ants were favorite predictors as well. When they start building mounds or tiny "dikes" around the entrance
to their tunnels, watch for rain. All animals are
more active in the twenty-four-hour period be-

"THE HIGHER THE CLOUD, THE FINER THE WEATHER."

fore a storm. The larger ones, such as deer, elk,
and moose feed heavily, while the smaller animals such as mice scurry to higher ground. All
activity will usually stop at least an hour before
the storm is due to hit. A still morning with lots
of dew or frost on the grass usually indicates a
clear day. A dry morning usually means rain is
moving in.

Many of us old-timers can also predict the
weather—although unwittingly. As humidity increases before a storm, it increases pressure in
joints such as knees and elbows, which results in
pain. Those with sinus problems can also predict
the weather because of the increased pressure
caused by the storm front.

Knowing how to cope with various weather
conditions can have a lot to do with your enjoyment, as well as your ability to survive in the outdoors. In case of rain, keep as dry as possible. Wet
clothing causes excessive body heat loss and can
lead to hypothermia. In a blizzard, do not travel.
Quickly find shelter until the storm subsides. Do
not travel in dense fog, either. In the desert do
not travel in the heat of the day; conserve your
energy. Find shade or improvise it. In case you're
caught in a lightning storm, leave high exposed
areas immediately. Get to a low, open area and
crouch down. Avoid trees, caves, and cliffs.

Staying Found

In these days of GPS, the olden-day methods of traveling in the wilderness are pretty well forgotten. They can, however, be handy if you're not into high-tech.

The Time-Honored Methods

Locating north by the North Star is a time-tried method of finding your way on a cloud-free night. The North Star, or Polaris, may be located by following an imaginary line extending from the outside edge of the Big Dipper. On a sunny day, watching the sun as it moves from east to west is an old-time woodsman's easiest method of determining direction. You can also tell direction by the shadow of a stick pushed into the ground. Mark the tip of the shadow. Wait fifteen minutes and then mark the tip of the new shadow. Draw a line between the marks and you have an east-to-west line. The first mark made indicates west.

It's important to keep looking around you as you travel. Note what it looks like behind you as well as in front. You'll find your way home more easily.

One of the best ways to avoid getting lost is to use a good map of the area you plan to explore, even if you think you know the area well. The best map is a topographical map. These maps show not only all streams, swamps, lakes, towns, and buildings, but also all mountains, valleys, and ter-

THE STARS HAVE BEEN A MEANS OF NAVIGATION FOR AGES. SHOWN HERE IS THE BIG DIPPER AND NORTH STAR.

rain changes. All water areas are shown in blue. Intermittent or dotted lines show streams that are dry for a part of the year. Swamps are indicated by blue symbols of marsh grass. The shape of the land is shown by contour lines printed in brown. Successive contour lines that are far apart indicate a gentle slope. Lines that are close together indicate a steep slope such as a cliff. All manmade works, such as cities and houses, are printed in black. Road types are indicated. Many maps also indicate forested areas by green shading.

A woodsman carrying a topographical map and compass needn't get lost, nor stay lost for long. When buying a compass, buy two and make sure they're high quality. The reason: A lost person tends not to believe in one compass. The second compass is assurance that the direction is correct. Three basic types of compasses are available and each works somewhat differently. Make sure you read the instructions for your particular compass and practice in your backyard or the city park to learn how to use it before heading into the wilds.

ON A SUNNY DAY, THE SHADOW FROM A STICK CAN INDICATE DIRECTION.

Trapping

One of the most important traditional primitive skills was trapping. And, in fact, without trapping our country wouldn't have been settled. Trapping has been and still is a very vital skill, not only for controlling specific predator or nuisance animals around the farm or ranch, but as a moneymaker as well. Many a youngster in years past, myself included, made spending money by trapping. Trapping is also easily learned and fun. Make sure you read your state rules and regulations regarding trapping and follow all rules pertaining to limits as well as trapping methods and tools that can be used.

TRAPPING IS ONE OF HUMANKIND'S OLDEST SKILLS. IT'S ALSO AN IMPORTANT SKILL THESE DAYS, AS WELL. TRAPPING CAN REMOVE NUISANCE ANIMALS OR PROVIDE FOOD OR FURS.

Tools

One of the simplest forms of trapping, and an excellent method of controlling nuisance animals, is with a box trap. I trapped rabbits with these as a kid and they'll still take rabbits and other small game.

Four other types of traps are available: the foothold or leg-hold; killer or body grip; snares; and cage traps. Foothold traps have a pan in the center. When the animal steps on the pan, the trap is triggered and the jaws snap shut to grip the animal. Foothold traps are available as coil spring, long spring, and underspring jump. Long spring traps are more stable when set on land. Coil spring traps, however, are smaller and more easily concealed. Underspring traps are also small, but not as common these days as coil springs. Body-grip traps, such as the Conibear from Woodstream, consist of two metal frames with a spring. A trigger in the center releases the spring-loaded frames and the animal is caught around the body. The animal is usually killed quite quickly. Killer traps are designed to be used in underwater sets for semi-aquatic animals, such as muskrats or beavers. These traps should not be set on upland areas where pets or livestock might be caught and killed. Snares are the simplest traps and commonly kill by choking the animal. They are outlawed in some states and should not be set on upland areas where pets, hunting dogs, or other non-target animals may be snared. Cage or live traps are made of wire cages with a door that closes behind the animal when it enters. These are commonly used in places with high populations of pets to trap and remove nuisance animals such as raccoons, opossums, and skunks.

Traps are constructed in various sizes and it's important to match the size to the target animal. The charts shown indicate the sizes for different animals (courtesy Woodstream Corp.). Cage trap sizes chart courtesy Havahart.

Body-grip Traps

Size Reference	Jaw Spread	Animal to be Trapped
#110-2 (single spring)	4½"	muskrat, mink, skunk
#120-2 (single spring)	4½"	muskrat and animals of similar size
#220-2 (double spring)	7"	raccoon, badger
#330-2 (double spring)	10"	beaver

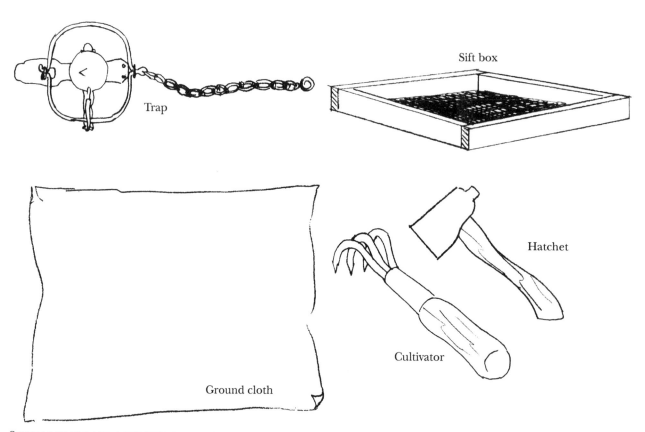

Trap

Sift box

Ground cloth

Cultivator

Hatchet

SEVERAL TOOLS AND A VARIETY OF TRAPS ARE NEEDED.

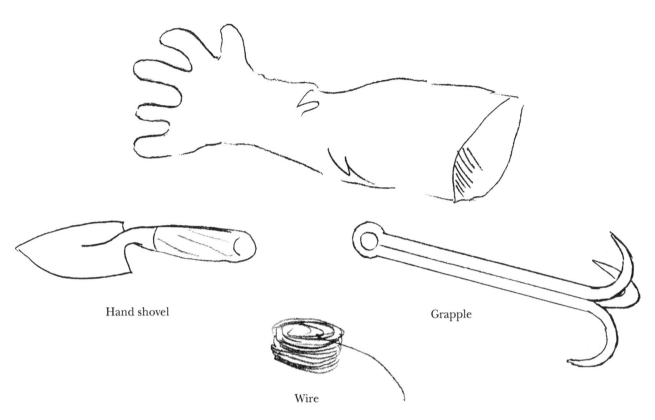

Hand shovel

Grapple

Wire

Coil Spring Traps

Size Reference	Jaw Spread	Animal to be Trapped
#1	3⅝"	mink, muskrat, skunk
#1½	4⅞"	fox, skunk, mink, raccoon
#2	5⅜"	fox, raccoon, skunk
#2 OS	5⅝"	fox, raccoon
#3	6"	bobcat, coyote, beaver
#3 OS	6"	coyote, bobcat

#2 (double spring)	4¾"	fox, raccoon, opossum
#3 (double spring)	5½"	beaver, badger
#3N (double spring)	5½"	coyote, wolf
#3 OS (double spring)	5½"	coyote, fox, badger, beaver
#4 (double spring)	5⅞"	beaver, coyote, wolf
#4 OS (double spring)	5⅞"	coyote, wolf

Long Spring Traps

Size Reference	Jaw Spread	Animal to be Trapped
#0 (single spring)	3½"	gopher
#1 (single spring)	4"	muskrat, mink
#11 (double spring)	4"	mink
#1½ (single spring)	4¾"	mink, muskrat, opossum, raccoon, muskrat

Jump Traps

Size Reference	Jaw Spread	Animal to be Trapped
#1	4½"	muskrat, skunk, mink
#1½	5⅛"	muskrat, skunk, mink
#3	6½"	coyote, fox, beaver
#4	7¼"	beaver, coyote, badger

Cage Traps

Size	Animal to be Trapped
24 × 7 × 7	squirrels, muskrats, cottontail rabbits, gophers
30 × 7 × 7	large squirrels, rabbits, skunks, mink
42 × 11 × 13	raccoons, cats, opossums, jack rabbits
55 × 12 × 12	large raccoons, bobcats
70 × 30 × 30	dogs, coyotes

In addition to traps, you'll need other equipment. For upland trapping, this consists of a hatchet, hand cultivator, and small trowel. A sift box is needed for sifting fine dirt over the trap. A setting tarp is used to kneel on when setting the trap and to place excess dirt that must be carried away from the set. Pliers and metal stakes or drags are also necessary. A half-inch concrete reinforcing rod with a five-eighths-inch nut welded on the top makes an excellent homemade stake. A lap-link added to the chain anchoring the trap to the stake allows freedom of movement and prevents an animal from binding or twisting the chain and pulling free. Pan covers of waxed paper are also necessary to keep dirt and other obstructions from the pan when setting the trap. For wetland trapping, wooden stakes are used more often than metal stakes. You'll also need a hatchet for cutting and driving stakes. For rocky stream bottoms, you may need drags rather than trying to drive stakes. A roll of wire and pliers with a wire-cutting edge are also necessary. Chest waders, hip boots, and shoulder gauntlets can keep you dry and warm. You'll also need scents, lures, or bait. Urine, gland, and natural scents are the best choices. A trapping basket for holding traps is also handy.

Trap Care

New traps must be pre-rusted by soaking them six to eight hours in a solution of water and vinegar. This washes the oil off. Hang them outside until they are completely covered with a light rust. The next step is to dye the traps. Fill a large container with enough water to cover the number of traps you have. Bring the water to a boil and add a commercial trap dye. You can also use walnut hulls to dye the traps. The final step is to wax the traps to prevent further rusting and also to improve the action of the trap. Conibear traps, however, should never be waxed because it makes them too slick and dangerous to handle. Bring clean water to a boil in the container used for dyeing. Melt trap wax over a double-boiler arrangement. Never melt wax directly over a fire. Pour the melted wax into the water. The wax will float. Lower and then pull the hot traps up slowly through wax. Hang the traps outside to dry, but away from strong odors. Scrape wax away from the pan notch and trigger before setting the traps.

Sign and Location

Before you set traps, you must determine what animals are using an area, or find an area animals are using. Learn the habits of the animals you wish to trap and then look for tracks, droppings, hair, scat, or disturbed ground or vegetation. Traps are most commonly set where animals frequently travel, but should never be set near a den or home. Most frequently used places include along a stream, around a pond or lake, near shelters such as brush and woods, fencerows, or near old building ruins.

Trap Sets

Specific sets are normally made for specific animal species. Following are some basic sets.

Coyote and **fox:** A scent post set is a very common and productive set for coyotes. If possible, find a natural scent post coyotes are using. If not, create your own. Set a post or cut off a sapling and squirt it with coyote urine. Do this once or twice a week for several weeks. Use three or four leg-hold traps, well bedded and concealed. The traps should be fastened to a drag or grapnel. When the coyote comes in to smell the scent post or leave scent, he steps on a trap, triggers it, and is then caught. As he pulls the grapnel or log, it catches on bushes. This provides

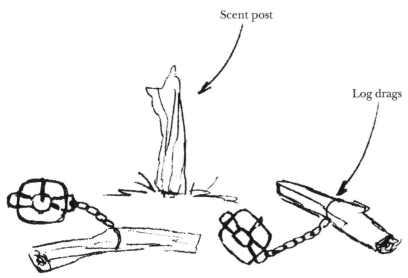

TRAPS ARE SET IN SPECIFIC PATTERNS FOR DIFFERENT ANIMALS. SHOWN HERE IS A TRAP FOR COYOTE AND FOXES.

overhang. A foothold bank set with a drowning stake is also good. The trap is placed close to the bank and in a few inches of water. When the trap captures the muskrat, it will immediately head for deep water. It will then head right or left and wrap the trap chain around the drowning stake. Muskrats like to crawl up on objects to sun and rest. A wooden float of an old plank can be used with two or more foothold traps anchored to the bottom of the float. An anchor is used to hold the float in place. Commercial muskrat scent adds to the set. When the muskrat is caught, it dives off the float and drowns by the weight of the trap. More than one muskrat can be caught at the same time with this method.

restraint without a solid resistant and prevents the animal from pulling out of the trap. A fox or coyote trail set is made on routes coyotes or foxes commonly use. Place a fairly large log over the trail and place a leg-hold trap on either side of the log. Bed the traps fairly deep over stakes driven well into the ground. Cover each pan with sifted dirt and carry all excess dirt away from the set. Do not use a lure or scent.

Raccoon and **opossum:** Both of these furbearers may be taken with a dirt hole set or artificial hole set. For a dirt hole set, dig a hole at a 30-degree angle from the surface. Place a bit of tainted meat in the hole and then lightly cover it with earth to keep the crows from stealing it.

Muskrat: In areas with lots of vegetation, such as cattails, muskrats create runways along banks, often creating overhanging banks. A Conibear trap fastened to a forked stick or stake and placed under the overhang is very productive. Use other sticks to "corral" or guide the muskrat toward the

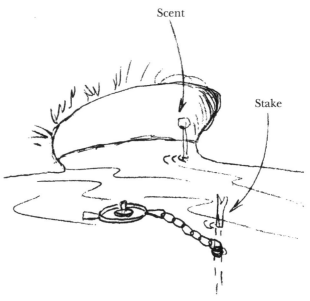

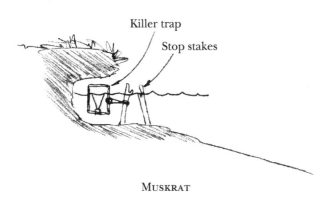

MUSKRAT   RACCOON AND OPOSSUM

Place a few drops of red fox scent near the back of the hole. Bed the trap near the hole so it is slightly below ground level and is held in place with a bedded, well-driven stake. Cover the trap with about a half-inch of sifted dirt. Sprinkle a few more drops of fox urine around the trap. When the animal comes to investigate the scent from the hole, it circles the hole and steps on the trap.

A stump set is also effective. It consists of a leg-hold trap set across an opening in a stump or tree roots with bait placed in the back. The trap should be nailed to the stump or staked. An artificial hole set is used along streams or the banks of ponds and lakes for raccoons. Dig a hole at least a foot deep with about an inch of water in the opening. The hole should be sloped so the back is dry. Place a bit of fish or fish oil in the back and place the leg-hold trap across the entrance. Stake the trap or anchor it well in deep water. This set will also take mink. Snares, where legal, are also good for raccoon. They can be set on trails or cross-under areas of fences.

Knots

Anyone who spends much time on a farm, ranch, or the outdoors will have to learn to make various knots. From tying up horses to tying down tarpaulins, it's an essential skill.

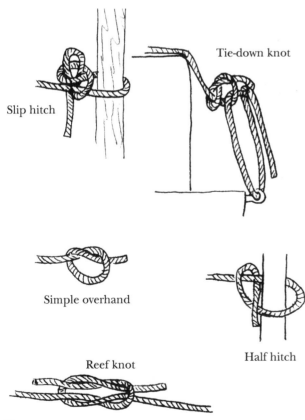

KNOWLEDGE OF A VARIETY OF KNOTS CAN BE INVALUABLE.

Slip hitch

Tie-down knot

Simple overhand

Half hitch

Reef knot

Basic Knots

When tying up a boat, especially in current where there might be some danger and you want to be able to untie quickly, use a slip-hitch knot. One quick pull of the end of the rope and it's free. I also use this knot when fastening portable electric polywire fencing. I simply pull on the tag end to loosen.

One of the toughest problems is tying anything down snugly, whether it's a guy for a load of furniture or a tent guy. Normally by the time the knot is tied, the rope has loosened. My dad taught me how to make the tie-down knot shown. The lines can be tied as taut as you can pull, yet will come free with a quick yank on the end. Other knots you should learn include simple overhand, reef knot, and half hitch. The latter is used for tying to an object, such as a post.

Whipping

To stop the end of a manila rope from unraveling, it can be whipped or wound with smaller cord or string. Lay a loop of string along the

217

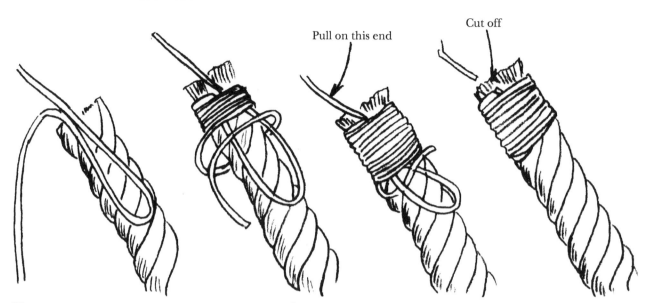

WHIPPING IS A MEANS OF FASTENING A ROPE SO IT WON'T UNRAVEL.

rope end and then wrap one free end tightly around the rope. When you've wrapped about one-half inch, place both free ends in the loop and pull on the ends. This will pull the ends under the wrap. Then trim the ends. To stop a nylon rope from unraveling, merely hold a match or flame to the end to melt the fibers together.

PART ELEVEN

Home Butchering

Butchering our own livestock as well as wild game has been a tradition in our family for generations. As a kid, I remember the neighborhood hog butchering as nothing more than a festival as neighbors came in to my grand-dads and spent an entire day, sometimes butchering up to a dozen hogs. With our own farm, Joan and I decided to butcher a beef and my dad came down to help. I was going to hoist the just-killed beef up to a limb with a chain fastened to my old 9-N Ford tractor so we could gut and skin it. The ground had patches of ice and the wheels were slipping. I poured on the gas; suddenly the wheels got traction, and the tractor leaped forward. Before I could get the clutch and brake in, I had pulled the beef off the ground, over the limb, and it hit the ground with a loud thump. My dad was laughing so hard he was practically rolling on the cold, wet ground. On his deathbed he began to chuckle, then reminisced: "Remember how you "tenderized" that beef with your tractor?" Butchering livestock and wild game is not a particularly difficult skill to learn. It does take work, but the results are more than worth it.

HOME BUTCHERING OF LIVESTOCK AND WILD GAME WAS A NECESSITY IN THE PAST AND CAN PROVIDE ECONOMICAL MEAT, CUT AND PREPARED AS DESIRED BY THE HOMESTEADER. THE AUTHOR'S BROTHER AND FATHER SCRAPING A FAT HOG MANY YEARS AGO.

Butchering Tools

Having the proper tools, as well as a place that can be kept clean for butchering and preparing meat is extremely important. Butchering poultry, small livestock, and small game doesn't require much in the way of tools. Butchering and properly preparing pork, beef, and venison or big game requires more.

Knives

The most important tools are knives, and they should be high quality. You'll need an assortment: skinning knives with rounded points; "sticking" knives with double-edge blades for bleeding hogs; long, thin, pointed knives for boning out meat and trimming cuts; and long, heavy-bladed knives for slicing steaks and other cuts. A sturdy cleaver is also important. A hand meat saw is required for numerous chores, such as quartering and making the traditional butcher cuts such as chops and ribs. A knife with a gut-hook is extremely handy for initial cutting when skinning as well as for gutting larger animals. The more knives you have the better off you are. When one gets dull, simply pick up another. Knives are available in a variety of steels, ranging from stainless through several grades of carbon steel and combinations. Stainless steel knives are the hardest; soft carbon steel is the softest. Stainless steel requires a great deal more effort in sharpening, but holds the edge longer than carbon metals. My favorite kitchen and butcher knives are the Chef's Choice Trizor Professional 10X Cutlery. They are made of Trizor, a unique stainless steel, containing twice the carbon and ten times the molybdenum, an extremely tough metal that stays sharp ten times longer than any other kitchen knife. It's also essential to keep the knives extremely sharp. A wide variety of sharpening devices are also needed. (Knife sharpening is covered in Part VIII.) I use the Chef'sChoice EdgeSelect Professional #120 Diamond Hone Knife Sharpener for major sharpening. Touch up while working is done with an AccuSharp. This is extremely handy and quick. If you're field dressing game, you'll need a sharp knife with a gut hook that's sturdy enough to cut the aitchbone, or a saw. The Katz Safari Kit includes a knife handle with detachable blades including a skinning blade, boning blade, and fillet blade, a bone/meat saw, a wood saw blade, and a hatchet, all in handy leather sheaths. With this, you can take care of any in-the-field butchering chores. You should also have a piece of twine for tying off the bung, disposable gloves, and a plastic bag.

Location

You'll need a place to hang animals for skinning and other chores. For hogs, beef, and big game, you'll need a sturdy game pole. This can be made from saplings lashed together, even a sturdy tree limb. A game pole with steel transfer hooks is a good idea if you do several animals at a time. Gambrels are also needed for hanging livestock and game. These can simply be sturdy wooden saplings cut and their ends sharpened or purchased or homemade metal gambrels. A block and tackle, hand or electric winch, or even ATV or tractor is necessary to hoist the carcass up on the game pole. Transfer hooks can be used to hold more than one animal at a time. Spreader sticks are required to prop open the cavity.

You'll need lots of clean tubs or pans to hold the various cuts of meat while you butcher and trim. Large plastic buckets or tubs are required to hold meat to be ground. Cutting boards or surfaces are also extremely important. The best to use are the newer plastic surfaces since they don't score as easily as wood and they are easier to clean and sanitize. Plenty of soft rags for wiping your hands, cleaning surfaces, and equipment are also needed. You should also have access to water and have bleach and soap to clean and sanitize surfaces and utensils as you work.

Work Surfaces

One of the most important items is a good, sturdy work surface. You'll need several solid tables that can easily be cleaned. We have a few old tables that we cover with plastic tablecloths. These are used to hold the quarters or large cuts of meat waiting to be cut up or processed. The actual meat cutting is done on a stainless steel table, which is easily kept clean. The work surface should also be at a comfortable working height so you don't have to bend over. The normal height for most people is about thirty-six inches. An excellent stainless steel butcher table is available from Cabela's.

In the olden days, most butchering was done in the winter months so the meat could be cooled

STURDY TABLES WITH EASY-TO-CLEAN SURFACES ARE ESSENTIAL FOR HOME BUTCHERING. (PHOTO COURTESY OF CABELA'S.)

naturally. This is still a good idea, although sometimes, and in some climates, hot weather will still prevail. Meat should be cooled fairly quickly and a meat cooler can be an asset. We have one made from an old refrigerator truck. We can hold a dozen deer-sized animals in it if necessary. You can also use an old refrigerator to chill a deer- or hog-sized animal. Remove the shelves, quarter the animal, and place the quarters on end in the refrigerator.

Specialty Tools

For grinding meat into sausage or burgers, you'll need a meat grinder. This can be done with a hand grinder, but it takes quite a bit of time. If you have a fairly good-sized animal or animals, you'll greatly appreciate a powered meat grinder. I inherited one from my granddad that originally ran off the jacked-up back wheel of his Model-A. It still works, but is somewhat dangerous. I now have a model from the SausageMaker. Cabela's has several excellent models including heavy-duty professional ones. Most of the newer models also offer sausage-stuffing attachments. Another extremely handy item is a powered meat slicer. The Chef's-Choice Professional Electric Food Slicer Model 667 is rugged, with a tilted design for fast and efficient slicing. The commercial quality, fully hardened stainless steel blade precisely cuts meat, cheese, bread, vegetables, and fruits. Round steaks often require tenderizing and the Cabela's Meat tenderizer and cuber make short work of this chore. I have cut chops and beef steaks with a handsaw or chops with a heavy cleaver, but it's hard work. One item is fairly expensive, but if you plan to do beef on a regular basis, a butcher's band saw is mighty handy. One commercial grade model is available from Cabela's. A vacuum-packing system, such as the Professional II Food-saver from Tilia does an excellent job of vacuum packing meat for longer life. If you intend to make jerky or summer sausages, you'll need a smoker, and the Bradley, Luhr-Jensen, Sausage Maker, and L.E.M. smokers are all excellent quality.

TODAY'S MEAT GRINDERS MAKE THIS ONCE-ONEROUS CHORE QUICK AND EASY. (PHOTO COURTESY OF CABELA'S.)

Butchering Poultry

When our kids were little, and I was just beginning as a freelance writer and author, the food on our table was pretty much grown on our farm. And that included chickens. We purchased 100 baby chicks each spring, raised them through the summer months, and butchered them in late summer or early fall. It was a family chore, but we made it fun and the kids still talk about those days.

Getting Started

Before slaughtering, the birds should be kept without feed for twenty-four hours, but keep plenty of fresh water in front of them. This makes eviscerating easier.

Dressing poultry such as chickens and turkeys is fairly easy, but it's also messy. Even in chicken slaughtering plants, it's messy. This is where the proverbial "chopping block" comes into play. In home butchering, the most common method of killing the bird is to chop off its head. This requires a sturdy wooden block, usually a chunk cut from a log and stood on end. You'll also need a sharp hatchet. Grasp the chicken legs, pull the wings down, and hold them tight with the legs. Place the head and neck on the chopping block and with a well-directed blow, decapitate the chicken. This is where it gets messy. Blood will spurt from the neck and the bird will start to flop. We tossed the carcass into a cardboard box where the blood

was contained and the bird kept "clean." After a day's work, the box was burned. A method considered more humane by some is to hang the chicken, insert a sharp knife into the roof of the mouth where the groove is, and then push the knife point into the brain. Immediately withdraw the knife, insert it blade out into one side of the neck, and then push it out and through the other side, slitting the throat. Use something to catch the blood that will immediately flow. A coffee can with a wire bail can be slipped around the neck. A rock for a weight in the bottom helps prevent flopping.

The next step is plucking the feathers. This again, is a messy chore. If you are dressing only one or two birds, they can be dry-plucked. As soon as the bird has been killed, grasp the carcass by the neck and pluck, beginning with the breast feathers. Pluck by grasping a few feathers at a time and gently pulling in the direction of the feathers. Be careful not to tear the skin by

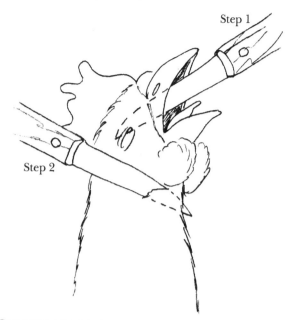

Step 1

Step 2

CHICKENS AND OTHER POULTRY CAN BE KILLED BY CHOPPING OFF THEIR HEADS OR BY INSERTING A SHARP KNIFE INTO THE ROOF OF THE MOUTH AND INTO THE BRAIN, AND THEN CUTTING THE THROAT.

grasping too many feathers or pulling too hard. Continue plucking over the back, down the legs, upper wings, and neck. Wet plucking is easier and less time consuming, especially if you're doing a number of birds. Use an old pan or tub and heat the water (best done outside) to 128°F or 130°F. Do only one bird at a time. Grasp the legs and dip the carcass in the scalding water. Use a stick to swirl it around and make sure the entire bird is well dunked. Move it around to make sure all feathers are soaked, but do not leave in the scalding water for more than half a minute. The feathers of old birds take longer to loosen than the feathers of young birds. Use the same plucking method as for dry-pluck. The feathers, however, will come out much more easily. Most pinfeathers, especially on young birds, can be rubbed out with your fingers. Holding the carcass under running water can help. Pinch stubborn pinfeathers with a knife blade and your thumb and pull out. Hairs on the bird are singed off using a propane torch.

Cutting Up

If the head hasn't been cut off, do so. Next, cut off the oil gland on top of the tail. Start the cut in front of the oil-gland nipple and cut out the gland in a scooping motion. Make sure you get all of it. Cut off the feet at the joint. Bend the feet to stretch and show the tendon. Then cut through the tendon at the hock joint. With the carcass lying on its back, cut through the skin and muscle of the belly from the tip of the breastbone to the top of the anus. Do not cut through the intestines. Cut around the anus. Reach in under the keel bone of the breast and scoop out the intestines. Keep the intestines intact and do not squeeze them during the process. You may have to repeat the step to get the gizzard, liver, and lungs. Use your fingertips to scrape away the lungs and the gonads of cockerels from the underside of the backbone. Cut

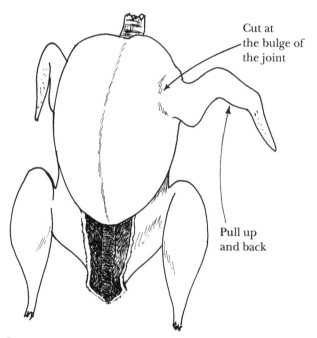

Cut at the bulge of the joint

Pull up and back

CHICKENS CAN BE LEFT WHOLE FOR BAKING, CUT INTO FRYING PIECES, OR CUT INTO HALVES FOR BAKING OR BARBEQUING. WITH THE BIRD ON A FLAT SURFACE, PULL A WING UP AND BACK TO REVEAL THE ROUNDED JOINT INSIDE THE MUSCLE. CUT THROUGH THE MUSCLE AT THE JOINT. REPEAT FOR THE OPPOSITE WING.

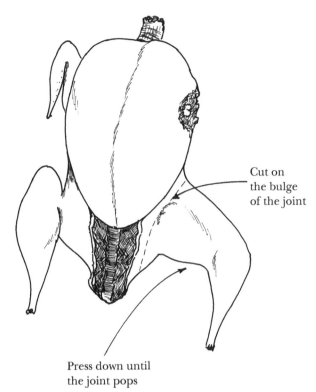

Cut on
the bulge
of the joint

Press down until
the joint pops

PRESS DOWN ON A LEG UNTIL THE JOINT POPS FREE, THEN
CUT THE MUSCLE SURROUNDING THE JOINT. REPEAT FOR
THE OPPOSITE LEG.

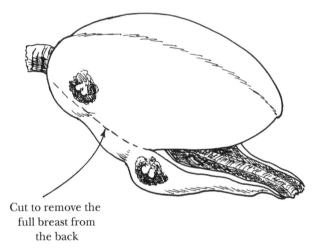

Cut to remove the
full breast from
the back

PULL THE BREASTBONE UPWARD AND CUT THROUGH THE
RIBS ON BOTH SIDES TO REMOVE THE IN-BONE WHOLE
BREAST.

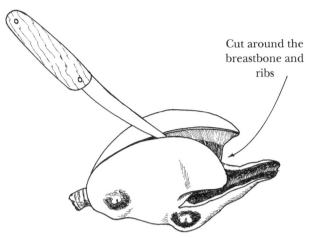

Cut around the
breastbone and
ribs

YOU CAN ALSO BONE OUT THE BREAST MEAT USING A BONING
KNIFE.

and peel the gall bladder or bile sack from the liver, being careful not to cut or break the bile. Slice the gizzard through the center, peel out the inner lining, and wash the liver, heart, and gizzard in cold water. Place in a small plastic bag. Wash the carcass for at least a couple of minutes in cold running water. Place the carcasses in a tub of ice water and cool them down to 40°F as quickly as possible. Once cooled down, remove from the ice water and drain for about ten minutes. Place in plastic bags. Bread sacks are an excellent choice. Place the liver, gizzard, and hearts inside the cavity before sealing off with plastic ties. The chickens can be kept refrigerated at 29° to 30°F for a couple of days before cooking fresh or freezing.

Turkeys are butchered in the same basic method, although they are normally dry picked. Allow to cool for at least twenty-four hours in 29°F refrigerator before freezing. Turkeys are normally left as whole birds, but they can also be cut into pieces if desired.

Wild game birds are drawn in the same manner as chickens. They are usually dry plucked or skinned.

Butchering Pork

Butchering a hog or two is an American tradition in the country. It really isn't difficult, although the work can be strenuous. When I was first learning how to cut the meat, my wife quipped, "Didn't matter how precise my meat cuts were, it all ate." Hogs are normally butchered between 160 and 180 pounds. It's a good idea to choose a day with temperatures hovering between 20° and 40°F. Colder and it's harder to cool the meat without freezing it. Warmer and it's harder to keep the meat cooling properly.

Killing

In days past, hogs were scalded and the hair scraped from the hide, leaving the skin intact. The skin was left on for protection of cured hams, sides, and shoulders. Scalding is both an art and the hardest part of hog butchering. We used to have a scalding vat and table for the chore, and it did provide the easiest means of scalding. The vat was set on concrete blocks over a fire pit. An alternative is to use a fifty-five-gallon steel drum set on blocks and positioned next to a sturdy wooden table. Water is placed in the tank and brought to between 145° and 160°F with the fire pit. On cold days make sure you get the temperature up around 160°F. Make sure you have plenty of wood on hand to keep the water hot. As soon as the water is hot, the hog is killed. This is normally done by placing a bit of food in a corner of the pen and shooting the animal between the eyes with a .22. As soon as the

animal drops, grasp the two front legs and pull them apart. Insert the sticking knife just ahead of the breastbone and make a two- to three-inch cut. Use a tilting motion of the knife handle to force the knife point up and under the breastbone at about a 45-degree angle. Then make a cut in the opposite direction, tilting the handle to point the blade toward the mouth. Done correctly blood will immediately spurt from the cut, properly bleeding the animal. Even a properly shot and stunned hog can do a lot of thrashing around and you can be injured in your attempt to bleed the animal. A helper to hold the animal on its back with its front legs spread is a good idea.

Scalding and Scraping

The hog is then dragged or hoisted out of the pen and carefully lowered into the scalding water. A hay hook can be used in the hog's

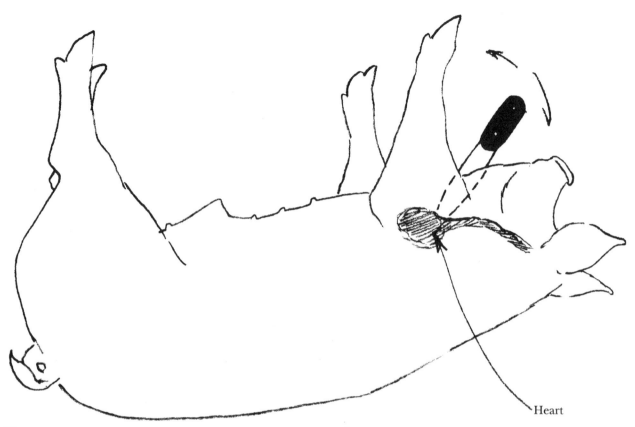

Heart

HOGS ARE TRADITIONALLY KILLED BY FIRST STUNNING WITH A .22. A STICKING KNIFE IS THEN USED TO PIERCE THE JUGULAR AND HEART AND ALLOW THE HOG TO BLEED OUT.

mouth for the initial hoisting and dipping. Be careful not to splash the scalding water on you or drop the hog into vat. Swirl the rear end around in the hot water, but do not allow it to remain for more than four or five minutes. If it gets too hot, the hair will "set" and be harder to remove. Then carefully pull the hog out onto the wooden tabletop and using large bladed knives, or better yet hog scrapers, scrape off all the hair. Once you have the rear end scraped, shackle a hind leg, lower the front end into the scalding water, and scrape the front. No matter how you do it, scalding and scraping is messy and hard work.

Skinning

I've done my share of scalding and scraping but these days, I prefer to skin the critters. I can skin a hog in the time it would normally take to get

the water hot enough for scalding. This is especially easier when just one or two persons are doing the butchering. It is also the method most commercial shops use these days. The hog is hoisted onto a sturdy pole, head down with gambrels inserted in the tendons at the hocks. A sharp knife is used to make a cut behind the jowls and head encircling the neck. The head is then twisted off and set aside in a pan in a cool spot for later work. I also like to cut off the front feet just in front of the hock joints with a meat saw. This makes for easier skinning. Hog skin is especially thick on the neck and back. To make the skinning chore easier, make scoring cuts about two to three inches apart and from the hips the full length of the body. Hog skin won't peel off like most other skins, which have an inner layer. The skin must be cut off, but the task is still easier than scalding and scraping. Use a

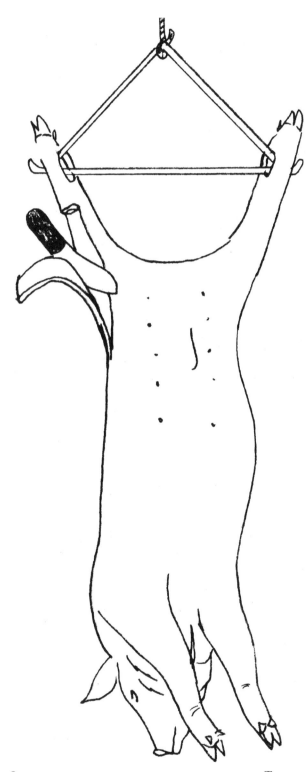

IN THE PAST, HOGS WERE SCALDED AND SCRAPED. THESE DAYS, MOST HOME BUTCHERS, AS WELL AS SLAUGHTER PLANTS, SKIN THE ANIMALS.

skinning knife with a rounded blade and keep it sharp.

Eviscerating

Regardless of whether scalding and scraping or skinning, the next step is to eviscerate the carcass, or you may choose to eviscerate before skinning. Use a knife to cut through the neck up to the point of the breastbone. Reach in and pull out the gullet and windpipe. Cut them off. Using a meat saw, continue splitting the chest cavity, splitting the ribs. If you're gutting a hog that has been scalded, this task is best done with the hog still on the scraping table and lying on its back. In any case, be careful not to cut into the intestines.

The next step is to open the belly. Make a short cut in the top of the abdominal wall near the rear of the pig and to one side of the penis and/or scrotum if a male. It is extremely important not to cut through the thin muscle and membranes and into the intestines. With a good gut-hook knife, you can make a short incision near the anus, insert the hook in the belly wall, and very simply and quickly rip the belly open to allow the paunch and intestines to fall out. If you don't have a gut-hook knife you can insert two fingers of one hand, position the knife blade facing outward and make the cut, pushing the intestines and organs back away from the cut. The traditional method, however, is to place your hand inside the opening cut made with the knife blade facing outward and down. Position your fist so the knife is pointed slightly upward. The cut is then made with the heel of the knife blade as your fist pushes the intestines away from the cut. When you cut through the belly wall, the intestines will fall out and downward. They will, however, be held in place by the muscles and membranes attaching them to the inside of the ribs.

At this point, the intestines will still be attached to the bung. The next step is to cut through the aitchbone or pelvic arch. I also like to cut around the penis and allow it to drop down over the back of the carcass. Then make a cut between the hams to locate the white line indicating

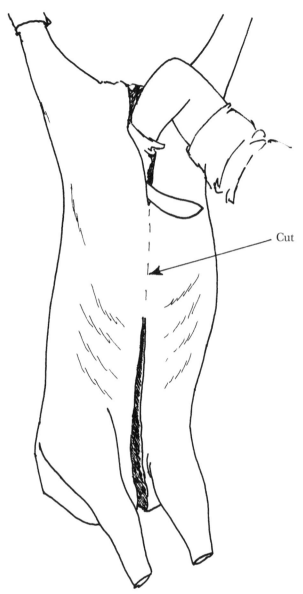

Cut

THE CARCASS IS EVISCERATED.

Once the bung gut has been loosened, the entire mass of entrails will fall further forward and down. Once the diaphragm is exposed, cut it and the gullet to allow the entrails and organs to drop away from the carcass. Have a clean tub beneath to collect the organs such as liver and heart. These should then be cut free, the bile sack removed from the liver, and the organs placed in a pan of cold water in a cool place. Rinse out the inside of the carcass with buckets of cold water or a hose.

The carcass can then be cooled as one piece if it's cold enough to hang outside or in a barn or shed. Make sure it's high enough and protected from varmints and pets. A better method is to halve the carcass. Two methods can be used. The carcass can be cut down the center of the backbone resulting in two sides with pork chops, or you can cut on either side of the backbone leaving the backbone intact and have boneless pork loins. The latter is a preferred southern method. Hogs are not left to hang and age as are other animals, but the meat must be chilled down quickly not only for quality meat but also to make it easy to work up the hog. Our process is to kill, skin, and split the hogs, and then leave them overnight in cold weather. The actual butchering chores are then done the next day. While the carcass is cooling, you can work on the head. Remove and clean the tongue. Cut off the jowls. These can be sliced into fresh jowls by lightly freezing in a freezer until just about stiff. Then slice into bacon thickness and serve with black-eyed peas for New Year's Day. The remainder of the head can be skinned out and the skull split to remove the brains. Our family left nothing but the "squeal" to waste, as my grandmother used to say. The brains were cooked the next morning with scrambled eggs. Mom cooked the heads and tongues and made "head cheese." This is one meat dish that definitely takes some getting used to.

The next step is to quarter the halves. Before quartering, remove the tenderloins located on either side of the backbone inside the body cavity. Use a knife to loosen one end and the ten-

the pelvic bone. Use a sharp knife to saw or cut through the bone.

Completely encircle the anus or bung gut with a sharp, pointed knife, much like coring an apple. If a female, encircle the genitals as well. Pull these upward and tie off to prevent feces and urine from the bladder from contaminating the meat. Then pull the bung gut down and out through the slit in the aitchbone. You will have to use a knife to cut the bung gut away from the backbone as well.

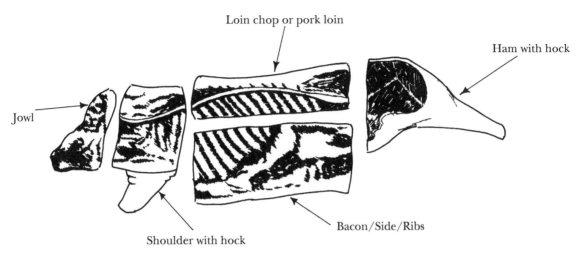

Loin chop or pork loin

Ham with hock

Jowl

Shoulder with hock

Bacon/Side/Ribs

CUT UP INTO THE DESIRED MEAT CUTS.

derloins will normally peel out easily. If the half has been cut to produce pork chops, lay the half down on a clean surface meat side up. Use a hand meat saw to cut off each hock from both front and rear legs. Then cut through the backbone and ribs just behind the front leg. This produces a long-cut shoulder that can be cured or you can debone the shoulder or a portion of it for ground meat. To remove the ham, use the hand meat saw to make a cut at right angles to the hind shank and about two and a half inches in front of the aitchbone. Once you've cut through the backbone, finish the cut with a knife. The ribs are then cut away with a handsaw just below the backbone to produce a row of chops and slab ribs. The chops can then be cut apart using a hand meat saw and sharp knife or with a power meat band saw. I've also chopped them apart with a hatchet or cleaver, but the results are not as clean looking. The sides are then peeled and cut away from the ribs. The slabs can be left as is or cut into baby-back ribs.

If the sides are cut to produce boneless pork loins, the first step is to remove the boneless loin. Cut and peel out the loin, and then cut the shoulder and ham away. Finally, peel the side away from the ribs.

The pork loin, ribs, pork chops, and backbone are normally wrapped and frozen after first being cut into serving-size pieces. The trimmings from the ham and shoulder are normally used to make sausage. You can add portions of the sides, but this normally creates a fattier sausage. We like to make our sausage extremely lean and cut away a great deal of the fat. The meat must then be cut into one-inch cubes and ground with a grinder. My mom packed sausage into muslin bags she sewed. The sausage was then sliced into patties, bag and all, and the cloth removed before cooking. We've discovered sausage lasts the longest if it's vacuum packed. The shoulders, hams, and even the sides can be sugar cured and/or smoked. See Part VI on preserving foods for instructions on curing and smoking.

Butchering Beef

Home-butchering a beef is the next step up. It's strenuous work, mostly due to the weight of the animal and the need to move the carcass around for the various chores. You will need sturdy equipment for hoisting and holding the carcass. The actual butchering process, other than the hefting, however, is not particularly difficult.

Choosing the Right Time

In days past, butcher beef was raised to about thirty months or 1,800 pounds or so. The last three months the animal was confined to a pen and grain fed; hence, "corn-fed" beef. In the past few years, more consumers and home-butchers have begun to butcher at an earlier and smaller age. This is usually from sixteen to twenty-four months and at around 1,000 to 1,400 pounds. Meat from animals of this size and age does not have the fat marbling, but contains less cholesterol and is extremely tender. Some growers have taken it a step further with "grass-fed" beef. These calves don't get any grain and there's even less marbling and cholesterol, but the meat is "healthier."

Beef is best when aged and unless you have a large cooler for aging, it's important to time the butchering to cold weather, in mid to late winter or very early spring, depending on your locale. A period of weather with temperatures in the upper 30s to low 40s is ideal.

Killing

One of the hardest chores is killing. This is traditionally done in slaughterhouses with a stun gun or in the olden days by stunning with a blow to the head. The animal must be secured and the blow delivered properly just above the eyes and off to one side of the centerline of the skull. A gun can also be used. Some people use .22 long rifles, however, this is iffy. Some use higher caliber rifles or pistol bullets. My neighbor insists that a shotgun with a slug, held about eighteen inches from the skull is deadly. Regardless, make sure of your aim and make the kill as humane as possible. As soon as the animal is stunned, immediately cut the throat with a sharp knife. Grasp the underside of the jaw and cut the neck completely through below the jaw to the backbone.

Allow the animal to bleed thoroughly. Drag or hoist the animal to the skinning/hanging pole. Cut across the tendons behind the foot, between the hoof and dewclaws of a rear leg. Then make an encircling cut around the foot and a cut

BUTCHERING A BEEF IS HARD WORK AND DOES REQUIRE MORE IN THE WAY OF TOOLS. THE FIRST STEP IS TO STUN THE ANIMAL BY SHOOTING IT OR DELIVERING A BLOW JUST ABOVE THE EYES AND OFF TO ONE SIDE. THE THROAT IS IMMEDIATELY CUT TO ALLOW THE ANIMAL TO BLEED OUT.

from this cut to about eight inches above the hock. Skin out the lower leg to just above the hock and cut off the lower leg at the lowest hock joint. Cut with a knife to loosen the tendons, and then you can twist the joint apart and finish cutting with the knife. Separate the large tendons behind the rear legs and use a knife to make a hole for the gambrels.

Split the belly and chest skin, but do not cut the belly lining. Make the cut from just below the anus to the neck, cutting to one side of the penis. Slit the skin on the inside of the front legs, and remove the feet at the lowest point of the hocks. Skin out the front legs down to the shoulders and continue skinning to the slit in the breastbone.

Skin out the rear legs and thighs down to the tail and skin down to the cut through the lower belly area. Cut through the muscle between the thighs to expose the white line marking the aitchbone. A slight seam will be exposed in the bone. Cut through the aitchbone with a saw, being very careful not to cut into the rectal tube. Using a saw, cut through the breastbone

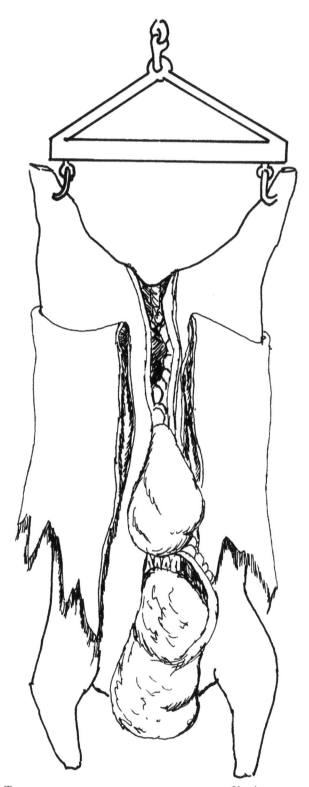

THE CARCASS IS SKINNED AND EVISCERATED. YOU'LL NEED A STURDY MEAT POLE AND GAMBRELS.

from the point of the last rib up to the juncture with the neck.

At this point, the gambrel is inserted and the carcass hoisted so the rump of the animal is at a convenient working height. With a sharp knife, continue skinning down the thighs to the rump on the back. Leave the skin around the anus, but skin to the tail and cut it off, leaving it with the skin.

Loosen the bung gut by cutting down it from the three unexposed sides. Tie off the anus, bladder, and vagina, if a female. Place a container under the carcass to receive the viscera. As you cut the tissues that hold the bung gut inside the carcass, the intestines and paunch will fall down and out. Remove the gall bladder from the liver and place the liver in a pan of cold water. The heart and lungs will stay in the carcass, connected by the diaphragm. Cut the diaphragm to allow the heart and lungs to fall out. Remove the heart, cut it in quarters, and place in a pan of cold water. Then cut away the gullet from inside of the throat.

Continue skinning the hindquarters of the carcass. Pull the hide down and use a skinning knife to cut it free. Continue skinning the remainder of the carcass. You can skin the head and remove the cheek meat for stew or dog food. Remove the tongue and clean it thoroughly. You may prefer to cut off the head before skinning. Unless you're using the head, this makes skinning much easier. In this case, continue the bleeding cut encircling the head. Once you've cut through all the muscle and ligaments, you can twist off the head. Use a prop stick to prop open the chest cavity. Rinse out the carcass with buckets of cold water or water from a hose.

The carcass is then split down the middle of the backbone for quicker cooling and to hang and age. A hand meat saw can be used, but it takes a great deal of effort. I've used an electric chainsaw kept just for that purpose. The chain is cleaned thoroughly after each use and kept in a jar with vegetable oil between uses. The carcass should be split down to leave a section of neck meat to hold them together and balance on the gambrel for hanging.

Hanging

Ideally, the meat should be hung in a dry, protected area such as an enclosed barn or shed for a week to ten days. The temperature must remain in the upper 30s and lower 40s for proper aging. If the temperature rises above 50°F for any period of time, start cutting up the meat.

Butchering

The first step in butchering is to finish cutting the halves into quarters. You will definitely need help with this task. As you cut the carcass into quarters, there's a lot of weight to handle, and it's awkward weight. The quartering cut is made between the last two ribs of each half. Begin this cut about two inches in from the front or flank, leaving a strip of meat intact in that location. Then saw the backbone to separate the quarters, leaving the strip of flank meat on the last rib to hold the quarter in place. One person can then grasp the quarter while another cuts the strip to separate the quarters. But, when you cut off a quarter, the full half will immediately swing down. One way of preventing this is to use a transfer hook on each half.

Lay the front quarter on a clean cutting table with the skin side down. Starting about halfway down the exposed rib, make a cut across the carcass and across the shank. Use a knife to make the cut, and then a meat saw to complete cutting through the bones. This removes the brisket, plate, and foreshank. The foreshank can be cut crosswise into soup bones, while the upper portion of the shank can be cut into arm roasts. The rib section can be sawed into short ribs, cutting across the ribs. Cut the brisket from the bone. All of these cuts can also be trimmed and be ground for hamburger if you prefer.

The neck is removed by cutting crosswise at the juncture of the shoulder. The neck meat is most often boned out and can be used as a rolled neck roast or boneless neck, or most often, the neck meat is ground. Boning the neck is fairly easy, but it's important to cut away all the yellow cartilage surrounding the windpipe.

The upper portion of the shoulder is divided just behind the withers to create the chuck and

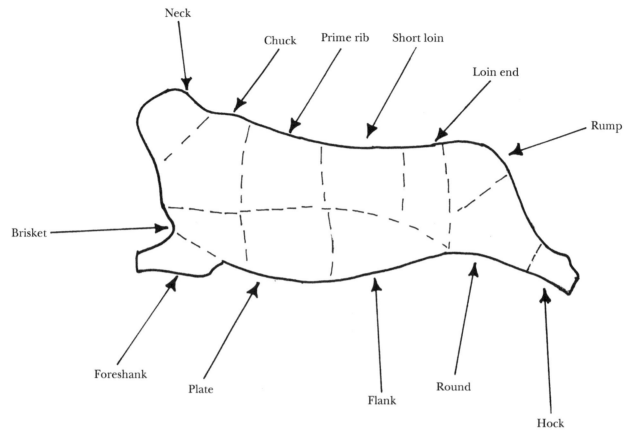

rib sections. Using either the hand meat saw or a powered meat band saw, the chuck or shoulder is then cut into roasts producing chuck roasts, cross arm, or round bone chuck roasts. Short ribs are cut from the lower part of the rib section and the upper section is cut into standing rib roasts, rolled boneless rib roasts, or rib steaks.

Hindquarter

Lay the hindquarter on a table with the skin side down. Remove the flank, the triangular shaped piece of meat on the lower front portion. The flank contains the flank steak, which can be peeled away. The rest of the flank, as well as the flank steak piece can be used in burgers.

Cut away the kidneys and kidney fat from the backbone. The hindquarter is first divided into two sections, the loin and the round. Sepa-rate these two sections at the ball-and-socket hip joint. Start the cut with a knife and then complete the cut with a handsaw. The loin is then divided into a short loin and loin end, making the cut at the hip joint. The loin section produces the most popular steaks. The short loin produces the club, T-bone, and porter-house steaks, while the loin end produces sir-loin steaks.

The round section is divided into two pieces, the round and the rump. The rump is cut away from the round across the top of the section by sawing across the bone. The rump makes a rump roast or a boneless rolled rump roast. The hind shank is cut away from the round section leaving a section that is cut into round steaks. Meat from the hind shank is used in burgers while the lower shank leg is used as soup bones.

Butchering Lamb and Goats

There really is no difference in the initial killing and dressing of lambs and goats. Cutting up the meat, however, differs somewhat.

Killing, Skinning, and Gutting Lambs

A spring lamb grown until November or late fall is one option. An Easter lamb is butchered between one and three months of age. As with most livestock to be butchered, the animal should be confined to a clean pen for twenty-four hours prior to being butchered. Do not provide feed, but supply plenty of water. Again, pick a cool day unless you have a refrigerated area to hang the meat.

The lamb may be stunned or shot with a .22 in much the same manner as other livestock. As soon as the animal falls, cut its throat just under the jaw and from ear to ear. Continue the cut around the back of the head where the skull joins the neck. Twist the head to remove it, cutting attachments free as you twist. Once the animal has bled out, skin out the front legs and remove the feet and lower portion of the leg, cutting at the knee. With a skinning knife, blade facing out, make a cut on the inside of the legs and down to the center of the breastbone. Continue the cut on the bottom of the neck to where the head was cut off. Go to the rear of the animal and skin out the rear legs. Cut off the rear feet at the last joint above the hoof. Insert a gambrel in the rear legs and hoist the animal up. Make a cut with the blade pointing inside out or with a gut-hook knife in the skin from the anus to the previous cuts made at the bottom of the breastbone. The skin will come off fairly easy if you use your clenched hand to "fist" the skin away. Cut with a sharp skinning knife where necessary.

The next step is to split the breastbone. On small animals this can be done with a sharp knife, however, a hand meat saw is best for larger animals. Make sure you don't cut into the intestines. The bung should be cut around, much like coring an apple. Then pull the bung up and out and tie a string around it. Using a gut-hook knife or knife with the blade out and your fingers to push back the intestines, make a cut from just forward of the pelvis down to the cut on the breastbone. The intestines and organs will start to fall out. Once they have fallen forward, reach up, grasp the bung from the inside, and pull it through the pelvis. This will allow all the paunch, intestines, and organs to fall farther downward. Use a knife to further cut the diaphragm and further loosen the intestines and organs. Allow them to fall into

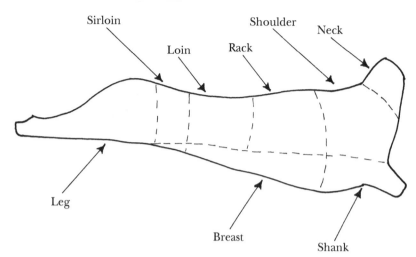

TYPICAL CUTS FOR GOAT OR LAMB.

a clean tub. Remove the liver, cut away the gall bladder, and remove the heart and cut it open. Place both in a pan of cold water to soak out the blood. Prop open the chest cavity and allow the carcass to cool.

Butchering

On small carcasses, the entire carcass is handled as one piece rather than in quarters. The carcass is usually not split, but in hot weather, the carcass may need to be halved to cool as quickly as possible.

If the carcass has not been halved, the first cut is made by sawing off the front shoulders

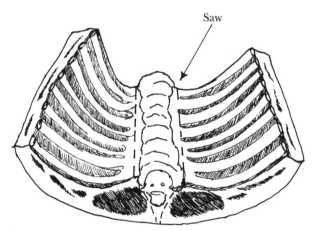

A RACK OR STANDING RIB ROAST CAN BE CREATED BY SAWING THE RIBS FROM EACH SIDE OF THE BACKBONE.

between the fifth and sixth ribs. Once the shoulders have been removed, the neck is cut flush with the front of the shoulder. Next, separate the left and right shoulders by sawing down the backbone, creating two small roasts. These can be left bone-in or the bone can be removed, creating a rolled roast. The shank, flank, breast, and neck are all boned and can be diced and made into lamb stew meat.

With the carcass on its side, remove the breast piece by cutting forward across the flank with a saw. The rack portion is then cut from the loin between the two ribs. The rack can be made into a standing crown roast or it can be split into chops. The first step is to separate the two pieces, a left and right side with a hand meat saw.

TRIM BACK THE MEAT ABOUT 2 INCHES FROM EACH RIB END, THEN BEND THE RIB SECTIONS TOGETHER AND TIE WITH A STRING.

To create a standing crown roast, lay the crown section on its back and saw the ribs from each side of the backbone, but leave the meat attached. Using a boning knife, trim out the backbone. Leave the ribs attached and do not separate the two rib sections. Remove about an inch or so of meat between the ribs on their outer ends. The last step is to bend the sections into a round shape and tie the two ends together with string.

The loin is removed from the leg at the small of the back or pin bone. Begin the cut with a knife and complete the cut with a saw down through the backbone. After removing the loin, the legs are separated by sawing them down the center of the backbone with a saw. Leg of lamb can be prepared American or French style and will bring out the connoisseurs. The majority of the shank bone is removed in American style, allowing it to fit in a smaller pan. The shank is removed approximately two inches from the shank joint.

Goats can be killed and eviscerated in the same manner as for lambs. The meat cuts can be similar or different depending on your choice.

Butchering Venison and Big Game

When we first moved back to the country, along with a big garden, venison provided the majority of our food. We learned to cook deer in just about every way you can imagine. And we still love it. With liberal bag limits and grown kids, along with grandkids and friends, we kill a good number of deer these days. We have venison on the grill, in chili and taco meat, fried, browned in gravy, in roasts, baked, smoked, and dried into jerky and sausages. Venison is good and it's good for you, but the same care and attention must be given in butchering deer as with domestic livestock in order to have quality meat.

Field Dressing

The first step is to field dress the deer as soon after it has been killed as possible. Do not cut off the scent glands or cut the throat to bleed it. Whether shot with an arrow or bullet, the animal will already pretty much have bled out internally, if shot placement has been correct.

Wearing plastic gloves, roll the deer over on its back on a flat, smooth surface. Position the head slightly higher than the rest of the body if possible. Make a shallow, two- to three-inch long cut to one side of the penis, if a buck, or the udder, if a doe. You're now ready to open the lower body portion of the animal and this must be done properly, from the inside. Slicing from the outside of the skin will not only slice through the hair and get hair all over the meat, but may also allow you to slice through the paunch or intestines and contaminate the meat. Stand straddling the animal and facing toward the head, and then extend the index and second finger of your hand, palm up, into the shallow cut made in the muscle and skin of the belly. Position the blade with the edge up between your two fingers and very carefully slit the belly muscle and skin all the way up to the sternum of the ribcage or to where the last or bottom ribs join. Keep pushing the paunch and intestines away as you cut and make sure the knife point doesn't protrude too deeply and cut the paunch. Another tactic is to

243

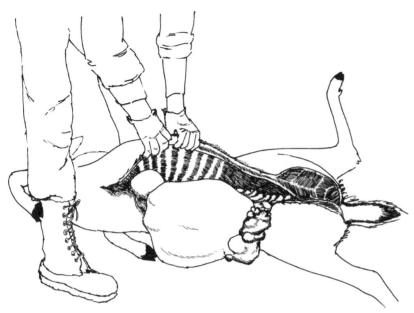

FIELD DRESS THE ANIMAL AS SOON AS POSSIBLE AFTER IT HAS BEEN KILLED.

on its side and the intestines and paunch will begin to roll out. You will have to cut through the diaphragm to allow the lungs and other organs in the ribcage to fall out.

Cut away the liver and remove the bile sack. Remove the heart. Place both in a clean plastic bag. Lift or prop up the head to allow blood to drain out of the cavity. If you have water nearby, wash out the inside of the body cavity. Prop open the body cavity to allow it to cool.

The carcass should be hung and allowed to cool. A rope can be tied around the antlers or neck. Hoist the carcass up onto a game pole. If the weather stays between the upper 30s and lower 40s, allow the carcass to hang for a week to ten days. If the temperature rises above 45°F, you may have to skin out the deer or proceed to butchering. Some may prefer to skin out the carcass before hanging. This is especially so if you have a cool garage, other enclosed building, or refrigerated cooler to hang the carcass. This is actually my preferred method. I usually allow the carcass to hang with the skin on overnight if the weather is cold, then skin the next day, and re-hang for aging.

use a gut hook knife. In this case, stand facing the rear and hook the gut hook into the opening made. Pull the knife toward you, ripping the belly open.

The next cut is through the ribcage to the neck of the animal. If the animal is small, you can use the knife to continue slicing through the center of the ribs toward the throat. On larger animals, you may have to use a packable, field-dressing saw to cut through the sternum. Reach in and cut through the windpipe and gullet.

At the rear of the animal, use the point of a sharp knife to completely encircle the anus and vaginal opening of a doe. Cut around as if coring an apple and then pull the rectum piece outside the body and tie it off with a piece of string.

The next step is to split the pelvic arch. Use a heavy-bladed knife or packable meat saw. The Katz Safari Kit contains everything you need in one package. Then push down on both legs. You'll hear a snap when the arch breaks, leaving an open channel between the arch. Grasp the anus and pull the entire viscera including the genitals through the pelvic arch. In most instances, you will have to do some cutting to release them from the body walls. Turn the carcass

Skinning

The first step in skinning is to saw off the back legs just below the hocks. Then skin out the hind legs past the hocks. Insert the point of a knife from the side opposite the scent glands and make a cut that will allow the ends of the gambrel to slip in place. Fasten a rope to the gambrel and hoist up the carcass to a comfortable working height.

Saw off the front legs just above the knees. Make a cut on the inside of each front leg to the field-dressing cut in the chest and skin out the front legs to the brisket.

Skin out the carcass and allow it to hang to age, if weather permits.

Starting back with the hind legs, make a cut on the inside of the legs, cutting with the skinning knife blade facing outward down to the opening made in the arch bone. Begin skinning with the legs, down over the rump and around the tail. Once you get a start, you can "fist" or pull off a great deal of the skin. Once you skin down past the tail, cut it off with the hand meat saw.

Continue skinning down the back and sides, fisting and cutting with the skinning knife to release the skin. Once you skin down past the shoulders, continue skinning down the neck. Cut off the head by cutting through the neck just below the jaw with a sharp knife and then encircling the neck where the neck and skull join. Twist off the head.

Butchering

Two methods can be used for cutting up the carcass. You can use a meat saw and cut the carcass in the traditional manner, or you can simply cut all the meat from the bones. The latter is easier to do, requires less equipment, and takes up much less freezer space. Or, you can use a combination of the two methods. In the traditional method, the carcass is suspended by the hocks and a meat saw or fine-toothed carpenter's saw is used to split the carcass down the centerline to the backbone starting at the point where the tail was removed. Slicing the muscle down to

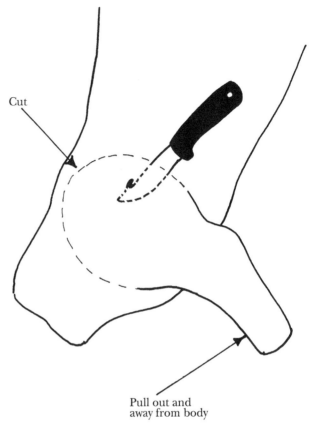

Cut
Pull out and away from body

Cut up the carcass to create the desired cuts. Completely boning out the carcass saves on freezer space. Remove the front shoulder. Pull the shoulder out and away from the chest, then slice down through and it will come off.

the bone with a knife will reveal the centerline starting point. Then quarter the halves, by making a cut between the two last ribs, but leaving a bit of muscle at the starting point. Next, saw through the backbone. Holding the front quarter with one hand, cut through the meat piece between the two ribs and release the front quarter. Both the front and rear quarters can then be cut into the various traditional butcher cuts.

I prefer to bone out deer, and often do this with the carcass intact, rather than halved. With the carcass still hanging, use a long sharp knife to slice off the shoulder. Start the slice at the lower junction between the leg and the brisket, slicing toward the top of the back of the animal. The shoulder comes off quite easily. Using

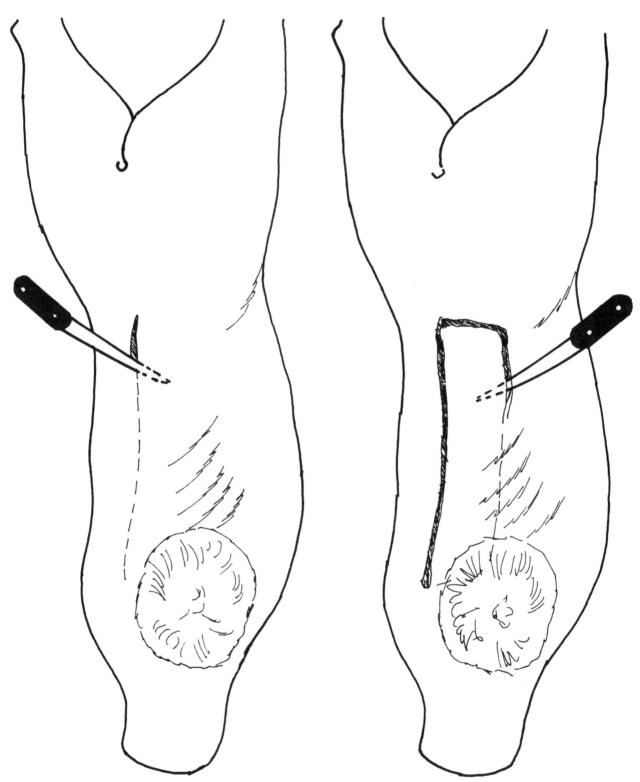

TO REMOVE THE BACKSTRAPS, SLIDE A BONING KNIFE ALONG THE SIDE OF THE BACKBONE DOWN TO THE RIBS.

TURN THE KNIFE AND MAKE A CUT FOLLOWING THE RIBS TO JOIN THE FIRST CUT. THE BACKSTRAP WILL PEEL OUT.

Cut part way through

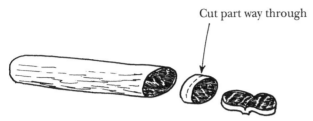

THE BACKSTRAP IS SLICED AND CAN BE BUTTERFLY CUT TO PRODUCE BIGGER PIECES.

a boning knife, bone out the shoulder. This should be set aside for ground meat. Repeat for the other shoulder. The next step is to remove the tenderloins from the inside of the ribcage. A sharp knife can be used to start them, and then simply peel them out. The next step is to remove

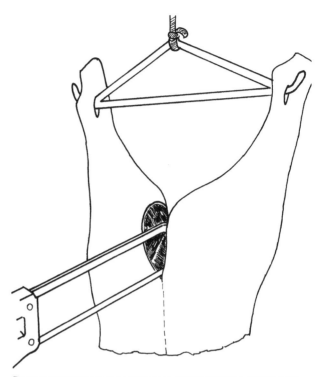

SPLIT THE HIND HALF INTO QUARTERS WITH A MEAT SAW.

the boneless loins. Make a cut along the backbone from where the rear leg joins the backbone. Then make a starting cut from against the ribs to meet the first cut. Follow along the ribs to meet the first cut. Once you make the initial cuts, the loin will simply peel out from along the backbone. Cut into two-inch-thick pieces; wrapped with bacon, and lightly grilled, it makes some of the best steaks you'll ever eat.

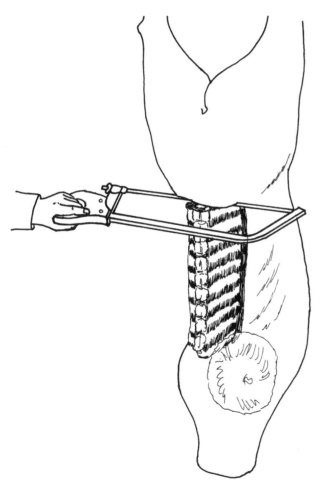

REMOVE THE FRONT HALF BY SAWING THROUGH THE BACKBONE AND CUTTING THROUGH THE FLANK.

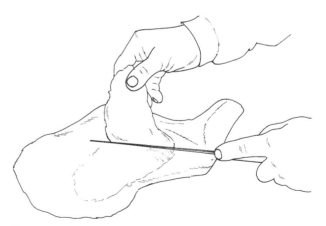

BONE OUT THE RIBS, NECK, AND SHOULDERS.

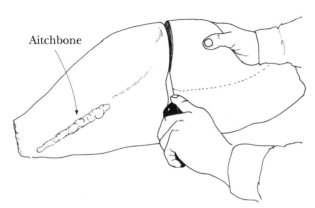

Aitchbone

YOU CAN MAKE A ROAST OR STEAKS FROM THE HAM BY
BONING IT OUT.

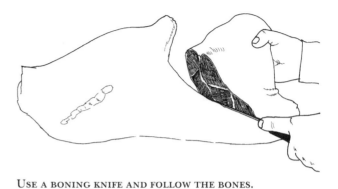

USE A BONING KNIFE AND FOLLOW THE BONES.

At this point, I like to use a meat or pack saw to cut off the front half through the backbone. This allows me to lay the section on a table and completely bone out all meat pieces from the neck and ribs. I then bring down the rear half and lay it on a table. It's easiest to cut this section into two "quarters" with a saw down the backbone. Then simply bone out both halves. I've also left the rear half hanging and boned out when I didn't have a table to work on, but the latter is more of a chore.

Most other larger game, such as elk or moose, is handled in the same manner. Smaller game, such as antelope or sheep, can be handled like sheep or goats.

Index